DUTCH PAINTING

by the same author

★

THE MODERN MOVEMENT IN ART

ENGLISH PAINTING

MODERN FRENCH PAINTERS

AN OUTLINE OF ENGLISH PAINTING

Van Huysum: 'Flowers in a Vase'

R. H. WILENSKI

DUTCH PAINTING

FABER AND FABER

First published in Mcmxxix
by Faber and Faber Limited
Second impression February Mcmxxix
Reprinted September Mcmxxxvii
Revised edition Mcmxlv
Reprinted Mcmxlvi and Mcmxlvii
Revised and enlarged edition Mcmlv
Printed in Great Britain
by the Shenval Press Limited
London, Hertford, and Harlow

PREFACE

to the 1955 *edition*

As originally written this book was mainly concerned with Dutch figure painting; but at the end of the Preface to the 1945 edition I expressed a wish to extend it to other aspects; and in this new edition I have added a chapter called *Dutch Flower Painting*.

This additional chapter is illustrated by eight new plates in monochrome and a coloured Frontispiece; and I should like to thank Miss K. McDouall, Major the Hon H. R. Broughton and Captain E. C. Palmer for their courtesy in providing me with photographs of pictures in their collections.

As all the monochromes and colour plates in the earlier editions are retained, the book now has a hundred and thirty monochrome plates and five colour plates.

The text has been revised throughout, and in the lists of 'Characteristic pictures' I have noted some recent changes in location.

Cookham Dean. 1954

7

PREFACE

to the 1945 edition

This edition contains four new colour plates (*cf.* pp. 28–30). As before there are a hundred and thirty monochrome illustrations; Honthorst's *St. Sebastian*, acquired by the National Gallery in 1930, has been substituted for his *Susanna and the Elders* in Rome; in one or two cases where the reproductions were unsatisfactory new blocks have been made.

I have revised the text throughout, adding some facts, recording changes of ownership, adjusting points of detail and improving the writing to make it clearer and so easier to read. If modern archivists find documents showing this or that date or factual statement to be inaccurate I hope they will inform me with a view to further improvements.

Recent happenings have underlined the significance of the Dutch revolution in the sixteenth and seventeenth centuries. We have been witnessing efforts made by authority to enslave the human mind by propaganda, intrigues, and tortures only comparable with the efforts made to the same end and by the same means in the Netherlands when the Inquisition was established in 1522, when the 'placards' of 1555 were followed in 1564 by the demand that the population should accept the doctrines of the Council of Trent, and when Alva's legions arrived in 1567. The destruction of that tyranny was a human need in the sixteenth and seventeenth centuries. The names of the men who fought in that period for mental freedom in England and France, as well as in Holland, are the period's great names; and the basic character of the Dutch contribution was typified not only in the individualist romantic art of Rembrandt but also in the art of the Dutch painters who portrayed Dutch citizens as plain men enjoying mental freedom in their own little houses and farms.

I laid stress in this book on that aspect of Dutch painting in the seventeenth century; and if I were planning the book now the stress might be greater still. In our own age, till the terrible counter-revolution, against which this war is being fought, revived the old machinery of repressions, all European painters were so free to concentrate on pictorial problems and so free to publish their solutions whatever they might be, that students of art history were led to a parallel absorption in such problems. When, after the camera's advent, all the most intelligent artists turned their main attention to the construction of a new art from which the camera's functions would be eliminated, the students of art history were usefully employed in finding precedents in earlier paintings for these later developments of the painter's art; and thus when this book was written the emphasis in most art criticism was on the artist as aesthetic experimenter rather than on the artist as human individual or social man. I largely avoided that tendency when I wrote this book, since I drew attention to many social factors which affected the artists at the time. But even so I may here and there have underrated the social meaning of certain pictures—the *tableaux de modes* for instance and van Ostade's records of 'grimy and pathetic dwarfs'. But for the rest I stand by the earlier diagnoses and assessments.

One word more. When first published this book was called *An Introduction to Dutch Art*, and, though it is now more conveniently and in one sense more accurately titled *Dutch Painting*, it still makes no claim to cover the whole subject. In particular, the omission of references to the Dutch descriptive painters of landscapes and animals and to the Dutch flower painters will doubtless strike all students. I had intended to discuss these subjects in another book. I have not yet done so—but perhaps one day I shall.

London. January 1945

PREFACE

to the first edition

When we speak of 'Dutch Art' we usually mean the painting produced in Holland between approximately the year 1580 and approximately the year 1700; and it is this art, in some of its aspects, that I have discussed in this book.

If we base our impressions of this art on the examples in the National Gallery we must describe it as consisting of (*a*) popular art —pictures of gay life, low life, and bourgeois life, descriptive portraits and landscapes, (*b*) the art of Rembrandt and his school, and (*c*) the art of Vermeer of Delft and his associates.

But Dutch art of this period is only partly represented in the National Gallery. Rembrandt and Vermeer were not, as they appear there, unheralded apparitions in Dutch art, but rather two peaks, each the summit of a great mass of preparatory production. Rembrandt's art not only embodies the art of Frans Hals, but it also embodies and crowns the whole *œuvre* of the Dutch Romanists; Vermeer's art not only embodies the art of Dutch popular painters of bourgeois life like Terborch and Metsu, with the elements which they themselves had derived from Dutch popular painters of gay life like Willem Duyster and Duck, but it also crowns the whole *œuvre* of Dutch painters of the picturesque, like Nicolas Berchem and Adam Pynacker.

The works of most of the Dutch Romanists are still little known in England, because the National Gallery has nothing by Cornelis of Haarlem, who was considered a much greater swell by the Haarlemers than Frans Hals, nothing by Bloemaert, whom Rubens thought an artist of such importance that he called upon him when he was in Holland, and nothing by Lastman or Jan Pynas, the personal masters of Rembrandt.

In the same way the works of the Dutch painters of the picturesque are little known here or largely forgotten. There are a few pictures by Poelenburgh, Berchem, and Pynacker in the National Gallery, the Wallace Collection and the Dulwich Gallery, but they are hung for the most part in inconspicuous positions or relegated to storerooms or private galleries which are only accessible to those who take the trouble to obtain permission to see them.

11

Then again the pictures by the Dutch painters influenced by
Poussin and Lebrun are hardly known here. The National Gallery has
no pictures by Gerard de Lairesse, who stood for Poussin and the
classical theory in Amsterdam in the last years of Rembrandt's life,
who was painted by Rembrandt, and who described him when he
died as 'a master capable of nothing but vulgar and prosaic subjects
who merely achieved an effect of rottenness'; the Gallery also has only
a minor work by Van der Werff, the most highly paid of all Dutch
artists at the end of the seventeenth century and one whose pictures
were almost unobtainable by ordinary collectors because the Elector
Palatine paid him a retaining fee for all his pictures painted during
nine months of every year.

I have, therefore, thought it essential in the first place to draw
attention not only to the Dutch Romanists and picturesque painters
who must be regarded, respectively, as forerunners of Rembrandt and
of Vermeer; but also to the works and careers of Gerard de Lairesse
and Adriaen van der Werff.

In *The Modern Movement in Art* I referred to Rembrandt as the
herald of the nineteenth-century Romantic Movement, and to Vermeer as an artist of the architectural kind and so one of the heralds of
the Modern Movement of our day; I also expressed the view that
Dutch popular art of the seventeenth century—the prolific production
of which was largely the result of social conditions in Holland after
the Dutch Revolution—must be assessed from standards of descriptive popular art which are not applicable to a romantic artist like
Rembrandt or an architectural artist like Vermeer.[1]

In the studies involved in the preparation of the present book I have
found no grounds for revising the general terms of those comments
and I have tried here to amplify and explain them.

The number of pictures produced in Holland between 1580 and
1700 is overwhelming. Dr. Hofstede de Groot's 'Catalogue of Dutch
Painters', which is based on John Smith's, and which deals with only
thirty artists, describes more than fifteen thousand pictures; and Sir
Robert Witt's library contains more than fifty thousand photographs
of Dutch works. Hundreds of thousands of pictures were, in fact,
painted in Holland at this time. No man living is acquainted with as

[1] Throughout this book I have used the words 'popular', 'original', 'architectural', 'romantic', 'descriptive', and so forth in the senses defined at length in
The Modern Movement in Art. As those definitions occupy a large proportion of
that book, readers who are familiar with them will absolve me from repeating
them here; and if the meaning I attach to the words is not clear from the con-
text in all passages in this book I must refer the reader to the other book as an
introduction.

many as half the surviving pictures, and no man can ascribe a third to the correct individual artists. The reader of a book of this kind has, therefore, the right to ask at the outset what pictures the author has in mind when he speaks of any category of Dutch art or of the art of any individual man. I have, accordingly, placed a list of 'characteristic pictures' at the head of my comments on each artist. These lists do not pretend to be exhaustive or even to represent exhaustively my own acquaintance with the artists' works; but as they consist exclusively of pictures of which I have seen the originals or of which I have had reproductions before me when I prepared my notes, they may fairly claim to represent the works I had in mind when I wrote my comments.

Except in a few special cases I have not entered into questions of attribution. It has appeared to me reasonable to accept in the main and for working purposes the attributions of men like Dr. Bredius, Dr. Bode and Dr. Hofstede de Groot. I have, however, entered to some extent into the discussions about Rembrandt's *œuvre* because the conception of Rembrandt as an artist which arises from the generally accepted *œuvre* of about six hundred and fifty pictures, three hundred etchings and two thousand drawings, is quite different from the conception which arises from the Rembrandt portrayed by Professor van Dyke, who would reduce the oil paintings to less than fifty, and the etchings and drawings, presumably, in a similar proportion. It was necessary to take a stand on one side or the other of this discussion, and I have explained why I feel it impossible to accept the idea of Rembrandt set up by Professor van Dyke.

I have also touched on some points of attribution in connexion with the work of Judith Leyster, who has hitherto been regarded merely as a follower and *pasticheuse* of Frans Hals, because an ingenious German student, Dr. Dangers of Hamburg, has suggested that she was the mistress of Rembrandt, by whom she became the mother of the boy shown in the Cook Collection picture *Titus as a Child*, and that she collaborated with Rembrandt in certain of his most famous works. I have set down Dr. Dangers's suggestions without attempting to assess their worth.

Dutch art of the seventeenth century is habitually described as essentially 'national'. But this does not apply to Rembrandt and Vermeer. Such national elements as appear in the works of these masters are merely incidental, and they have purely a local or historical interest to-day. The essential content of Rembrandt's work is romantic in character because Rembrandt had a romantic mind. The essential content of Vermeer's work is architectural because Vermeer's mind was architectural. Rembrandt's works and Vermeer's survive as masterpieces because both the romantic and the architectural attitudes of mind are permanent and universal attitudes, and the original contributions of both these masters in their respective fields are thus not national or temporary but universal and of all time. It is also not possible to apply the term 'national' to the art of the Dutch Romanists, of the Dutch picturesque painters, or of Gerard de Lairesse or Adriaen van der Werff. In Holland in the seventeenth century—as elsewhere at all times—it was, in fact, only popular art which was national; and the term can only be properly applied to the Dutch popular painters of gay life, low life and bourgeois life who were primarily concerned with recording their familiar experience of the national life around them.

The student of seventeenth-century art cannot fail to be struck by the curious fact that whereas Rubens dominated much Flemish painting in this period, his influence is scarcely perceptible a few miles away in Holland. The explanation is that pageantry provided the circumstantial content of the art of Rubens, and pageantry and pageant art were associated in the minds of the Dutch people with the pomp and persecutions of the Spanish regime. To understand Dutch art of this century it is therefore essential in the first place to realize the extent to which pageantry and pageant art were bound up with life in the Netherlands at the end of the sixteenth century and to realize how much gaiety, fantasy and colour the Dutch artists sacrificed when they refused to avail themselves of material which had been used by countless European artists all through the Renaissance and was finally exploited in a brilliant climax by Rubens and his school; and I have, therefore, recalled some typical instances of pageantry and pageant art in two chapters called a 'Prologue'. In this 'Prologue' also I have drawn attention to some protests against the Spanish persecutions which can be found in contemporary Netherlands art.

One other section of the book calls for mention. In the chapter headed 'Vermeer's Mirrors' I have suggested that Vermeer and certain other Dutch artists may have established their compositions or actually painted their pictures with the aid of mirrors or other mechanical devices analogous to the reducing glass which, it is recorded, was used by Gerard Dou. For this theory I have nothing but the internal evidence of the pictures; and I have, therefore, illustrated this chapter with as many photographs as possible in order that the reader may be able to judge the theory for himself.

In the preparation of this book I have received much help from Sir Robert and Lady Witt, who allowed me to use their library daily for weeks on end, and to examine some thousands of their photographs; I acknowledge this help, and that of their clever and courteous librarians, with grateful thanks. I have also been helped by Mr. W. F. Mansell, who kindly lent me several hundred photographs from his own collection and allowed me to keep them by me from the beginning of my work to the end.

I am aware that a comparison of photographs is less satisfactory than a comparison of actual paintings. But I have found that the photographs in many instances have recalled to me details of composition in the case of pictures in foreign galleries which I had forgotten, and that a comparison of photographs in other instances has suggested lines of inquiry which bore fruit. I make, therefore, no apology for having supplemented my acquaintance with pictures in the Dutch and other Continental museums and the museums in this country, by the study of photographs which I trust I have been able to use with the necessary discretion.

Heston. October 1928

CONTENTS

PROLOGUE

PART I. FOREIGN INFLUENCES

PART II. FRANS HALS AND HIS SCHOOL

PART III. REMBRANDT VAN RYN

PART IV. MORE FOREIGN INFLUENCES

CONTENTS

ILLUSTRATIONS

COLOUR PLATES

MONOCHROME ILLUSTRATIONS

Plates 1-16 between pages 48 and 49

19

ILLUSTRATIONS

Plates 17—32 between pages 64 and 65

ILLUSTRATIONS

ILLUSTRATIONS

ILLUSTRATIONS

ILLUSTRATIONS

ILLUSTRATIONS

ILLUSTRATIONS

ILLUSTRATIONS

NOTES ON THE COLOUR PLATES

FRONTISPIECE

VAN HUYSUM: *Flowers in a vase*

This picture is an attractive example of the decorative manner of Jan van Huysum who died in 1749 and is still the most famous of Dutch flower-painters.

Many, however, will prefer the simpler styles of the first three quarters of the seventeenth century which are recorded here, with notes on the artists' careers and characters, in Part VII 'Dutch Flower Painting' (pp. 195-206).

PLATE A

DE HOOCH: *Courtyard of a Dutch House*

The correct title of this picture is *View into the Courtyard of the former Cloister of Hieronymusdale in Delft* as is shown by the inscription on the tablet.

Painted in 1658, when De Hooch was twenty-nine, it shows all his talents in a high degree, and in particular his power of rendering the sensation of clear outdoor atmosphere and the pale sunlight of northern climes (*cf.* Pl. 117). It shows a space concept bridging that of Rembrandt with that of Vermeer (*cf.* p. 187) and also a characteristic compromise between genre painting and architectural art (*cf.* p. 177).

The picture was acquired for the National Gallery in 1871 as part of the Robert Peel Collection. Constable wrote of it: 'The best pictures I have seen are some of the works of De Hooge, particularly one of an outdoor subject at Sir R. Peel's. His indoors are good, but less difficult, as being less lustrous.'

PLATE B

REMBRANDT: *Woman Bathing*

The model for this study was doubtless Hendrickje Stoffels who came into Rembrandt's house as a pretty servant girl of twenty-three in 1649 and lived with him till her death in 1662 or 1663 (*cf.* pp. 93 and

94). The picture, painted on oak, is signed *Rembrandt f.* and dated 1654, the year in which Hendrickje's daughter Cornelia was born. Rembrandt at this time was forty-eight.

The resemblance of this work pictorially to the *Flayed Ox* (Louvre), painted in 1655, is a measure of the transformation of both 'subjects' into terms of art. Rembrandt when he painted the *Woman Bathing* was as remote from the lascivious or anecdotic painter as he was remote from genre painters when he painted the *Flayed Ox*. In each case he was concerned to enlarge his experience of an emotive fragment of life—the experience including the light and shade pattern on a group of forms and its record in certain qualities of colour and impasto. At the same time he has imbued both works with romantic sentiment of the deepest kind (*cf.* pp. 99 and 103).

This fine work was bequeathed to the National Gallery by the Rev. William Holwell Carr in 1831.

PLATE C

MIERIS: *Lady with a Parrot*

Frans van Mieris (called the Elder) was born at Leyden in 1635 and lived there till he died in 1681. He was the son of a goldsmith and diamond cutter and one of a family of twenty-three children. He was famous in his lifetime not only in Holland but also abroad—his patrons included the Archduke Cosimo of Tuscany and the Archduke Leopold Wilhelm who vainly invited him to become his court painter in Vienna. Mieris was a close friend of Jan Steen (*cf.* pp. 156–161) whose work he is said to have influenced though Steen was his senior by ten years. He is well represented in the galleries of Munich, Vienna, Florence and The Hague.

This picture is typical of Dutch *tableaux de modes* (*cf.* pp. 162–169). It is in the National Gallery and painted on copper; a signed version on canvas is in the Munich Old Pinakothek; and there are other versions in Buckingham Palace and in the Cook Collection, Richmond. Mieris, like Metsu, was a pupil of Gerard Dou (*cf.* pp. 124, 125, 135, 168).

PLATE D

VERMEER: *Lady standing at the Virginals*

I have discussed in the text the architectural qualities which make Vermeer's work so exceptionally attractive to those in sympathy with the modern Cubist-Classical renaissance. There, too, I have drawn attention to Vermeer's feeling for a defined and bounded picture space with a closing backcloth in the Claude tradition (*cf.* pp. 68, 107, 172, 187), which distinguishes his paintings from those by De Hooch (Pl. A) and the painters of *tableaux de modes* (Pl. C) on the one hand and by Rembrandt (Pl. B) on the other (*cf.* p. 170 *ss.*). The serenity and finality of this most precious example (which the National Gallery bought in 1892) are the direct results of this classical approach; and, incidentally, the painting is a masterpiece of craftsmanship, since it gives us almost incredible precision in the details (the high light on each separate nail in the chair is set at exactly the right angle to the source of light) without any disturbance of the monumental structure of the whole.

PROLOGUE

i. Pageants and Pageant Art

Living in the modern world where pageants and processions are of rare occurrence and generally conducted on a modest scale, we are apt to forget the frequency and splendour of the pageantry which began in the late Middle Ages and steadily increased in western European lands till it reached something like a climax in the sixteenth century. This pageantry has a history of its own; and the part played by artists in designing the pageants and the influence of the pageants on pictorial art are also separate subjects in themselves; my purpose here is merely to remind the reader of the close connexion which existed between pageantry and art, and to look for a moment at the gay fantastic art on which the Dutch artists of the seventeenth century deliberately turned their backs.

There is evidence that pageantry in the early stages was intimately connected with ecclesiastical ceremonial on the one hand and with the development of theatrical performances on the other; and in Gothic times if the artist was not employed in the service of dogma he was employed in the service of pageantry or ritual. Moreover, from Gothic times onwards princes and noblemen provided secular pageants of their own. Hundreds of courts, large and small, formed points of focus where the people were daily entertained by cavalcades and processions. This aspect of pageantry again called for the service of artists, and from it the artists also drew material for pictures not only of wedding processions, hunting scenes, triumphs and so forth, but also for the processions of the Magi in which contemporary costumes were regularly introduced. The influence of secular pageantry is seen, indeed, all over the Early Renaissance, or, as it is now called, 'International Gothic,' art. To recall it I reproduce a detail from Gozzoli's frescoes in the Riccardi Palace in Florence (Pl. 1).

In the sixteenth century pageants increased in frequency, in scale and in splendour; and it would seem to have been the Republic of Venice, then at the height of its wealth and influence, which set the standard and, as it were, the pace. In Venice the Doge took part in

31

thirty-six prescribed processions every year in addition to the ceremonies attendant on his own coronation and on that of the Dogaressa. He also took part in numerous extra pageants organized to celebrate military or naval victories, special events such as the end of an outbreak of the plague, the foundation perhaps of a new church or other public building of importance, or the reception of some distinguished foreign visitor whom Venice thought it wise to entertain with special magnificence. The Venetian populace also saw the pageants and processions of the Venetian Carnival, where cars with *tableaux vivants* depicting the Virtues and Vices, the Triumph of Venice, and other fantasies paraded St. Mark's Square; and they saw a good deal in one way or another of the magnificent entertainments in the private palaces, since it was not unusual in Venice, after a banquet followed by a masque or dance, for the entire company to finish the revels on a barge on the Grand Canal or on foot in the Piazza. At the coronation of the Dogaressa Morosina Morosini a triumphal arch adorned with figures, ornaments, mottoes and trophies was erected near the Ponte della Paglia; the Dogaressa proceeded down the Grand Canal in a Bucentaur accompanied by a fleet of boats 'fantastically decked'; and when she landed at the Piazzetta a thousand youths dressed in silks went before her to St. Mark's. When Henri de Valois left Poland to ascend the throne of France as Henri III he stayed on the way in Venice; at San Niccolo on the Lido he was greeted by an immense triumphal arch; in Venice itself public and private fêtes were organized in his honour; at a banquet given him in the Hall of the Great Council in the Ducal Palace there were three thousand guests; the tables were adorned with gold and silver candlesticks and beakers, exquisite glass from Murano, elaborately chased wine coolers, gold spoons and knives, gold tooth-picks and even the new luxury of forks. At another banquet in the Palace all the table appointments, plates, knives, forks, table-cloths, were made so naturalistically of sugar that the royal guest was startled when his napkin broke beneath his hand. The dish set before the King at this banquet represented a queen riding on two tigers who bore on their breasts the arms of France and Poland; and all the tables bore statuettes of popes, kings, doges, deities, allegorical figures of the planets, the arts, and the virtues, and representations of animals, fruit, flowers, and trees which likewise were all made of sugar.[1]

In all the Italian pageants and festivities, artists played a cardinal part. Leonardo da Vinci at the very beginning of the century had

[1] *Cf.* Molmenti, *Venice, The Golden Age.*

made designs for Ludovico il Moro's festivities in Milan; Piero di Cosimo was in great demand in Florence as a designer of pageants, as we know from Vasari:—

'In his youth Piero, possessing a capricious and extravagant invention, was in great request for the masquerades of carnival-time, and was a great favourite with the noble Florentine youths, because by his inventive mind he greatly improved those amusements in ornament, grandeur and pomp. He is said to have been one of the first to give the character of triumphs, and at any rate he greatly improved them with his scenes, with music and appropriate speeches, and a grand procession of men on horses and foot, in costumes adapted to the subject. . . . It was certainly a fine sight at night to see twenty-five or thirty couples of horses, richly caparisoned, with their masters dressed in accordance with the subject of the invention; . . . footmen in the same livery, in single file, carrying torches in their hands, sometimes more than four hundred, and then the car of triumph full of ornaments spoils and curious fancies, which enchanted the people and instructed their minds.'

Moreover, in the entertainments for Henri III in Venice, referred to above, the triumphal arch on the Lido was designed by Palladio and it was painted with scenes by Veronese and Tintoretto, and the sugar statuettes at the banquet were designed by no less an architect than Sansovino himself.

These pageants also yielded as much to art as the artists had contributed. Venetian art is unthinkable without this source of inspiration. It was Venetian pageantry that provided Gentile Bellini with material for his processions, Carpaccio with material for his St. Ursula pictures, Titian with his sumptuous colour, and Veronese with the circumstantial content of his glorious decorations.

Outside Italy the spirit of pageantry was similarly developed throughout the sixteenth century. Francis I received Henry VIII at Calais in 1520 with the pomp and ceremony which has survived in history as 'The Field of the Cloth of Gold'. When Henri III ascended the French throne, fresh from Venice, he organized a ceaseless round of gorgeous festivals, tourneys, processions, masquerades, and banquets; at Court balls, to the delight of his 'mignons', he not infrequently attired himself like a woman 'with silken flounces, jewelled stomacher and painted face, with pearls of great price adorning his bared neck and breast and satin-slippered feet of whose delicate size and shape he was justly vain'[1]; when Henri IV recon-

[1] Motley, *History of the United Netherlands.*

ciled himself with Rome at the end of the century all Paris turned out to see him proceed arrayed in white satin with a brilliant entourage to the Cathedral of St. Denis and watch him dine in public when the ceremony was complete; and when the Emperor Rudolph II entered Vienna in 1577 he passed under arches designed by Batholomaus Spranger and Carel Van Mander, the art historian.

The London pageants of the period had a characteristic of their own; for it was customary on these occasions to regale the populace with wine. At Anne Boleyn's coronation procession the Great Cheap Conduit ran with white wine and claret all the afternoon. When Queen Mary rode in state through London the day before her coronation she was received with ceremonies all over the city; at the corner of Greenchurch the Hanseatic merchants had built up a hillock on which four children dressed in allegorical raiment were posed as statues round a fountain that poured wine; and in front of the Steelyard there was a fountain of wine from which the populace drank to the tune of £1,000 in the money of the day.[1]

Queen Elizabeth was notoriously devoted to pageants. When she went on the Royal Progress each year and quartered herself with her suite on the house of some favoured nobleman in the country, the most elaborate pageants, masques and diversions had to be prepared to welcome her. The entertainment provided for the Queen at Elvetham by the Earl of Hertford in 1591 was typical. Lord Hertford had caused large temporary pavilions to be erected to house the Queen's retinue; he had dug a lake, or, as the old chronicles have it, a 'pond', in the park and placed in the centre a fort and other devices, and on the edge of the pond there was a throne for the Queen covered with silver lace, and plumes spangled with silver. As the Queen approached Elvetham she was met by Lord Hertford with three hundred attendants arrayed in yellow and black; and a poet recited a speech of welcome, while six virgins, arrayed in costumes apparently modelled on some engraving after Botticelli's *Spring*, strewed flowers before her feet. At Elvetham the Queen also witnessed a water pageant in which, as the old chronicler tells us: 'A pompous array of sea persons waded breast high or swam till they approached near the seat of her Majesty. Nereus, the prophet of the sea, attired in red silk and having a cornered cap on his curled head, did swim before the rest as their pastor and guide. After him came five Tritons breast high in the water all with grisly heads and beards of divers colours . . . all five cheerfully sounding their trumpets.' While the

[1] This heartening custom continued right into the eighteenth century. In 1727 at the Coronation of George II, Lamb's Conduit ran with wine.

Tritons played their trumpets three virgins in a pinnace played Scottish jigs on cornets; and we are told that the 'melody was sweet and the show stately'. Meanwhile, from a wood beside the pond another group of performers representing Silvanus and his attendants began to join in the action. Silvanus was attired 'from the middle downwards to the knee in kids' skins with the hair on, his legs, body and face naked but dyed over with saffron'; he was hooded with a goat's skin and had two little horns over his forehead; his followers were all covered with ivy leaves. When all the performers had handed gifts to the Queen and recited laudatory verses the denizens of the wood fell to comic combat with the denizens of the water, and finally Nereus ducked Silvanus in the pond. At a banquet on this occasion, in the pavilion in the park, the plates were served by two hundred of Hertford's gentlemen attended by a hundred torch-bearers, and Henri III's banquet was rivalled in the variety and profusion of the ornaments made of sugar, for they represented 'Castles, Forts, Drummers, Trumpeters, Lions, Unicorns, Bears, Horses, Camels, Antelopes, Rams, Dogs, Tigers, Dromedaries, Elephants, Snakes, Adders, Vipers, Frogs, Toads, and all kinds of Worms. Eagles, Cranes, Bustards, Pigeons, Pheasants, Cocks and Owls. Mermaids, Whales, Dolphins, Congars, Sturgeons and Pikes'. When the Queen departed through Lord Hertford's estate she came at every turn upon groups weeping and wringing their hands, and as she left his confines a concealed musician sang:—

'O come again fair Nature's treasure,
  Whose looks yield joy exceeding measure'.

James I and his Queen were even more devoted to masques and pageants than Queen Elizabeth, and English pageantry reached its high-water mark in the first years of the seventeenth century with Ben Jonson's masques designed by Inigo Jones. In these masques and pageants, where many of the performers were amateurs, the women's parts were performed by women, though in the theatre, as is well known, the women's parts were performed by boys. In these circumstances it is curious to observe that in Inigo Jones's designs for the costumes in his masques many of the female figures have their breasts exposed; and it is probable that many of the allegorical figures in masques and pageants were very lightly clad (Pl. 3).

The employment of nude and semi-nude figures seems indeed to have been a feature not only of the art influenced by pageants, but also of the pageants themselves, particularly in France and the

Netherlands. Thus when Louis XI entered Paris in 1461, and was welcomed at the city gates, he listened to three panegyrics on his greatness recited one after another by three naked girls; and when Charles the Bold entered Lille in 1468 a *tableau vivant* representing the Judgement of Paris was staged for him in the open street.

Wherever the Emperor Charles V went his arrival was celebrated by a pageant. When he arrived in Rome on his return from Africa in 1536 all the artists in Rome, native and foreign, were employed in designing the triumphal arches. One of the foreign artists was the Dutchman Martin Heemskerk, who had charge, with a number of Dutch, Flemish and German artists, of the arch at one end of the Corso. The 'Germans', as they were called, were slow at their work until, as Vasari relates, the pageant masters began to supply them with wine, when being *sempre ubriachi* and *riscaldoti dal furor del vino* they became enthusiastic and *feciono cose stupende*. The Netherlanders organized elaborate preparations for the Emperor's tour in 1519, the year before his coronation. In that year the Emperor entered Antwerp through a triumphal arch which had cost 4,000 gulden and he was welcomed with *tableaux vivants* which included entirely naked girls; and when in 1549 he again toured the Netherlands to introduce his son Philip, who was later to cause such misery in those regions, he entered Antwerp through arches designed by Pieter Coeck van Aelst, the master and father-in-law of Pieter Brueghel.

After the separation of Holland from Flanders, the 'obedient' provinces continued this tradition of pageantry. All the successive Viceroys appointed by Spain made triumphal processions through Brussels, Antwerp or Ghent. For the pageant on the arrival of the Archduke Ernest in 1594, the cities of Brussels and Antwerp voted enormous sums, and it was devised by a celebrated 'rhetorician' and pageant master named John Baptist Houwaerts; it is so amusingly described by Motley that I cannot refrain from quoting it at length:—

'The day came at last, and the exhibition was a masterpiece. . . . A stately procession of knights and burghers in historical and mythological costumes, followed by ships, dromedaries, elephants, whales, giants, dragons, and other wonders of the sea and shore, escorted the archduke into the city. Every street and square was filled with triumphal arches, statues and platforms, on which the most ingenious and thoroughly classical living pictures were exhibited. There was hardly an eminent deity of Olympus, or hero of ancient history, that was not revived and made visible to mortal eyes in the person of Ernestus of Austria.

'On a framework fifty-five feet high and thirty-three feet in breadth he was represented as Apollo hurling his darts at an enormous Python, under one of whose forepaws struggled an unfortunate burgher, while the other clutched a whole city; Tellus, meantime, with her tower on her head, kneeling anxious and imploring at the feet of her deliverer. On another stage Ernest assumed the shape of Perseus; Belgica that of the bound and despairing Andromeda.[1] On a third, the interior of Etna was revealed, where Vulcan was seen urging his Cyclops to forge for Ernest their most tremendous thunderbolts with which to smite the foes of the provinces, those enemies being of course the English and Hollanders. Venus, the while, timidly presented an arrow to her husband, which he was requested to sharpen, in order that when the wars were over Cupid therewith might pierce the heart of some beautiful virgin, whose charms should reward Ernest—fortunately for the female world still a bachelor—for his victories and his toils.

'On yet another stage a Poet, played by Houwaerts himself, so soon as the approach of Ernest had been announced, fell straightway into a trance. While he was in that condition, a beautiful female apparition floated before his eyes, and, on being questioned, announced her name to be Moralization. . . . The spirit informed the poet that the forests of the Low Countries—so long infested by brigands, wood-beggars, and malefactors of all kinds—would thenceforth swarm with nymphs, rabbits, hares, and animals of that nature.

'A vision of the conquering Ernest, attended by eight-and-twenty noble and pleasant females, marching two and two, half naked, each holding a torch in one hand and a laurel-wreath in the other, now swept before the dreamer's eyes. He naturally requested the "discreet spirit" to mention the names of this bevy of imperfectly attired ladies thronging so lovingly around the fortunate archduke, and was told that they were the eight-and-twenty virtues which chiefly characterized his Serene Highness. Prominent in this long list were Philosophy, Audacity, Acrimony, Virility, Equity, Piety, Velocity, and Alacrity. The two last-mentioned qualities could hardly be attributed to the archduke in his decrepit condition, except in an intensely mythological sense.'[2]

This performance was witnessed by a youth of seventeen called Peter Paul Rubens. Two years later, when he was working as an

[1] A fancy repeated by Rubens in 1639 as a special commission for Philip IV, left unfinished at the artist's death and now in the Prado.

[2] Motley, *History of the United Netherlands.*

assistant to Otto van Veen, his master was designing, and he was doubtless helping in the execution of, triumphal arches intended for yet another pageant—the Archduke Albert's entry into Antwerp; and it was from this experience of the Antwerp pageants and from other experiences of pageants in life and art gained during his travels in Italy and Spain, that Rubens evolved his own imposing pageant art.

When pageants were required in Brussels and Antwerp in Rubens's day he was of course the obvious person to design them, and in so doing he had but to translate his pictures into pageant form. In 1634 he designed in fact a whole series of triumphal arches adorned with hundreds of painted figures and a series of statues carved by sculptors in white sandstone which were used to adorn the streets for the Infante Ferdinand's state entry into Antwerp; this pageant cost 78,000 gulden, and the designs are preserved in the Hermitage at Leningrad. In 1638 he designed a triumphal car which was paraded in the streets of Antwerp to celebrate a victory of the Viceroy's troops over the Dutch at Calloo in that year; for this he received a cask of wine from Paris costing 48 gulden and presumably a fee as well; his design is preserved in the Museum in Antwerp (Pl. 2).

While Rubens was thus engaged on art of this character, the Dutch artists were developing on other lines; and we must now consider why the Dutch artists abandoned the movement, the gaiety and the colour, the fantastic imagery, and the engaging absurdities, which pageantry and pageant art had presented to the world.

ii. Pageants and Pain

In the year 1519, when Charles V was regaled in Antwerp with the tableau of the naked girls, Martin Luther wrote his 'Address to the German Nobles' wherein he asked why 300,000 florins should be sent each year from Germany to Rome; in 1520, when Charles was crowned, Luther burned the Papal Bull in the market-place at Wittenberg; and the history of the Netherlands from this date to the end of the century is the history of a struggle between the spirit of Charles V and the spirit of Luther. With that struggle we are not here concerned, except in so far as the extortion and persecutions inflicted by Charles and Philip, Alva and Titelmann, were accompanied with pageants of the sort I have described.

That they were so accompanied we have the testimony of history. In 1540 the prosperous and important city of Ghent refused to

Plate A. De Hooch: 'Courtyard of a Dutch House'

collect a tax levied by the Spanish Crown, and Charles himself sent to Ghent to consider the dispute. He was accompanied by four thousand lancers, one thousand archers, five thousand halberd men and musketeers, cardinals, archbishops, bishops and other ecclesiastics, dukes, princes, earls, barons, and a contingent of the Knights of the Holy Fleece with their respective attendants, who were all quartered on the city for the period of his visit. The pageant of his entry occupied six hours. He investigated, or pretended to investigate, the point at issue, and some weeks later a second pageant was arranged, this time in the Town Hall, where the Emperor announced a verdict which confiscated almost the entire property of Ghent, annulled the city's charters and privileges, and ordered that, on a date named, a third pageant—a pageant of repentance—should take place. In this pageant the senators, their pensionaries, clerks and secretaries, thirty notable burghers, the great dean and second dean of the weavers, were to appear dressed in black robes, bareheaded and without their chains: fifty persons from the guilds, and fifty others were to come dressed only in their shirts with halters upon their necks; and these representatives of the city were then to fall upon their knees before the Emperor, and 'say in a loud and intelligible voice, by the mouth of one of their clerks, that they were extremely sorry for the disloyalty, disobedience, infraction of laws, commotions, rebellion and high treason, of which they had been guilty, promise that they would never do the like again, and humbly implore him, for the sake of the Passion of Jesus Christ, to grant them mercy and forgiveness'. This humiliating pageant on the appointed day was accurately performed.[1]

I referred in the last section to the Emperor's tour of 1549 when he introduced Philip II to the Netherlands. Brussels on that occasion organized a procession that filed past the visitors and stopped for some time before them while a musician performed upon an organ. The sounds emitted from this organ were of an unusual character, for a cat with its tail tied to a key was imprisoned in each pipe and as the musician struck the notes the tails were pinched and the cats screeched and howled. We can well believe that Charles and Philip enjoyed this interlude which heralded the howls of agony that their lordship of the Netherlands was about to wring from thousands of human throats.

In the following year Charles published the terrible edict which was republished by Philip when he succeeded in 1555. The edict included the following provisions:

[1] Motley, *History of the Rise of the Dutch Republic*, Introduction.

PROLOGUE

'No one shall print, write, copy, keep, conceal, sell, buy, or give in churches, streets, or other places, any book or writing made by Martin Luther, John Ecolampadius, Ulrich Zwinglius, Martin Bucer, John Calvin or other heretics reprobated by the Holy Church; . . . nor break, nor otherwise injure the images of the Holy Virgin, or canonized saints; . . . nor in his house hold conventicles, or illegal gatherings, or be present at any such in which the adherents of the above-mentioned heretics teach, baptize, and form conspiracies against the Holy Church and the general welfare. . . . Moreover, we forbid all lay persons to converse or dispute concerning the Holy Scriptures, open or secretly, especially on any doubtful or difficult matters, or to read, teach, or expound the Scriptures, unless they have duly studied theology and been approved by some renowned university; . . . or to preach secretly, or openly, or to entertain any of the opinions of the above-mentioned heretics; . . . such perturbators of the general quiet are to be executed, to wit: the men with the sword and the women to be buried alive, if they do not persist in their errors; if they do persist in them then they are to be executed with fire; all their property in both cases being confiscated to the crown. . . .We forbid . . . all persons to lodge, entertain, furnish with food, fire, or clothing, or otherwise to favour any one holden or notoriously suspected of being a heretic; . . . and any one failing to denounce any such we ordain shall be liable to the above-mentioned punishments. . . . The informer, in case of conviction, shall be entitled to one-half the property of the accused, if not more than one hundred pounds Flemish; if more, then ten per cent. of all such excess.'

The atrocities committed by Titelmann's Inquisition on the strength of this edict, the tortures regularly inflicted to extort confessions and information and the special tortures inflicted in special cases of defiance,[1] are described by Motley and the other historians of the period; in their works we can read of the year 1566 —the year of the first revolt against the Spanish tyranny, of the destruction of the sculpture and works of art in Antwerp Cathedral,

---

[1] One Le Blas, guilty of an act of flagrant defiance in Tournay Cathedral, was thrice put to the torture to extract information of his associates. He was then dragged on a hurdle, with his mouth closed with an iron, to the market-place. Here his right hand and foot were burned and twisted off between red-hot irons and his tongue was torn out by the roots. With his arms and legs fastened together behind his back he was then hooked by the middle of his body to an iron chain and made to swing to and fro over a slow fire till he was entirely roasted.— Motley, *History of the Rise of the Dutch Republic.*

and of the open-air preachers of the reformed faith, whose sermons were attended by thousands in fields outside the towns and cities both in Flanders and Holland; and in their works also we can read of the still more terrible years when Alva arrived to punish the revolt and make a final effort to stamp out the reformed faith and to drain the Netherlands of their wealth; and all these horrors were accompanied by pomp and pageant even in the darkest days.

Alva arrived in 1567. The troops who arrived with him were equipped with engraved and gilded armour; and their attendant services included two thousand prostitutes. Alva neglected no occasion for pageants. When he gained military successes against the rebels, the populations of Brussels and Antwerp were treated to triumphant progresses in which his horse's hoofs trampled on carpets of strewn flowers. The famous fortress at Antwerp was erected as much as a gesture of pomp and pride as a measure of defence; and the colossal statue of himself, attired as a Roman conqueror with a torch-bearing angel on one side and a gentle shepherd on the other, which he erected in the same city, was a gesture of the same kind.[1] In 1569 he staged a pageant to proclaim an amnesty. This amnesty proclaimed a general pardon, but excepted 'ministers, teachers, dogmatizers, and all who had favoured and harboured such dogmatizers and preachers; all those in the least degree implicated in the image-breaking; all who had ever been individually suspected of heresy or schism; all who had ever signed or favoured the compromise or the petition to the Regent; all those who had taken up arms, contributed money, distributed tracts; all those in any manner chargeable with misprision, or who had failed to denounce those guilty of heresy'. To proclaim this amnesty—which the list of exceptions rendered a purely empty form of words—Alva appeared with his suite on the square in front of the Town Hall:—

'Here a large scaffolding or theatre had been erected. The platform and the steps which led to it were covered with scarlet cloth. A throne, covered with cloth of gold, was arranged in the most elevated position for the Duke. On the steps immediately below him were placed two of the most beautiful women in Antwerp, clad in allegorical garments to represent Righteousness and Peace. The staircase

[1] The statue depicted Alva with his foot on a prostrate figure with two heads, four arms and one body—representing presumably Heresy and Sedition in one body corporate. It bore an inscription reading 'To Ferdinand Alvarez de Toledo, Duke of Alva, Governor of the Netherlands under Philip the Second, for having extinguished sedition, chastised rebellion, restored religion, secured justice, and established peace'. It was the work of a Flemish sculptor named Jacob Jongeling.

and platform were lined with officers, and the square was beset with troops.'[1]

Alva wore the sword and the jewelled hat presented him by the Pope as 'a helmet of righteousness' to encourage him in stamping out heresy; and he sat on the golden throne while the herald read the document, the true nature of which was brought home later to the people when the persecutions and executions continued with little perceptible decrease.

But they were not to continue for ever. Four years later Alva left the Netherlands, and from the conflicts with his successors the Dutch Republic gradually arose.

As noted in the last section, when Charles and Philip entered Antwerp in 1549 the triumphal arches were designed by Pieter Coeck van Aelst, who lives in art history as the master and father-in-law of Pieter Brueghel the Elder.

The extent to which Pieter Brueghel's work was a comment on the times has not, I think, been very generally observed. Brueghel was born at the village of that name about 1525. In 1553 he went to Italy and he then returned and settled in Antwerp. In 1563 he married Coeck's daughter and moved to Brussels, where he worked till he died in 1569. The pictures which won him his title of 'Peasant' Brueghel—such as the famous *Village Wedding* in Vienna—are everywhere recognized as one of the sources of the Dutch popular pictures which I shall presently discuss; and Sir Charles Holmes has suggested that his *Adoration of the Magi* in the National Gallery (painted in 1564 when the Netherlanders were on the verge of their outbreaks of two years later) shows a freedom and audacity in the treatment of the Magi and other attendant figures indicating 'a reaction not wholly unnatural from a religious observance too rigidly enforced'.[2] But Brueghel made many more daring comments than these in other pictures, some of which, thinly disguised as allegories or scriptural illustrations, are nothing less than tragic comments on the Spanish persecutions.

His *Road to Calvary* in the Vienna Gallery (Pl. 6) is a record of a procession of Titelmann's victims to the barren space outside the city where those condemned by his tribunal were broken on the wheel, strangled, burned alive, and hanged. The figure of Jesus, almost lost in the crowd in the middle distance, is conventionally

[1] Motley, *History of the Rise of the Dutch Republic.*
[2] *The National Gallery, The Netherlands, Germany and Spain,* by Sir Charles Holmes. (Bell.)

treated. So, too, are the holy figures in the foreground. But the rest of the picture is merely a record of a scene which the artist had witnessed dozens of times himself. The Spaniards ride on horses towards the place of execution, where a crowd has already collected in a circle waiting for the victims. The two crosses are already in position and a hole in the ground is being made for the third. On a hillock near by there is a double gallows on which a corpse, the victim of yesterday's procession, still swings (Pl. 5). A second gallows in the far distance is also furnished with its corpse; the crowd passes by a double row of wheels on high poles on which other victims will be exposed to-morrow. Jesus has just fallen beneath the cross. Some way behind, the Spanish soldiers seize Simon the Cyrenian, portrayed as an ordinary peasant, to help to bear the cross; Simon's wife, who, with her rosary at her waist, doubtless intended to go to market after the execution was over, was carrying a lamb and a pitcher; in her panic she has let both fall upon the ground, and she strives vigorously but vainly to rescue her husband while a soldier thrusts at her with a spear, and other peasants, fearing Simon's fate, take quickly to their heels (Pl. 7). The two thieves are seen bound in a cart, accompanied by priests who thrust the crucifixes into their hands and exhort them to repentance. Above, crows fly in the air, and in the background small boys make slides on the ice unperturbed by a scene which was of too frequent occurrence to arouse their interest.

In *The Numbering at Bethlehem*, in the Brussels Gallery, Brueghel describes the economic aspect of the Spanish persecution. The scene here takes place in winter on a village square; while children play in the snow and the Holy Family slips quietly away, the representative of Spain, seen through the window of a building which bears the arms of Charles V on the wall, is shown engaged in the census of the peasants, just as Brueghel had seen him many times assessing and collecting taxes and noting names and addresses; and at the back of the square a company of Spanish lancers is camped in readiness to enforce the civil officer's behests.

In the *Massacre of the Innocents* in the Vienna Gallery (Pl. 9) the Spanish lancers are drawn up on the square, and their leader is an old man with a white beard, possibly the terrible Alva himself. Here we see the children seized and slaughtered while the peasants on their knees in the snow entreat for mercy—as Brueghel had seen them entreat a hundred times. While this scene takes place in the snow-covered square, other soldiers, whose horses are tethered to the trees, make a house-to-house search and batter down the doors which offer resistance. Here only a pair of dogs are unconcerned and have the spirit to frolic together with waving tails.

In the engraving *Justice* all the horrors of the Spanish interpretation of the word are depicted. In the foreground a man stretched on a rack is suffering torture by water poured into his mouth through a funnel; his stomach is already swollen and a further pail stands ready at hand; at the same time he is being stretched on the rack while a man holds a lighted torch to be applied to his flesh. Behind him a man, cross in hand, is being beheaded; further back a man tied to a post is being flogged, while another is hanging in the air by his feet with his hands tied behind him; further back still a man is being burned alive; against the sky men hang on gallows and are trussed on wheels; within a building a man's right hand is being broken. While these operations are in progress judges in a court examine new prisoners or victims released for a moment from one of these ordeals. All the tortures and executions in this picture are represented as public 'shows' with crowds looking on, and in the scene of the *auto-da-fé* the crowd is kept in order by mounted guards.

In the *Triumph of Death* in the Prado, Madrid (Pl. 8), the death and devastation of the times are symbolized in a fantastic picture of mortals in combat with armies of skeletons—Death on a skeleton horse rides into a crowd of terrified peasants swinging his scythe; Death collects cartloads of victims, hangs them on gibbets, casts them into the sea; beneath solemn crosses, in the light of burning buildings and the great candles of the Inquisition processions, to the sound of the tolling of the dread Inquisition bell, every conceivable horror is depicted. No ghastlier indictment of a system has ever been set down by the hand of man. Travellers in Holland in the seventeenth century, E. Veryard, for example, remark with surprise that no bell tolled at Dutch funerals. When we look at Brueghel's picture we can understand the reason.

There must, I think, be some connexion between this picture of Brueghel's and Piero di Cosimo's *Triumph of Death* pageant for the Florentine carnival of 1511, which is thus described by Vasari:

'This particular device was the Car of Death secretly prepared by Piero in the Pope's Hall, so that nothing transpired until it was made public to all at the same time. It was a large car drawn by black buffaloes and painted with white death's heads and cross-bones. At the top of the car a gigantic Death held his scythe, while round the car were many tombs with their stones. When the car stopped, these opened, and figures clothed in black issued out, with the complete skeleton painted on their draperies, the white set off by the black. From a distance there appeared some of the torches with masks painted behind and before like skulls, including the throat, most realistic but a horrid and terrible sight. At the raucous, dead sound of some trumpets, they came half out of the tombs and, sitting on them, sang the following noble canzone to a music full of sadness:

> Dolor, pianto e penitenza, &c.

In front of and following the car were a great number of dead mounted on the leanest and boniest horses that could be found, with black trappings marked with white crosses. Each one had four footmen dressed as the dead, carrying black crosses and a great black standard with crosses, skulls and cross-bones. After the triumph they dragged ten black standards, and as they marched they sang the Miserere, a psalm of David, in unison, with trembling voices. This lugubrious spectacle, by its novelty and tremendous character, as I have said, at once terrified and amazed the whole city. Old people who saw this spectacle preserve a lively recollection of it and are never tired of talking about this curious invention. I have heard it said by Andrea di Cosimo, who helped him with this work, and by Andrea del Sarto, his pupil, who also had a share in it, that this invention was intended to signify the return to Florence of the house of the Medici, exiles at the time and practically dead. Thus they interpret the words:

> Morti siam, come vedete
> Cosi morti vedrem voi
> Fummo gia come voi sete
> Voi sarete come noi, &c.

The opinion was certainly entertained by many, and it was much discussed.'

It may well be that Piero's pageant, like Brueghel's pictures, was a secretly audacious satire on the times, covered up by the rumour circulated by his assistants, and that Piero had been influenced by Savonarola, who turned the carnival of 1497 into a holocaust of 'vanities'; and it seems to me possible that Brueghel, when he went to Italy, heard of this famous pageant or saw engravings of it, or even perhaps witnessed a repetition with some variations, since Piero's grim fancy is said to have entered the regular repertoire of carnival pageants.

Brueghel himself was certainly not uninfluenced by preachers; for his *St. John Preaching in the Wilderness*, of which versions exist in the Dresden and Vienna Galleries and other places (Pl. 10), is fundamentally a record of the open-air Protestant sermons in the Netherlands in 1566. The picture might be an illustration of Motley's account of these open-air meetings; the women are seated on the ground round the preacher, while the men, who carry such arms for protection as they can muster, stand and form an outer ring; but the historian has not given us Brueghel's characteristic touch of the small boys who have climbed the trees.

It is recorded that Brueghel destroyed a number of his works before his death in 1569, lest they should bring down trouble on the head of his wife and family. The precaution was surely a wise one. When we remember that Brueghel was painting these pictures just before and just after the arrival of Alva, it seems astonishing that he escaped molestation. In his last years he seems indeed to have become more prudent. In the celebrated *November*, in the Vienna Gallery, for example, where peasants drive their cattle up a slope, we have to regard the picture with great care before we notice the inevitable gallows with its corpse and the wheels on the high poles which the artist has placed on a low hillock far down in the valley. In his last picture we have the protest carefully disguised. Here a gallows is the centre of the composition; it has no corpse, but a magpie is perched upon it, and in the shadow of the emblem of oppression three peasants—two men and a woman—caper an uncouth dance.

Brueghel was not the only artist who thus recorded the impressions or the memories of the Spanish persecutions and the Netherlands revolt. Cornelis of Haarlem, who left his native town just after the siege, returned in 1583, and painted an *Auto-da-fé* and a *Massacre of the Innocents* (Pl. 11) where the slaughter takes place at the foot of a triumphal arch before the eyes of horsemen, one of whom has the white beard of Alva. Pieter Aartsen painted a *Road to Calvary* which anticipated some of the features of Brueghel's work and may have influenced it. St. John preaching in the Wilderness became moreover a favourite subject with Dutch artists of all kinds long after the reformed faith had churches of its own and was no longer banished to the fields. Cornelis of Haarlem painted a picture of this subject, which was engraved by Saenredam; Abraham Bloemaert of Utrecht painted several versions of it; so did Jan Molenaer of Haarlem; Adam Elsheimer, who had indirectly so much influence on Rembrandt, painted it in a picture in the Munich Gallery, and there is a picture of the subject in the Berlin Museum which is ascribed to Rembrandt. All the versions known to me seem to be based on Brueghel's, which may have been engraved and widely distributed in Protestant circles. Rembrandt, in his *St. John Preaching in the Wilderness* (Berlin, Kaiser-Friedrich Museum), characteristically abandons the wood for a strange wild place with the ruins of an amphitheatre and the bust of Caesar which occur in his *Christ Mocked* (Pl. 68), but he introduces Brueghel's boy perched aloft among the trees. In this connexion also it should be noted that in Rembrandt's *Entombment* in Dresden (Pl. 38) he shows the place of Crucifixion on a hill-top in the distance, and that the crosses, surrounded with wheels of torture, are silhouetted as in Brueghel's *Road to Calvary* against the sky. We must also remember that the French engraver Callot, who was in Holland in 1627 and was taken by Poelenburgh to see Bloemaert, engraved (and perhaps painted) a *St. John Preaching in the Wilderness* on the Brueghel-Dutch model, and that his grim plate *Les Supplices* is a protest analogous to Brueghel's *Justice*, which he doubtless knew.

To understand the Dutch rejection of pageant art we have thus but to realize that in 1609, when the Twelve Years' Truce was signed, there were still Dutchmen alive who remembered the Alva persecutions with horror, who looked on the continuation of pageantry in Antwerp and Brussels with contempt, and remembered the open-air sermons and the fury of the iconoclasts with pride. The Dutch 'Romanists' and the followers of Elsheimer were there to prepare the way for Rembrandt; the popular artists were there to produce a national Dutch art; but no Dutch artists had stomach to recall the group of naked girls who welcomed Charles V to Antwerp, the maidens who posed as Righteousness and Peace on the left and right of Alva when he proclaimed his mock amnesty, or the ships, dromedaries, elephants, whales, giants, and dragons which escorted the Archduke Ernest to hear the panegyric of John Baptist Houwaerts. The art of Raphael and the baroque masters the intellectual Dutch artists could try to apprehend; the art of the broadsheet they could develop and enjoy; but the art to which Rubens was faithful they rejected with memories of the Spanish domination which Dutch energy and Dutch Protestantism had buried in the past.

Part I
FOREIGN INFLUENCES

***

i. The Raphaelesque and Baroque Styles

Modern historians of Dutch art habitually ignore the Dutch seventeenth-century 'Romanists', as they were called in their day, and there is accordingly a widespread notion that Dutch art produced under foreign influences was stone-dead by 1600. But this notion is wrong. Of the Dutch Romanists Cornelis of Haarlem lived to 1636, Paul Moreelse to 1638, Abraham Bloemaert to 1651, Honthorst to 1656; when Cornelis died, Frans Hals was already over fifty; and Rembrandt was fifty and producing the works of his last period before Honthorst died. Dutch Romanism, moreover, was followed by Dutch picturesque art which likewise was the result of foreign influences. Of the Dutch picturesque painters Pynacker lived to 1673, Berchem to 1683, Gerard de Lairesse to 1711 and Van der Werff to 1722. When Rembrandt died Gerard de Lairesse was well on the way to a tremendous reputation, and when Vermeer died Berchem was still living. Dutch art under foreign influence was in fact produced in large quantities all through the century. The men who produced it were intellectual artists pursuing consciously held ideals of art; they were famous and they were patronized by people of taste and education; they all had numbers of pupils and followers and their works were regularly engraved and widely collected.

The prevailing habit of ignoring the whole of this aspect of Dutch art has its roots in an absurd prejudice which suggests that there is something disgraceful in art produced under influences from other lands. As a result of this prejudice Dutch art historians have not only exalted Dutch popular art at the expense of contemporary intellectual endeavour, but also omitted to mention what the Romanists contributed to the art of Rembrandt and what the Dutch picturesque painters contributed to the art of Vermeer. The French art historians have no such absurd prejudices. They do not ignore Poussin and Claude because they lived and worked in Rome and because, not being popular artists, their art was not national. Nor

Florence—Palazzo Medici—Riccardi   *Brogi Photo*

Plate 1. BENOZZO GOZZOLI: 'Lorenzo the Magnificent' (*detail*)

Plate 2. PETER PAUL RUBENS: Design for a Triumphal Car

Plate 3. CAREL DU JARDIN: 'Lady of the Court of Louis XIV as Diana in a Masque'

Carel du Jardin (born Amsterdam 1622, died Venice 1678) was a pupil of Nicholas Berchem

Plate 4. NICHOLAS BERCHEM: 'Allegory of the Growth of Amsterdam'

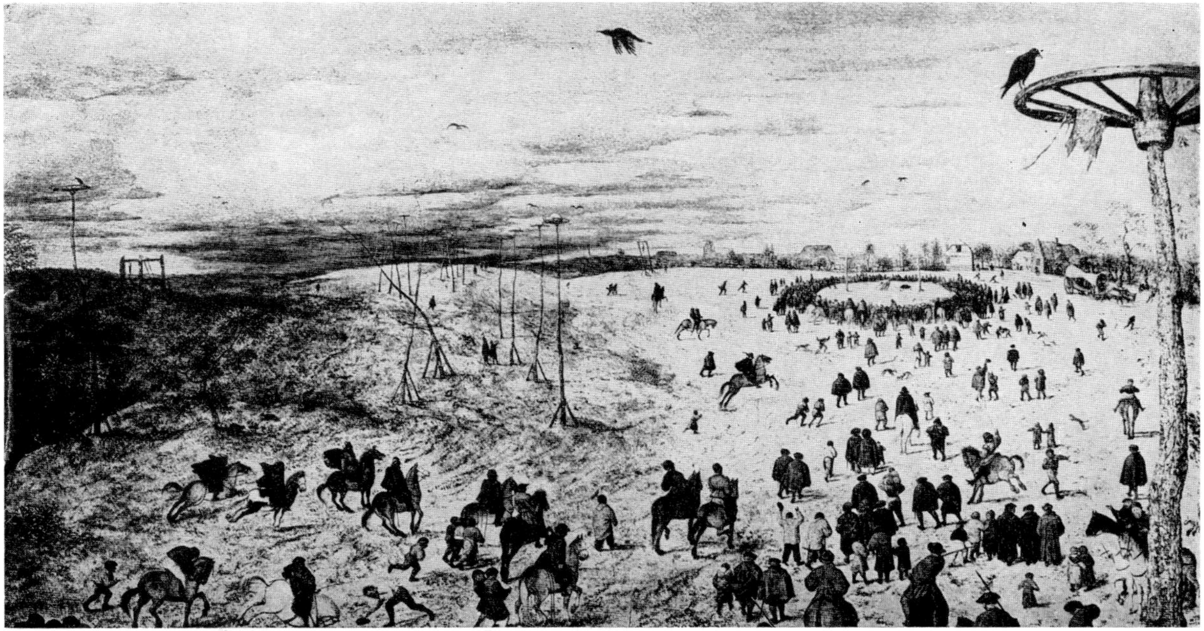

Vienna Gallery *Bruckmann Photo*

Plate 5. PIETER BRUEGHEL: 'The Road to Calvary' (*detail*)

Plate 6. PIETER BRUEGHEL: 'The Road to Calvary'

Plate 7. PIETER BRUEGHEL: 'The Road to Calvary' (*detail*)

Plate 8. Pieter Brueghel: 'The Triumph of Death'

Madrid—Prado

Anderson Photo

Plate 9. PIETER BRUEGHEL: 'The Massacre of the Innocents'

Plate 10. PIETER BRUEGHEL: 'St. John preaching in the Wilderness'

Plate 11. CORNELIS OF HAARLEM: 'The Massacre of the Innocents'

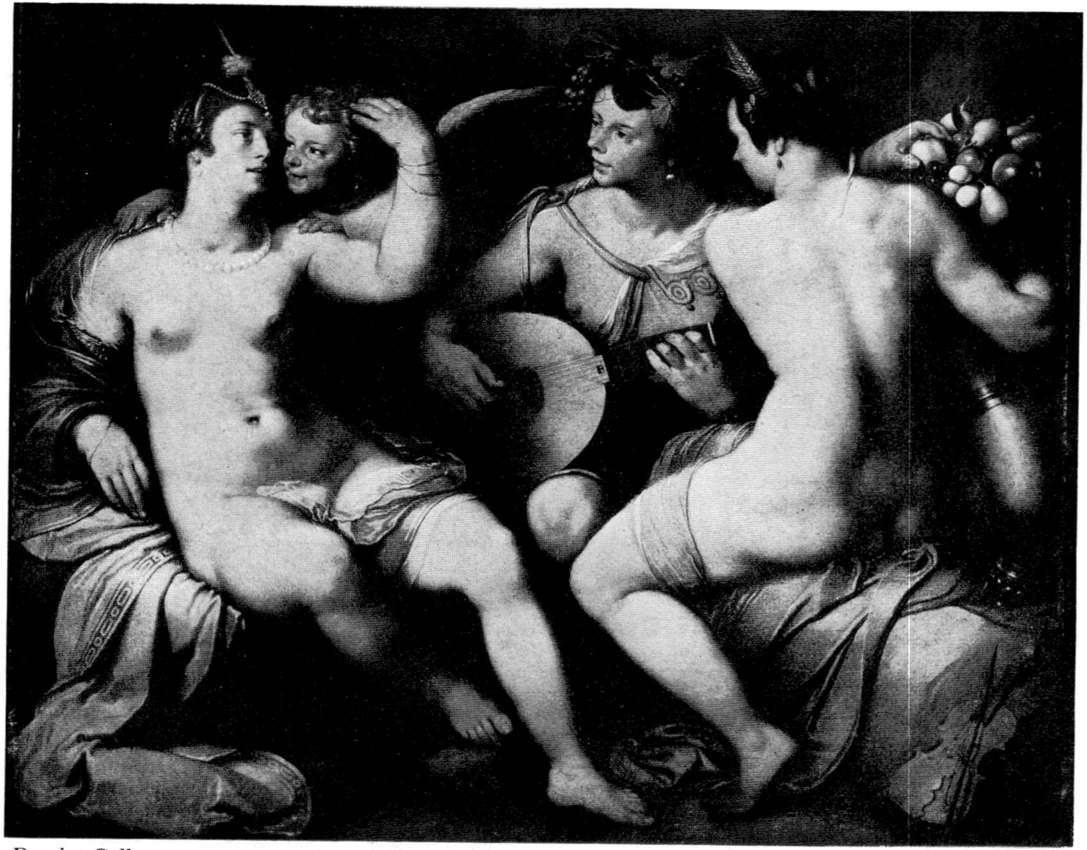

Dresden Gallery *Bruckmann Photo*

Plate 12. Cornelis of Haarlem: 'Bacchus and Ceres'

Plate 13. CORNELIS OF HAARLEM: 'The Golden Age'
(*Cf. Plates* 15, 17, 24, 28, 73, 75, 77, 78 *and* 79)

Plate 14. PAUL MOREELSE: 'Shepherdess'

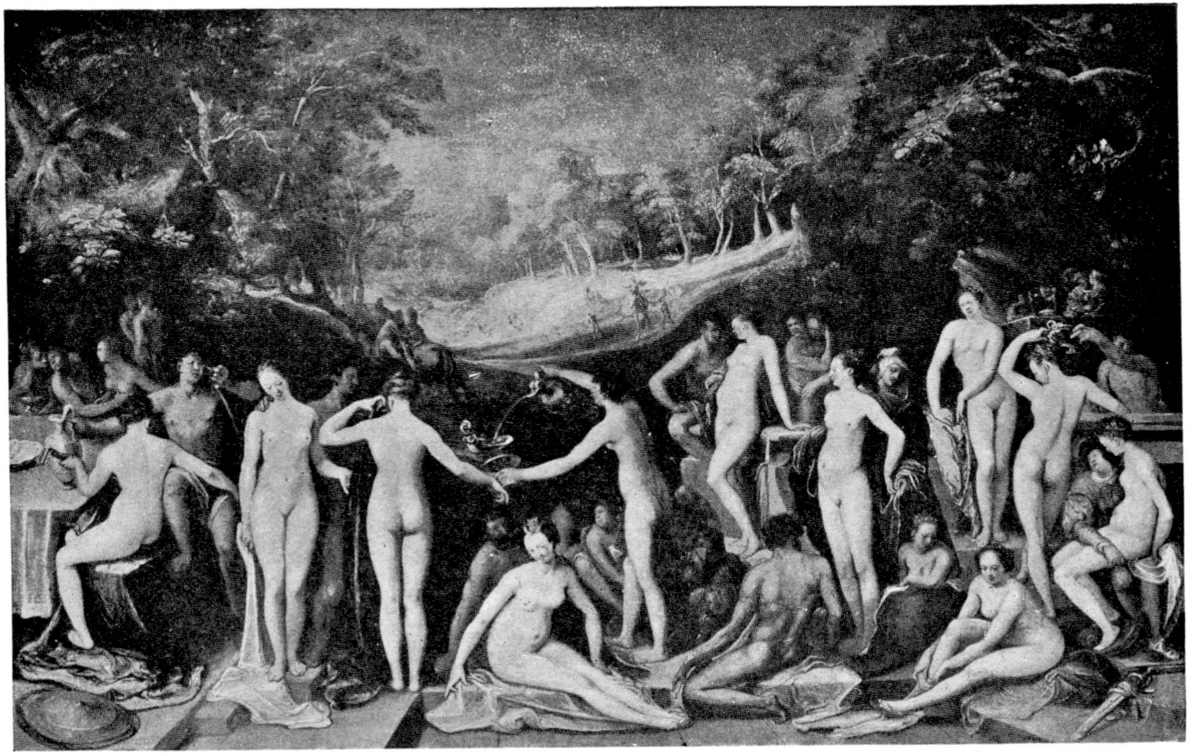

Leningrad—Hermitage *Bruckmann Photo*

Plate 15. Paul Moreelse: 'The Love Garden'

Plate 16. PAUL MOREELSE: 'Shepherdess'

indeed do English art historians ignore the Norwich school because it was based on Dutch painting, Gainsborough because he was influenced by Van Dyck, or Reynolds because, while exalting in his 'Discourses' the classical Roman masters, he tried secretly to combine the 'ornamental' style of Titian with Rembrandt's impasto and light and shade.

Most of the work of the Dutch Romanists is not of a kind to appeal strongly either to modern educated or uneducated taste. But its historical importance in relation to the art of Rembrandt cannot, I think, be overrated; and if only for that reason it should not, in my judgment, be ignored. The works of the Dutch picturesque painters are also not such as make a strong appeal at the moment. But they also, in my judgment, are worthy of far more study and appreciation than they now habitually receive.

The pageant art referred to in the Prologue was the art described by Reynolds in his 'Discourses' as 'ornamental'; and Reynolds drew a distinction between this ornamental art and the classical art of Raphael. This distinction must be borne in mind when considering the work of the Dutch artists who sought inspiration from classical Italian painting and made large compositions with nude figures. Also we must remember that the Dutch artists of the late sixteenth and early seventeenth centuries studied not only Italian Renaissance but also Italian Baroque art, and that Baroque art was exceedingly complex.

Italian influences on the art of the Netherlands began early in the fifteenth century when men like Rogier van der Weyden went to Italy. Jan Gossaert (Mabuse) and Bernard van Orley went to Rome quite early in the sixteenth century; Frans Floris, who was known as the 'Flemish Raphael', also went to Rome, and on his return he opened an art school in Antwerp in which problems of æsthetics were consciously studied and discussed. Jan Scorel, who was the master of Heemskerk and worked at Haarlem, Amsterdam, and Utrecht, visited not only Rome but also Venice where he saw the works of Giovanni Bellini, Giorgione, and some early works by Titian. Gilles Coignet, the master of Cornelis of Haarlem, who worked in Antwerp and Amsterdam, visited Rome and Naples, and copied pictures by Titian; and, as already noted, Martin Heemskerk, who died in 1574, drank wine in Rome to find inspiration for his paintings on Charles V's triumphal arch.

Italian production in the first period after Raphael's death in 1520 was staggered by the achievements of the great Renaissance masters. It was no easy matter to follow Leonardo, Michelangelo, and Raphael. The Venetian artists who developed pageant painting were at ease; but it was a harder task to follow the intellectual Renaissance masters because their work was difficult to understand. Michelangelo's achievements were taken to be no more than an affair of bulging biceps and large limbs; and Raphael from the outset was generally misunderstood because the easel pictures produced by Gianfrancesco Penni and Giulio Romano from his drawings and sent out from his studio with his name, and the large proportion of work done by these and other pupils on his frescoes in the Vatican, had caused much confusion from the start. The fine character of Raphael's real *œuvre* was as hard for his immediate successors to discover as it is to us to-day until we reduce the *œuvre* at present ascribed to him to works that were really by his hand[1]; and the Italian 'Raphaelesque' painters, while they successfully imitated the master's mannerisms, overlooked for the most part the basic architectural character of his work. It took the Italian artists, outside Venice, a full fifty years to work through the mannerisms of Michelangelo and of Raphael's assistants to the new conceptions to which we give the general title of 'Baroque'.

The Baroque conceptions were evolved to some extent in the celebrated Carracci art school at Bologna. The Bolognese 'eclectics' tried to work out a new kind of picture from the study of drawings by the Roman classical artists, the movement and colour of the Venetian pageant painters, the light and shade of Leonardo and Correggio, and various other elements in Renaissance art; these principles produced Guido Reni's *Hippomenes and Atlanta*, in the Naples Museum, where the pale limbs and flying draperies of the rapidly-moving figures form a rhythmic arabesque, and they also produced Domenichino's *Diana at the Pool* in the Casino Borghese in Rome.

In the Carracci art school the disastrous system of painting from the nude model in a life-class was established for the first time as the fundamental part of an artist's training; and one of the aims of this system was to achieve what I shall call baroque tactility, an ideal which entered Italian art from the Counter-Reformation of the Jesuits.

This is not the place for any detailed examination of the influence of the Jesuit Counter-Reformation on Italian and Spanish painting in the late sixteenth and in the seventeenth century. But I must

[1] A valuable attempt to do this has been made by Dr. Wanscher in *Raffaello Santi da Urbino: His Life and Work*. English Translation. Benn, 1926.

point out that the Jesuit concept of a propaganda art which would move the spectator to pity, terror and exaltation involved a presentation of the human body that would bring the spectator *right up* to the figures in the picture and make him feel that he could *touch* them; the Jesuits' aim was to induce the spectator to project himself into the situation of the holy figure, the saint, or martyr who was being crucified, burned, flayed, or tortured in the picture, so that the spectator could participate in the agony just as he was also intended to participate in the ecstatic joy of the angels and the blessed who floated above him on the painted ceilings of the new Jesuit churches. The system of drawing and painting from the nude in the Carracci life-school taught the students to use a thick impasto and effects of forced light and shade to achieve this quality of tactility which we find not only all over Italian baroque art—notably in Domenichino's *Communion of St. Jerome* in the Vatican and in paintings by Caravaggio and Ribera—but also in the Velasquez *Crucifixion* in Madrid, and in the works of Frans Hals, Honthorst and Rembrandt.

Italian post-Raphaelite art thus included:—(a) an attempt to rival the classic art of Raphael, (b) an eclectic attempt to evolve a new kind of picture and to develop it, and (c) an attempt to achieve the Jesuit ideal of tactility by the use of heavy impasto and vigorous light and shade; and all three developments had their influence on the artists of the North who visited Italy, or who were acquainted, through contact with paintings by the masters or through engravings, with the Italian efforts of their time.

We must further note that the Northern artists were also influenced by the *popular* continental art of the period which was disseminated largely in broadsheets and prints.

There has always everywhere been a popular art by the side of the work produced by artists engaged in more serious effort. Such art, generally descriptive, but often disguised as a moralistic art or as satire or as farce, aims at achieving contact with the spectator's familiar experience of everyday life. In Gothic times it crept into cathedral sculpture, where we find the months and seasons represented by peasants engaged in the appropriate agricultural pursuits, and where in odd corners we find coarse humour such as the most untutored peasant could enjoy. It crept into Gothic glass, where the guilds, when presenting windows, often inserted panels depicting the processes of their own trade; and it crept into the altarpieces, when the attendant figures in Nativities or Adorations are often crowds of *petits bourgeois* or peasants in contemporary clothes. In late

51

Gothic and early Renaissance times all the traditional forms of popular art continued to be produced in woodcuts and engravings, or in pictures intended to be reproduced on wood or copper, and, in the High Renaissance, popular art was more widely disseminated than ever before. In Gothic times the popular artists had been largely anonymous and obscure and their work was held of such small account that most of it has perished. But in the High Renaissance quite famous artists who painted and engraved sacred subjects, pageants, allegories and portraits of princes and eminent person-alities in prints that were collected by the rich, also produced paintings, popular woodcuts, and engravings showing peasants' festivals, scenes in taverns (discreetly labelled *The Prodigal Son*), or scenes in the public men's and women's baths (sometimes dis-guised as *The Fountain of Youth* or *The Golden Age*). They also pro-duced numerous pictures of an old man trying to seduce a young girl with offers of money, or of a procuress introducing a client, and so forth. All these characters appear not only in Dutch popular art of the seventeenth century but in the work of the Dutch 'Romanists' as well.

(a) CORNELIS OF HAARLEM
Born Haarlem 1562, died Haarlem 1636

CHARACTERISTIC PICTURES

Haarlem Gallery	*Civic Guard at a Banquet*
Haarlem Gallery	*Marriage of Peleus and Thetis*
Haarlem Gallery	*Auto-da-fé*
Haarlem Gallery	*The Haarlem Miracle*
Haarlem Gallery	*Christ Blessing Little Children*
Amsterdam Rijks Museum	*Adam and Eve*
The Hague—Mauritshuis	*The Massacre of the Innocents*
Brunswick Gallery	*The Flood*
Brunswick Gallery	*Venus and Adonis*
Budapest Gallery	*The Golden Age*
Kiev Gallery	*Diana and Callisto*
Wurzburg Gallery	*The Prodigal Son*
Berlin—Kaiser-Friedrich Museum	*Bathsheba*
Dresden Gallery	*Like unto Like*
Dresden Gallery	*Bacchus and Ceres*

Cornelis of Haarlem was born in Haarlem in 1562. He was eleven years old when Haarlem was besieged, and tradition has it that he was abandoned by his parents, who fled when the Spaniards entered, and that he was adopted and given his first lessons in drawing and painting by Pieter Aartsen the Younger, son of the Pieter Aartsen who painted the *Road to Calvary* anticipating Brueghel. Seven years after the siege Cornelis went to France, and it is recorded that he was at Rouen during an outbreak of the plague which drove him to Antwerp. In Antwerp he was attached to the studio of Gilles Coignet, who had travelled all over Italy and copied works by Titian. He returned to Haarlem in 1583, probably as a result of the 'French Fury' of the Duke of Anjou of that year; and he remained in Haarlem till he died in 1638.

Gilles Coignet was a Protestant, and when the Duke of Parma conquered Antwerp in 1585 he fled to Amsterdam. Cornelis was also a Protestant and, as already noted, when he returned to Haarlem he painted a number of protest pictures including *The Massacre of the Innocents*, with Alva in the background (Pl. 11), an *Auto-da-fé* and a *St. John Preaching in the Wilderness*. In Haarlem on his return at the age of thirty-one he was acclaimed as a master; and he held this position, amassing a considerable fortune, till he died. Hals painted his great Civic Guard groups of 1616, 1627 and 1633 in Haarlem in the lifetime of Cornelis, but he was never held in the same esteem as Cornelis, who from 1614 to 1619 was one of the Guardians of the Hospital for Old Men in which Hals was to end his days and of which Hals was destined at the age of eighty-four to paint another body of Guardians.

Immediately after his return to Haarlem, Cornelis was commissioned to paint a group picture, *Officers of the Civic Guard at Haarlem at a Banquet*, and this picture, produced when Hals was three years old, was a prototype for Hals's own groups at Haarlem. For *The Massacre of the Innocents*, together with the *The Haarlem Miracle*, Cornelis received 600 florins—a high fee in those days—from the Burgomasters. The subject of *The Haarlem Miracle* is a local legend, related as follows in the Haarlem Museum catalogue:—
'A nun of one of the Haarlem convents was accused of misconduct; a monk who was an expert in the knowledge of medicines undertook to examine her; he advocated as a test that, if the charge were correct, her breasts would be found to contain milk. Upon examination, however, fruit and wine were produced from them, which, being symbols of virgin purity, completely refuted the calumnious charge.' The *Auto-da-fé* was a commission from the St. Elizabeth Hospital, whose Guardians were painted by Hals in 1641. The *Christ Blessing Little Children* was a commission from the House of the Holy Ghost. The *Adam and Eve* was presented by the City of Haarlem to Prince Maurice of Orange, and it retained its honoured position over the fireplace in the Prinzenhof long after the artist's death.

FOREIGN INFLUENCES

Cornelis was closely associated with Carel van Mander and the celebrated engraver Hendrik Goltzius, and the three artists established an art school in Haarlem which was attended by numerous pupils including Frans Hals himself and Pieter Lastman, the master of Rembrandt. In this school, which was founded on the model of the Carracci school in Bologna, the students were grouped round a model in a life-class and attended lectures on æsthetics, as in Bologna. But the instruction was more 'old-fashioned' than in Bologna, because ideas in art travel slowly, and we have but to compare the Dutch-Italian pictures of the seventeenth century with those by Cornelis to realize that baroque principles and baroque tactility were still only partly apprehended in the North when this art school was founded. As was inevitable, when a dominant engraver like Goltzius was a director, the school stood for symbolic line as against the new system of statement by impasto and light and shade which was spreading everywhere. The Dutch professors lectured against the new tendency and talked to their students about Michelangelo and Raphael just as Reynolds did two hundred years later; but Cornelis —like Reynolds—did not practise what he preached, and he allowed baroque tactility painting, as the years passed, to creep into his work, as we can see in his *Bacchus and Ceres* (Pl. 12).

Van Mander was in Italy in 1573. Goltzius was there on more than one occasion. But Cornelis himself never saw the works of the Italian painters in the originals; he knew them exclusively from engravings; and in considering the development of Dutch-Italian art it is important to remember that engravings of pictures were then disseminated in just the same way that photographs of pictures are disseminated to-day; and that it was engravings of pictures rather than pictures which were held up as models to the students in the Cornelis-Goltzius-van-Mander art school and in the studios of all the art professors of the time. Thus several works by Cornelis were engraved by Goltzius, and Saenredam engraved his *St. John Preaching in the Wilderness* and his *Adam and Eve*.

In his purely 'Romanist' pictures, Cornelis made a real effort to capture the Raphaelesque style which had come to him through engravings. But in his later years he degenerated, and he seems to have been drawn to the subjects which crept into Renaissance art everywhere from popular broadsheets and so forth.

He was of course familiar with this type of production. He knew all the nude love-scenes by Goltzius and those engraved by the master of Goltzius, Philip Gallé, and by Jacob Matham who was the son-in-law and pupil of Goltzius. He must have known plates like

Saenredam's *Lot and his Daughters* after Goltzius, Jan Sadeler's *Intemperance* where Wine, Women and Song at a Renaissance banquet are depicted, the *Crapula et Lascivia* by Martin de Vos, and the public-bath scenes by Hans Beham and Aldegrever; and he may have known engravings after pictures like *The Love Feast* by Pieter Pourbus in the Wallace Collection, and after pictures showing the Prodigal Son in taverns by Hemessen, Joachim de Beuckelaer, and Pieter Aartsen whose son, as already noted, is said to have been his first master; and in his later works he shows a definite leaning to subjects in this borderland popular class.

The Dresden *Like unto Like*, where an old man offers a purse to a girl to induce her to leave the arms of a young man, and *The Prodigal Son* in Wurzburg, are examples of such works. The *Golden Age* (Pl. 13) is a sublimated Prodigal Son picture; and the *Bathsheba* in Berlin—also on the Prodigal Son model—shows a similar scene while an old man chalks up the reckoning on a slate— exactly as the tavern-keepers chalk it up in the avowed Dutch pictures of gay life by Dirck Hals, Buytewech and their school, and also in Metsu's picture, in the Dresden Gallery, usually called *The Painter and his Wife*.

Such was the end of this Dutch Romanist who never went to Rome, who painted Civic Guard pictures, Protestant protests, and popular scenes of gay life disguised as the art of Raphael, and who was esteemed by the Haarlemers far above Frans Hals.

(b) PAUL MOREELSE

Born Utrecht 1571, died Utrecht 1638

CHARACTERISTIC PICTURES

Edinburgh—Scottish National Gallery	*The Grecian Daughter*
Amsterdam—Rijks Museum	*The Pretty Shepherdess*
Amsterdam—Rijks Museum	*The Little Princess*
Amsterdam—Rijks Museum	*Civic Guard Group*
The Hague—Steengracht Collection	*Shepherdess*
Leyden Gallery	*Family Group*
Budapest Gallery	*Portrait of a Woman*
Berlin—Kaiser-Friedrich Museum	*Portrait of a Woman*
Leningrad—Hermitage	*The Love Garden*
Leningrad—Hermitage	*La Princesse de Rohan, Duchess de Chevreuse*
Rome—Corsini Palace	*Portrait of Man in high hat*

Paul Moreelse, the first real tactilist of the North, was born at

Utrecht in 1571; he worked most of his life in his native city; he visited Italy before 1604; as he lived till 1638 he was almost an exact contemporary of Cornelis of Haarlem and of Abraham Bloemaert in Utrecht, and he was also a contemporary of Frans Hals, Brouwer, and Mierevelt to whom he was attached as a pupil for a time in Delft.

His *Portrait of a Woman* in the Berlin Gallery, entirely in the style of Mierevelt, was clearly painted before his Italian tour; and I fancy that his *Love Garden* (Pl. 15)—in spite of the Italian grace of the figures—is also a sixteenth-century work done after studying engravings by Niccolo Nelli or some other Venetian engraver of the kind. The subject of the *Love Garden* is of the pseudo-classical lascivious order already discussed in connexion with Prodigal Son and Bacchanal pictures by Cornelis. But there is a great difference between the way Cornelis treated the subject and the way it is treated by Moreelse. The Haarlem painter was concerned with the subject as such and his Romanism was adapted to these ends. But Moreelse's picture reveals an artist for whom the subject is merely an excuse for the invention of an ingenious pictorial arabesque; with its pretty formula for the female nude it constitutes a link between Titian's *Diana and Callisto* at Bridgewater House and the art of Boucher and Falconet; and it even has elements foreshadowing the characters which preoccupied Cézanne in his compositions with nude figures.

In Italy Moreelse must have seen pictures by Titian—including the *Flora*—and also works by baroque tactilists; and when he returned to Utrecht he painted the *Shepherdess* (Pl. 14) and the similar picture, now in Amsterdam (Pl. 16), where the new tactility is seen. Both pictures show a feeling for pictorial form; there is nobility in the way the figures fill the canvas, and there is architectural grandeur in the disposition of the light; the student indeed will find it instructive to compare these pictures with Titian's *Flora* in the Uffizi, Bloemaert's *Shepherdess with Grapes* in Carlsruhe (Pl. 20), and Rembrandt's *Saskia as Flora* in the National Gallery. The same qualities, though not quite to the same degree, seem to be present in Moreelse's portrait *Princesse de Rohan*, in Leningrad, where the sitter has bare breasts and holds a Cupid in her arms.

Moreelse was mainly employed on portraits, and he painted many Dutch notabilities, including Coen. He was also an architect, and he designed the St. Catherine's Gate at Utrecht, which was not pulled down till 1845. He engraved and etched and printed plates in three colours. He was much esteemed in Utrecht, where he held various official positions, and in 1627 the Estates of Utrecht presented one of his pictures called *A Shepherdess* with another of his works to Princess Amalie de Solms on the occasion of her marriage to Prince Frederick Henry of Orange. He had a large school in which Dirck van Baburen was one of his pupils.

(c) DIRCK VAN BABUREN

Born 1570 (?), *died* 1624 (?)

CHARACTERISTIC PICTURES

Amsterdam—Rijks Museum	*The Procuress*
Cassel Gallery	*The Violinist*

Moreelse's pupil, Dirck van Baburen, painted *The Procuress* (Pl. 17), a version of the popular *entremetteuse* subject. This picture must have belonged to Vermeer of Delft and hung in his studio because it occurs on the wall in two of Vermeer's pictures: *The Lady seated at the Virginals* (Pl. 112) in the National Gallery and *The Concert* in the Gardner Collection in Boston; in the National Gallery the picture is shown in a gold frame; in the Boston picture it is shown in a black one. The use of this picture by Vermeer—which I have not seen noted in any comments on the National Gallery picture (though it is noted in the Rijks Museum's catalogue in connexion with Baburen's picture)—is at present Baburen's main title to fame. But he was highly thought of in Utrecht and he was employed by the Prince of Orange.

It is known that he went to Italy and was much impressed by Caravaggio; and it may be that some of the pictures now ascribed to Caravaggio's more celebrated disciple Gerard Honthorst (Gerardo della Notte) are really by his hand.

The dates of Dirck Baburen's birth and death are traditional, and they may arise from a confusion with another artist, Theodor Baburen, to whom they might apply. Dirck Baburen's name occurs in the list of Moreelse's pupils in 1611. We are thus asked to believe that he was still a student at the age of forty. This would be unlikely anywhere and quite impossible in Holland in the seventeenth century where students started their apprenticeship at thirteen or fourteen and were often established as independent artists before they were twenty. I suggest that Dirck Baburen was born about 1596, was apprenticed to Moreelse in 1611, that he was a more important artist than is commonly supposed, that he lived till at least 1650 and that he perhaps had contact with Vermeer.

FOREIGN INFLUENCES

(d) ABRAHAM BLOEMAERT

Born Gorcum 1564, died Utrecht 1651

CHARACTERISTIC PICTURES

Leamington—Gallery	*Return of the Prodigal*
Haarlem Museum	*The Message to the Shepherds*
The Hague—Mauritshuis	*Hippomenes Receiving the Prize*
The Hague—Mauritshuis	*Marriage of Peleus and Thetis*
Amsterdam—Rijks Museum	*Rest on the Flight*
Paris—Louvre	*The Nativity*
Paris—Louvre	*Man warming his hands by a Brazier*
Carlsruhe Gallery	*Shepherdess with Grapes*
Munich—Alte Pinakothek	*The Raising of Lazarus*
Utrecht—Central Museum	*The Adoration of the Magi*
Brunswick Gallery	*St. John Preaching in the Wilderness*
Schleissheim Gallery	*St. John Preaching in the Wilderness*
Lubeck Gallery	*Landscape with Cottage, a Tree, a Woman and a Goat*

Abraham Bloemaert was born at Gorcum in 1564. His father was Cornelis Bloemaert, a sculptor, architect, and engineer. As a result of political or religious difficulties Cornelis Bloemaert had to move from Gorcum to Bois-le-Duc and from Bois-le-Duc to Utrecht. Under his father's direction Abraham began his art training by the copying of drawings by Floris—a good 'Romanist' beginning—and later he worked with Hieronymus Francken, who was also a disciple of Floris. Like Cornelis of Haarlem he never went to Italy, but, again like Cornelis, he made one journey to France. For the rest he lived, worked and died in Utrecht.

Bloemaert had a great reputation in his lifetime; he held, in fact, much the same position in Utrecht that Cornelis held at Haarlem (for Moreelse, as noted, was mainly employed on portraits); and he was visited by Rubens, who made a special expedition for the purpose when he was in Holland in 1627. His *Hippomenes Receiving the Prize* was bought for the Château de Honselaersdijk, whence it was transferred, on the death of the Stadhouder William III, to the Château Het Loo, where it hung over the fireplace in the ante-chamber of the Princes of Orange; the Comte de Lippe commissioned a version of his *Marriage of Peleus and Thetis*; and the St. Elizabeth Hospital at Haarlem commissioned his *Message to the Shepherds*. His works were engraved by Matham and Saenredam, by his sons and many others.

It is difficult to-day to speak of Bloemaert's compositions with sympathy. The various versions that he painted of *St. John Preaching in the Wilderness* have not now the local and topical significance which was their main asset in Holland at the time; and his *Hippomenes Receiving the Prize* is a forerunner of the thousands of dreary and pretentious academic 'history' compositions which filled all the exhibitions of Europe in the nineteenth century. It is clear that Bloemaert was a victim of the then still relatively new habit of painting from the model posed in the studio instead of painting from drawings. His *Marriage of Peleus and Thetis* (Pl. 18), painted in 1638, contains two figures in the foreground—a nude woman and a half-nude man which are art-school studies and nothing more. Bloemaert in such works was but an eye-and-hand naturalist attempting to disguise his lack of pictorial imagination by imitating Italian compositions of which he failed to grasp the underlying principles.

But though he never understood the principles of Italian Renaissance or baroque design, he did master the technical procedures producing baroque tactility. His *Raising of Lazarus* contains a Lazarus based on Domenichino's *St. Jerome*, and in an old man's head twice repeated in the picture even the hair is massed in locks which, as the phrase goes, 'can be touched' and even lifted; and the same quality can be observed in his *Man warming his hands by a Brazier*.

His *Shepherdess with Grapes* (Pl. 20) is at first glance an attractive picture. It is related to Titian's *Flora* and Moreelse's shepherdesses and if it be compared with the works it resembles it will be found in some respects to hold its own; the rather masculine character of the hands, for example, makes the hands in Titian's *Flora* appear insipid, and there is something of Greek sculpture in the relation of the head to the fine full throat. But the picture falls short of the works by Titian and Moreelse because both Titian and Moreelse were able to achieve a unified vision all over the figures, to make them fill the canvas and to achieve an architectural ensemble. Bloemaert was unable to give his figure unified artistic form; the head and throat exhibit one conception of form, the shoulders and breasts another, the hands and the bowl of grapes a third, the drapery a fourth; the figure, moreover, does not fill the canvas, and the background, in lieu of architectural relation to the figure, contains descriptive details which have relation only to the title 'Shepherdess'.

Another tolerable picture by Bloemaert is the *Landscape with Cottage, a Tree, a Woman and a Goat* in the Lubeck Gallery. Here the artist was influenced by the school of Dutch-Italian picturesque painters whose works I shall discuss later, and as the picture was evidently painted from a drawing (which exists in a private collection in

London), it is free from the life-school atmosphere which depraves so much of his work.

Bloemaert taught the pernicious system of eye-and-hand painting from the posed model to a large number of pupils, including Terbruggen, Sandrart and Gerard Honthorst.

(e) GERARD HONTHORST

Born Utrecht 1590, died Utrecht 1656

CHARACTERISTIC PICTURES

London—National Gallery	St. Sebastian
London—National Gallery	Christ before Caiaphas
London—National Gallery	A Dutch Officer
London—National Portrait Gallery	George Villiers, 1st Duke of Buckingham, and family
London—Hampton Court	Allegory: The King and Queen of Bohemia
London—Hampton Court	Elizabeth, Queen of Bohemia
London—Hampton Court	Duke of Buckingham and family
Paris—Louvre	Pilate washing his Hands
The Hague—Mauritshuis	The Stadhouder Prince Frederick Henry with his wife Amelia of Solms
Dresden Gallery	The Dentist
Brunswick Gallery	Boy with Flute
Florence—Uffizi	The Fortune Teller
Florence—Uffizi	Adoration of the Shepherds
Florence—Uffizi	The Prodigal Son (Merry Party)
Florence—Uffizi	The Wedding Party
Rome—Borghese Gallery	Susanna and the Elders
Rome—Doria Gallery	Boy singing by Candlelight
Rome—Doria Gallery	Boy with head back singing by Candlelight
Rome—Doria Gallery	Girl catching a Flea in her Nightdress
Grenoble Gallery	The Supper at Emmaus

Till the National Gallery acquired Honthorst's *Christ before Caiaphas* (Pl. 23) in 1922 this artist was practically unknown to the general public in England, although the National Gallery already had his *A Dutch Officer* and the National Portrait Gallery had his portrait group *The 1st Duke of Buckingham and his family*. But when the *Christ before Caiaphas* was placed in the centre of a wall where it was seen by every visitor approaching the Dutch Rooms from the Italian Gallery, Honthorst became a famous 'old master' in England, especially as the subject of the picture is comprehensible to all, and both its size and its dramatic illumination combine to fix it in the memory. Since then the National Gallery has acquired a signed *St. Sebastian* (Pl. 22) and Honthorst's reputation here has still further increased. But even so, the extent of his prestige in his life-time and the influence of his work on his contemporaries are not generally realized.

As a native of Utrecht, Honthorst was naturally at first a pupil of Bloemaert, whose art school was then the most important in the city; and his training with Bloemaert can be seen in his drawings and in the art school figures of his *Susanna and the Elders*, which is probably an early work.[1] When he was about twenty (i.e. about 1610) he went to Rome, saw Raphael's *Liberation of St. Peter* (Pl. 21) in the Vatican and works by Caravaggio and then embarked on the exploitation of effects of concentrated or artificial light. A number of Italian baroque tactilists, known in their day as 'Tene-brosi', were influenced by Raphael's night-scene in the Vatican and by Caravaggio's development of spot-light effects; and Honthorst, who made a sensation in Rome with his first pictures in this manner and who was dubbed 'Gerardo della Notte' (Gerard of the Night) by the Italians, played a considerable part in the popularization of this style. In Rome he painted a *Beheading of St. John the Baptist*, where the scene was illumined by torch-light; and it was probably in Rome that he painted his *Christ before Caiaphas*, known to have been commissioned by Prince Giustiniani. In Rome, too, he painted *Scenes from the life of St. Paul* for the church of Santa Maria della Scala, which was built by Cardinal Scipio Borghese as a thank-offering for the gift he had received of the antique statue 'Hermaphro-dite' now in the Louvre. The success of these works was so great that Cardinal Spada commissioned a *Christ on the Mount of Olives* to be painted as a night effect, and Honthorst received many other commissions from Cardinals and princes, and found enthusiastic purchasers for small single figure candlelight studies like the *Boy singing by Candlelight* (Pl. 25) and the *Girl catching a Flea in her Nightdress*, both now in the Doria Gallery in Rome.

Caravaggio was among the Italian artists who painted the Prodigal Son drinking with women in a tavern, and Honthorst did the same. The three supper-parties of this sort in the Uffizi Gallery in Florence illumined by candlelight of which I reproduce one (Pl. 24) are characteristic of his personal contribution to this tradition. The

[1] Honthorst was obviously acquainted with Domenichino's picture of this subject (now in the Munich Gallery) or an engraving after it. In Domenichino's picture the water drips over the edge of the fountain and one of the Elders is pulling Susanna's drapery. The student should compare Honthorst's version of this subject with those by Domenichino, Lastman (Pl. 31), and Rembrandt (Pl. 35). Lastman must also have been acquainted with Domenichino's picture.

subject of *The Dentist* (Pl. 27) is in the same popular tradition, and Honthorst, as in his Prodigal Son pictures, has made the subject an excuse for a display of his favourite torchlight effect.

In 1622 Honthorst returned to Utrecht, and there he repeated his Italian successes and opened an art school where, in the time of Sandrart who wrote his life, he had over twenty-four pupils, all paying high fees. He seems to have been a man of good and accommodating manners. In Holland, as in Rome, he soon established relations in fashionable circles, and many of his pupils were amateurs of noble birth.

In 1627 he was visited by Rubens, and the year after he was invited to the English Court by Charles I. In London he planned some decorative pieces and painted *Charles I* and *Henrietta Maria*, and the portrait group *George Villiers, 1st Duke of Buckingham, and his family*. Charles I paid him £420 for the pictures painted to his command and settled on him a pension of £300 a year. Returning to Holland, Honthorst went to The Hague and took the portraits of Charles and Henrietta to Charles's sister, Queen Elizabeth of Bohemia, who had taken refuge in The Hague, where she held a miniature court after the defeat and flight of her husband Frederick V, Head of the Protestant Union of German Princes, in 1620.

Honthorst had been commissioned by Charles I to paint an allegorical group of the Queen of Bohemia and her family, and this picture, now at Hampton Court, was sent to England in 1630. At the same time the Queen of Bohemia's children, Princess Sophia, afterwards Electress of Hanover and mother of George I, and Prince Rupert, the Royalist hero of the Civil War, became his pupils. Prince Rupert is generally supposed to have been the inventor of mezzotint engraving, and it may well be that the process was evolved as a means of imitating Honthorst's 'night' effects.

Honthorst's success continued to his death. He painted a series of pictures for the King of Denmark, and he soon rivalled Mierevelt himself as a favourite painter of court and fashionable portraits in The Hague. When Mierevelt died in 1641 he became Court painter to the Princes of Orange and painted a number of pictures for the Honselaersdijck and Rijswick Palaces and for the House in the Wood, where the widow of Prince Frederick William—in defiance of the Dutch prejudice against pageant painting—had the walls of the Orange Salon entirely covered with flamboyant pictures in the manner of Rubens. In 1652 Honthorst retired to Utrecht, and he died there four years later.

In his later years Honthorst abandoned his torchlight effects, and imitated Van Dyck in many of his portraits; in so doing he revealed how much his art had relied upon violent chiaroscuro, and how tame and ill-composed it was without it. But his pictures with light effects play an important part in art history, because they contributed to Rembrandt's experience of pictorial light and shade.[1]

When Honthorst died at the age of sixty-six he was a very wealthy man. Hals at that time was seventy-six, Rembrandt was fifty; and they were both bankrupt.

ii. *The Elsheimer Influence*

In addition to the specifically Italian post-Raphaelite and baroque efforts in Italy there were yet others—the efforts made by the foreign artists resident in Rome. These efforts were of two kinds. The first was a romantic effort made by the German, Adam Elsheimer (1576–1610), and his circle, which, as far as Dutch art is concerned, culminated in Rembrandt. The second, a classical-architectural effort, was made in the picturesque art of Paul Bril (1554–1626), a Fleming, and of the Frenchmen, Claude Lorrain (1600–82) and Nicholas Poussin (1594–1665), which, as far as Dutch art is concerned, culminated in Vermeer of Delft.

As I have remarked in the Preface, only popular art is national, and we have seen how the Dutch-Romanists played their parts in the Italian baroque efforts to evolve a new kind of picture. In Germany and France, at the end of the sixteenth and the beginning of the seventeenth centuries, there were national productions of a popular kind; but the artists who felt impelled to more ambitious production turned inevitably in the same way as the Dutch to Italy, and many of them actually left their native countries and established themselves in Rome.

The foreign artists who lived in Italy had, of course, a great advantage over their countrymen who knew the Italian works only from engravings or from contact with native artists who had been there. Moreelse and Honthorst, for example, had an advantage over Cornelis and Bloemaert. The residents had an advantage also over

---

[1] Students of the torchlight tradition in seventeenth century art should take into account the work of the Frenchman Georges Dumesnil de la Tour, painter of *St. Sebastian mourned by Women* (Berlin, Kaiser-Friedrich Museum) and other notable pictures with such light effects. (*Cf.* my *French Painting*, Medici.)

artists like Moreelse and Honthorst, who were only in Italy for a short period and were frequently unable for that reason to acquire more than a tourist's knowledge of the art they had come to seek. The position of the intelligent foreigner living in Rome at this period was, indeed, much like that of the intelligent foreigner living in Paris in our own time. He was not only in contact with the living artists of the day who were attempting to enlarge their formal experience and to develop a new conception of pictorial space, not only in daily contact with the great achievements of the Italian Renaissance, but also while he was thus stimulated to rival the efforts of the present and the past, he enjoyed far more mental freedom than would have been possible at home where the claims of national popular art on the one hand, and of partly digested Italian art on the other, were bound continually to confuse him. I do not suggest that such conditions are essential to original production, but it does seem a fact of art history that the only original pictures painted by a German between 1570 and 1620 that are known, are those by Adam Elsheimer, who lived in Rome, and that the works by Claude and Poussin, who lived in the same city, are among the most eminent productions of the French mind.

I discuss later (in the section titled Picturesque Art, pp. 105–137) the influence of Claude and his circle on Dutch painting. Here I must consider the influence of Elsheimer and his circle. This has been much neglected till recent times by historians. But its importance in art history is very great, because Elsheimer was the master of Pieter Lastman and Jan Pynas, who in their turn were the masters of Rembrandt.

(a) ADAM ELSHEIMER

Born Frankfort 1578, died Rome 1610

CHARACTERISTIC PICTURES

London—National Gallery	*The Martyrdom of St. Lawrence*
London—National Gallery	*Tobias and the Angel*
London—National Gallery	*Shipwreck of St. Paul*
London—National Gallery	*Baptism of Christ*
Cambridge—FitzWilliam Museum	*Minerva, Patroness of the Arts and Sciences*
Cambridge—FitzWilliam Museum	*Latona converting Peasants into Frogs*
Cambridge—FitzWilliam Museum	*Venus and Cupid in a Landscape*
England—Methuen Collection	*The Death of Procris*
England—Elgin Collection	*The Liberation of St. Peter*
Paris—Louvre	*The Flight into Egypt*

Plate 17. DIRCK BABUREN: 'The Procuress'

Plate 18. ABRAHAM BLOEMAERT: 'Marriage of Peleus and Thetis'

Plate 19. HONTHORST OR BABUREN: 'The Concert'
(Cf. Plate 17)

Plate 20. ABRAHAM BLOEMAERT: 'Shepherdess with Grapes'
(*Cf. Plates* 14 *and* 16)

Plate 21. RAPHAEL: 'The Liberation of St. Peter'

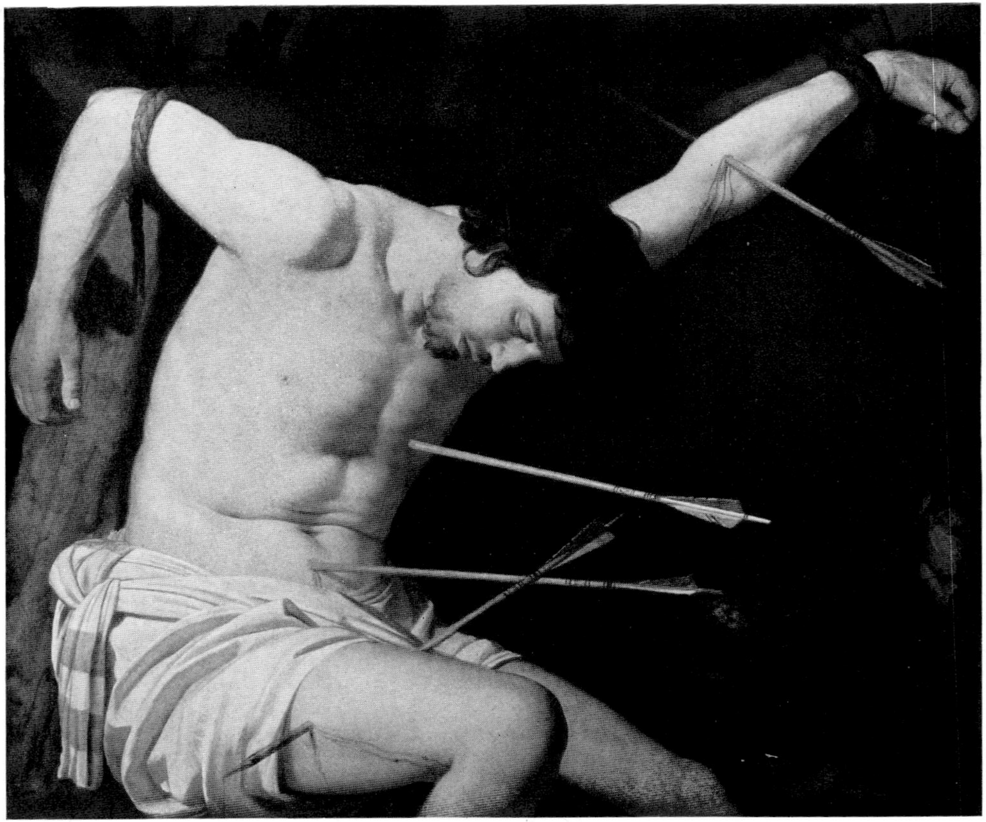

London—National Gallery

Plate 22. G. Honthorst: 'St. Sebastian'

Plate 23. G. HONTHORST: 'Christ before Caiaphas'

Plate 24. G. HONTHORST: 'The Prodigal Son'
(*Cf. Plates 13, 15, 17, 28, 73, 75, 77, 78 and 79*)

Plate 25. G. HONTHORST: 'Boy Singing by Candlelight'

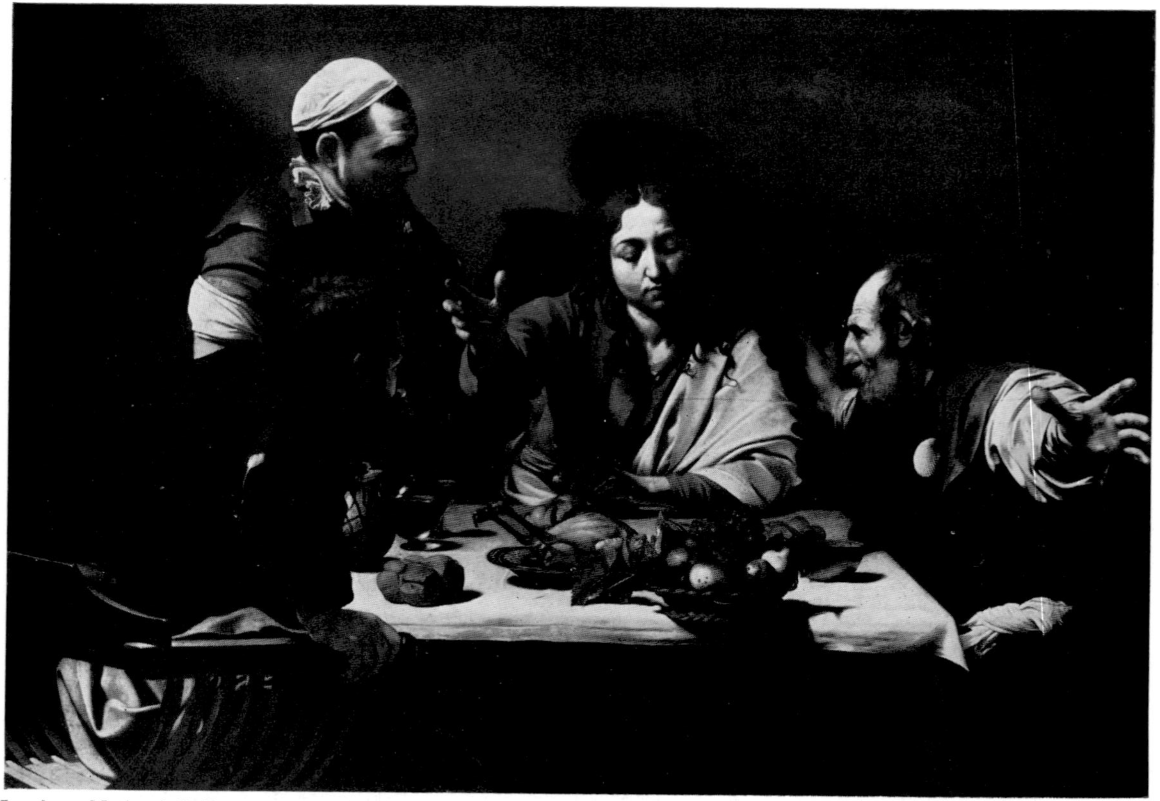

London—National Gallery *Hanfstaengl Photo*

Plate 26. Caravaggio: 'The Supper at Emmaus'

Plate 27. G. HONTHORST: 'The Dentist'
(*Cf. Plates* 70, 93 *and* 97)

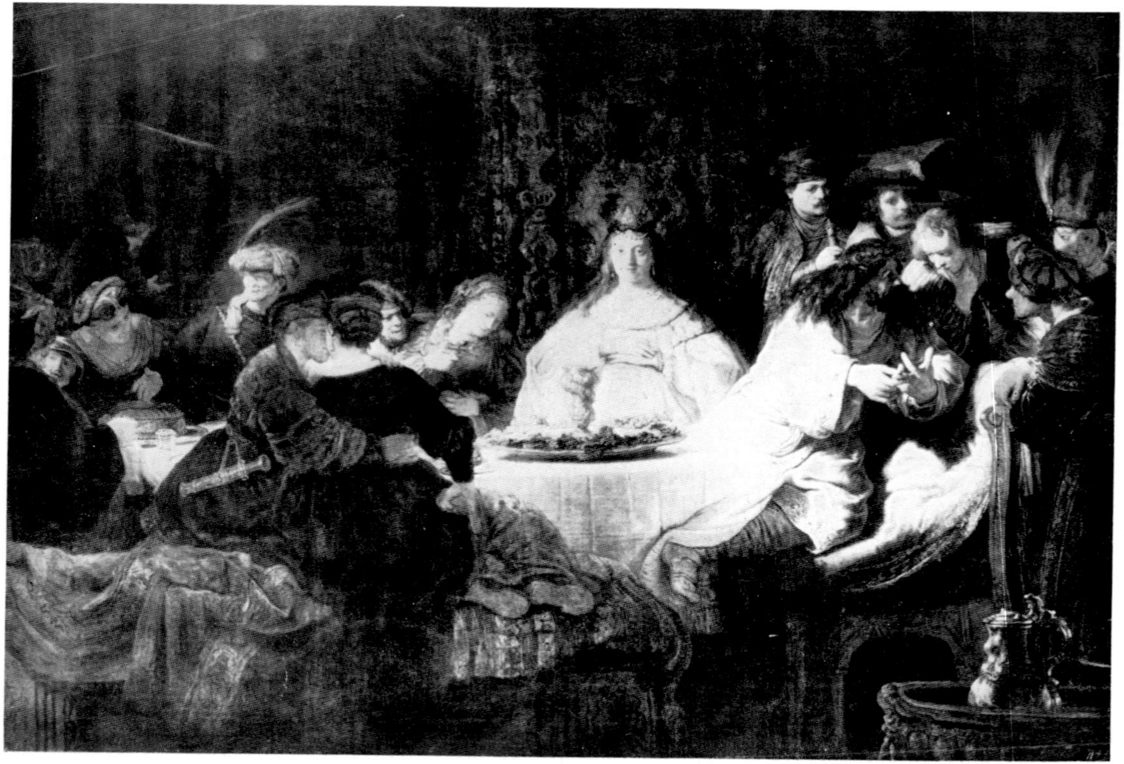

Dresden Gallery *Bruckmann Photo*

Plate 28. REMBRANDT: 'Samson's Wedding Feast'
(*Cf. Plates* 13, 15, 17, 24, 74, 75, 77, 78 *and* 79)

Plate 29. PIETER LASTMAN: 'The Raising of Lazarus'

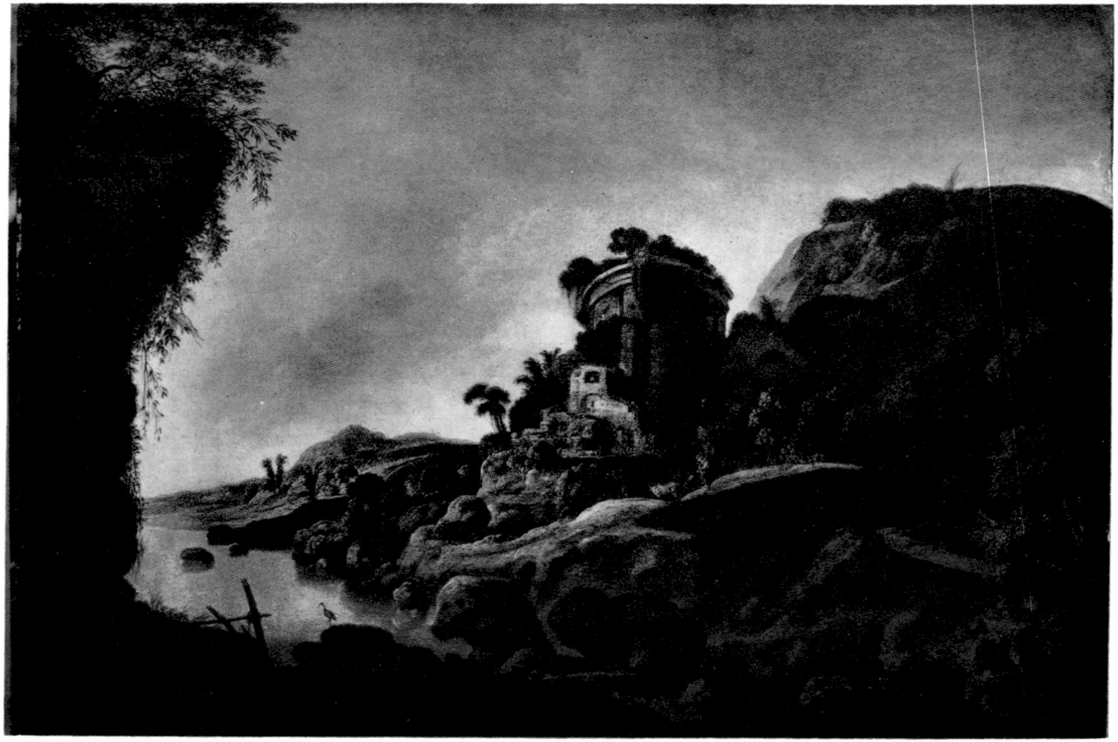

Brunswick Gallery *Bruckmann Photo*

Plate 30. ADAM ELSHEIMER: 'Mountain Landscape'

Berlin—Kaiser-Friedrich Museum

Plate 31. PIETER LASTMAN: 'Susanna and the Elders'
(Cf. Plates 22 and 35)

Plate 32. ADAM ELSHEIMER: 'The Flight into Egypt'
(*Cf. Plate* 33)

THE ELSHEIMER INFLUENCE

Munich—Alte Pinakothek	*The Flight into Egypt*
Munich—Alte Pinakothek	*St. John Preaching in the Wilderness*
Vienna Gallery	*The Flight into Egypt*
Brunswick Gallery	*Mountain Landscape*
Frankfort Gallery	*The Education of Bacchus*
Dresden Gallery	*Philemon and Baucis*
Naples Gallery	*Daedalus and Icarus* (four pictures)
Naples Gallery	*Ariadne Abandoned*

When Rubens heard of the death of Adam Elsheimer he wrote as follows:—

'Truly such a loss should plunge all our profession into deep mourning. It will not be easy to replace him, and in my opinion he can never be equalled in small figures, landscapes and many other things. He has died in the full course of his studies and his harvest was still growing, so that one could hope from him things which now will never be; destiny only showed him to the world.

'I have never felt my heart more torn with distress than when I heard this news, and I can never feel friendly towards those who have driven him to so miserable an end. I pray God to pardon Adam his sin of laziness, by which he has deprived the world of so many exquisite things, caused himself so many miseries, and reduced himself to despair; when he could have made for himself, with his own hands, so great a fortune and could have won the respect of the whole world.'

Elsheimer was born at Frankfort and is said to have been the son of a tailor. He was at first the pupil of one Philip Uffenbach, but before he was twenty he went to Venice and thence to Rome, where he settled. In Rome his personality was soon felt among the foreign artists, and he was also highly thought of by the Italian artists who came in contact with him. He received considerable prices for his pictures from collectors, and one of his patrons was the Count Hendrik Goudt of Utrecht who was studying art in Rome and who engraved a series of plates from his works.[1] For some reason, however, he became bankrupt in a few years and was imprisoned for debt; and his death at the age of thirty-two, shortly after his

---

[1] After the death of Elsheimer, Count Goudt returned to Utrecht. His engraving after Elsheimer's *Tobias and the Angel* in the National Gallery was etched by Hercules Seghers. Rembrandt acquired Seghers's plate and transformed it into his own etching *The Flight into Egypt*. Descamps relates that Count Goudt's memory was destroyed and his days shortened by an unfortunate accident: 'Une dame conçut tant d'amour pour lui qu'elle lui fit prendre un breuvage qui eut un effet contraire à ses désirs.'

E

release, is said to have been caused by a disease contracted in prison. He was presumably a Protestant, and he painted a *St. John Preaching in the Wilderness* to which I have referred in the Prologue (p. 46). He painted only small pictures, and they were mostly on copper.

By Rubens, who had a keen mind and who was sufficient of an art-historian to recognize the originality of Elsheimer's work, but who was essentially a man of action, Elsheimer's tragic debacle could be simply ascribed to laziness. But looking at the variety in the apparently small amount of work which Elsheimer produced in his short life, and the enlargements of experience which it represents, it seems more probable that he was not so much a lazy man as a man of thought rather than of action, a man driven more to ponder on the nature of art than to turn out pictures; and this character would, of course, not only account for his inability to cope with material affairs, but also for his position as the centre of an artistic circle where his influence was exerted as much by the spoken word as by the examples of his pictures.

Elsheimer's importance in art history has only recently been realized, and scholars are now working on his *œuvre*. Early biographers state that one of his pupils, Thomann von Hagelstein of Lindau, copied his style so closely that it was difficult to distinguish his works from those of his master, and Count Goudt is also said to have painted pictures in the Elsheimer manner in addition to his engravings. It is possible, therefore, that some of the works which stand to Elsheimer's credit—or are now being assigned to him by German scholars anxious to make the most of an opportunity to add to the short list of important German artists—are really by the hand of Hagelstein or Goudt or some other Elsheimer pupil or *pasticheur*. On the other hand, it is also possible that in the period of neglect between Rubens's day and our own, some of his pictures have been credited to more famous masters. It is impossible, for example, to dismiss the extremely close relation of the *Philemon and Baucis* in the Yerkes Collection, Philadelphia, now ascribed to Rembrandt, to Elsheimer's *Philemon and Baucis*, and though the Philadelphia picture would appear, from a photograph, to be looser in handling than was customary with Elsheimer, and may indeed be a work by Rembrandt or some member of his school who specialized in spotlight effects (van der Pluym, for instance), it may be that Elsheimer scholars will eventually find grounds for assigning it to the last period of Elsheimer's career.

It is not, however, likely that the Elsheimer *œuvre* will ever total a large number of pictures, because it is obvious from the records of his life and the short number of his working years that he actually produced only a few pictures, and because small pictures more easily disappear than large ones.

From the works now ascribed to him I have in mind three distinct types of production.

The first includes *St. John Preaching in the Wilderness*, which was based on an engraving of Brueghel's picture of the subject (Pl. 10) and *The Education of Bacchus*. In the first we have the preacher and his audience disposed in a shallow circle in the foreground; the wood in which the scene takes place is based on a large semicircle intersected by the bottom of the picture, the light is disposed on the foreground figures and on a mass of foliage in the front plane, and it forms a closing background behind the half-sphere of the wood. In *The Education of Bacchus* the proportion of the figures to the trees in the picture is much the same, but here we have the figures disposed in a small circle in the left foreground, a mass of trees in the centre, and left and right of the trees a vista into limitless space. In the genesis of these pictures, which I take to be early work, I suspect a contact with the Flemish artist Paul Bril, who was then at the height of his great reputation in Rome, and who probably introduced Elsheimer to engravings after his countryman Pieter Brueghel. Elsheimer's landscapes, in the pictures of this period, were evidently not painted from nature, but were put together, like those by Bril and all the picturesque landscape painters, from engravings, from their own drawings, and from recollections of the landscapes round Rome.

The second type of Elsheimer's production includes the series of pictures *Daedalus and Icarus* in the Naples Museum, which are tentatively ascribed to him, and the *Ariadne Abandoned* in the same gallery. These pictures suggest a contact with the works of Albani (1578–1660), who was in Rome at this time and painting small, picturesque pictures of the loves of Venus and Vulcan, Salmacis and Hermaphrodite, Apollo and Daphne, and so forth. In Elsheimer's pictures we have small nude figures of the Albani character, but they are set in a landscape in which there is a conception of space which differs alike from that of Albani and from that of Elsheimer's own earlier work. The tall trees and woods of the *St. John Preaching in the Wilderness* and the *Education of Bacchus* have now given place to a landscape that is all earth, water, and sky; the trees, seen from a distance, are disposed on the banks of estuaries or rivers, and the sky is not a closing backcloth but a symbol of sheer space. The landscapes suggest, in fact, that Elsheimer may have used for them some old sketches done before he left his native land. The qualities of these pictures appear to some extent in the work of Elsheimer's interesting pupil Cornelis van Poelenburgh (whose contribution I discuss later), and the attitudes of the figures in the *Daedalus and Icarus* picture, where the boy is about to start his flight from a hillock, evince a concept of the nude which is intimately related to the figures in Poelenburgh's *Women Bathing* (Pl. 59). Elsheimer was presumably painting these pictures at the time when Poelenburgh was his pupil, unless the figures in the Naples pictures were painted by Poelenburgh in Elsheimer's studio and the landscape by Elsheimer from his German sketches.

It is in the third group of works by Elsheimer, which I have in my mind, that the artist's important contributions to art occur. This group includes the *Mountain Landscape* (Pl. 30), the *Flight into Egypt* (Pl. 32) in Vienna, and the *Flight into Egypt* in Munich.

In the Brunswick picture Elsheimer painted a landscape which at the time was new in European art. It is a landscape which is essentially the record of the artist's reaction not to form, but to a mood; it is, perhaps, the first landscape in which all the constituent parts are deliberately stressed and distorted to express a sensation; it stands at the beginning of romantic landscape as we know it in the art of Rembrandt, and later in the art of the nineteenth century in France and England.

Also, we must observe that the characteristics of the early and the High Renaissance landscapes are absent from this picture. In landscape backgrounds by the Italian painters of the fifteenth century and before, the constituents were exquisitely observed and recorded and mutually related in clear structure; and since the essence of the classical mind is the architectural instinct, the sky was always of the nature of a painted backcloth—that is to say, a flat plane parallel with the imagined front plane of the picture. All the structure of an Italian Renaissance picture consisted in the disposition of elements between these two planes, and frequently side planes were added to complete, as it were, the stage 'set', or the imaginary box. In Elsheimer's *Mountain Landscape* the front plane is indicated by the line that runs from the bottom to the top of the picture on the left, but once the eye passes this point we are in a world of *undefined recession*; the sky is no longer a backcloth but a symbol for boundless space, the river which passes the tree-trunk on the left disappears into undefined distance and undefined direction, and all the sections of the earth structure indicated by the light converge towards this limitless recession. We find the beginning of this romantic feeling for infinite space in the Patinir landscapes in the National Gallery, and we find it, of course, also in the work of Leonardo da Vinci, whose scientific mind kept his romantic nostalgia in control. But Elsheimer goes much further in making the picture-structure serve as expression of a mood.

Elsheimer in fact has here symbolized his emotional reaction to the idea of remoteness in space, and with this reaction was bound up an emotional reaction to the idea of remoteness in time. In this work we see, not the clear coherent temple which a classical artist would have placed on the hill-top, but a crumbling overgrown ruin that spells an uncertain message from the past. This attitude of mind was the root of the later attitude of the artists of the nineteenth-century Romantic Movement who assumed that anything remote in time or space was *ipso facto* more emotive than anything near or present. It is for this reason that I have described the picture as the beginning of romantic landscape. For the student of Dutch art, moreover, this landscape by a German living in Rome, who died when Rembrandt was still a child, is of cardinal interest because it already speaks to us in the language which Rembrandt was about to develop and enrich.

The same interest attaches to Elsheimer's religious paintings. In the *Flight into Egypt* (Pl. 32) we have a compositional scheme resembling the *Education of Bacchus* in that there is a mass in the centre of the picture, and the eye travels into space on either side of it; but we are taken now into undefined light on one side and into undefined darkness on the other; or in other words we have here an attitude of mind reacting emotionally, not only to the idea of an escape from defined darkness into infinite light, but also to the idea of an escape from defined light into darkness and mystery.

The idea of depicting the *Flight into Egypt* as a night-scene was, I believe, in itself an innovation. As I have already noted, night-scenes and candlelight effects had appeared before in Italian art. There was, in the first place, Raphael's *Liberation of St. Peter* in the Vatican, and long before that there had been Simone Martini's fresco, in the Siena Palazzo Pubblico, of the condottiere Guidoriccio Ricci dei Fogliani riding across the country by night; and in Elsheimer's own day Caravaggio had developed spot-light effects —(Honthorst's candlelight pictures were later; he arrived in Rome about the year of Elsheimer's death). But both in Simone's picture and in that by Raphael the night effect is used in a purely decorative and architectural way, and the night sky in each case is the closing architectural backcloth, equivalent to the closing back-cloths of light sky in the ordinary Italian work; and both in Caravaggio's pictures and in those which Honthorst produced later, the torchlight effects are purely rhetorical tricks. In Elsheimer's picture we find for the first time a night effect used to symbolize a mood, and in this work—as original in its way as Brueghel's *Flight into Egypt*, where the Holy Family slips away from a crowded market-place in broad daylight—we find for the first time a concept of the scene which depicts the Holy Family leaving the warmth and comfort of a home and starting on a perilous night journey into undefined space beneath a starry sky.

Elsheimer's *Flight into Egypt* in Munich shows the same characters. But here the mood is different; for the Holy Family is here shown traversing a peaceful night landscape, with the moon reflected in the waters of a lake or river, and arriving at a place of temporary warmth and comfort where some shepherds have just made a wood fire in a sheltered corner of a wood; and this picture, like the Vienna *'Flight'*, was probably known to Rembrandt through engravings and exercised an influence upon his art.

Elsheimer's most distinguished pupils were Cornelis van Poelenburgh, who became an important picturesque master, Pieter Lastman and Jan Pynas, the immediate forerunners of Rembrandt (who was four years old when Elsheimer died) and Pieter van Laer, known as Bamboche.

(b) PIETER LASTMAN

Born Amsterdam 1583, died Amsterdam 1633

CHARACTERISTIC PICTURES

England—Leatham Collection	*Landscape with Mercury and Argus*
Dublin—Irish National Gallery	*Joseph selling corn in Egypt*
Paris—Louvre	*The Sacrifice of Abraham*
The Hague—Mauritshuis	*The Raising of Lazarus*
Amsterdam—Rijks Museum	*Orestes and Pylades*
Berlin—Kaiser-Friedrich Museum	*The Baptism of the Moor*
Berlin—Kaiser-Friedrich Museum	*Susanna and the Elders*
Brunswick Gallery	*Ulysses and Nausicaa*
Brunswick Gallery	*David in the Temple*
Brunswick Gallery	*The Massacre of the Innocents*
Carlsruhe Gallery	*The Baptism of the Moor*
Munich—Alte Pinakothek	*The Baptism of the Moor*

Pieter Lastman was the son of an Amsterdam jeweller. Cornelis of Haarlem is stated to have been his first master, and he is also said to have worked with one Gerrit-Pietersz Swelingh. At the age of twenty-one he went to Rome, and he was there for three years as a pupil of Elsheimer. He returned to Amsterdam in 1607, and had a career of uninterrupted success till he died at the age of fifty, when Rembrandt was twenty-seven. Rembrandt was his pupil in 1623, when Lastman was forty and Rembrandt himself seventeen.

The influence of Cornelis and the Dutch-Romanist school is apparent in many of Lastman's pictures; and this influence—to which we must add that of the chief Italian baroque artists—whose work he doubtless saw in Rome—was responsible for the rather dreary academic baroque pictures for which he was mainly famous in his day; and modern students will have the same lack of sympathy with his *David in the Temple* in Brunswick that they have for the more academic compositions by Cornelis and Bloemaert. But the very qualities which we find tiresome in these works to-day were the root of their success in official, artistic and literary circles at the time; and Lastman's *Orestes and Pylades* was celebrated in resounding verse by the Amsterdam poet Joachim Oudaen in 1657 (when Rembrandt was painting the great works of his later life), and his *Paul and Barnabas in Lystra* was celebrated in a poem by Joost Van der Vondel.

But there seems to have been a period in Lastman's career when these Dutch-Romanist and Italian baroque influences were overcome by or combined with the influence of Elsheimer. The pictures in my mind which represent this period are a small wooden panel *Landscape with Mercury and Argus* (where the rocky landscape is clearly derived from Elsheimer), the *Raising of Lazarus* (Pl. 29) which was painted the year before Rembrandt entered his studio, the *Susanna and the Elders* (Pl. 31), the *Massacre of the Innocents* in the Brunswick Gallery, and the *Baptism of the Moor* (Pl. 34). In all these pictures we see Lastman as a link between Elsheimer and Rembrandt.

In the *Raising of Lazarus* (Pl. 29) we see the background reft into an arched opening leading to infinite space, and if we draw a line down Lastman's picture from top to bottom, touching the left arm and hand of Jesus, and compare the composition of the left half of the picture with that of Rembrandt's *Entombment* (Pl. 38) in Dresden, we find the same semicircular sweep of the central group of figures from left to right, and we note that the sweep is repeated in the arched form enclosing the distant space. It would seem, moreover, that the drawings for Rembrandt's picture were made from some of the same models who sat to Lastman for his.

In Lastman's *Massacre of the Innocents* we have an animated scene in the foreground, an Italian building on the left, and on the

71

right, leading to undefined distance, a group of ruined towers and the romantic decaying architecture that comes from Elsheimer. More significant still is Lastman's *Susanna and the Elders* (Pl. 31), which shows Elsheimer recession, an Elsheimer romantic overgrown bridge, and a composition which is the obvious basis of Rembrandt's *Susanna and the Elders* (Pl. 35) in Berlin. There is also a close connexion between the art of Elsheimer on the one hand and that of Rembrandt on the other in Lastman's *Baptism of the Moor* (Pl. 34); and I cannot resist the suspicion that Rembrandt himself may have worked on this picture, which seems in some strange way to be imbued with his spirit.

(c) JAN PYNAS

Born Haarlem 1580, *died Amsterdam* 1631

CHARACTERISTIC PICTURES

The Hague—Mauritshuis	*Christ on the Cross*
Amsterdam—Rijks Museum	*Moses changing the Water into Blood*
Paris—Louvre	*The Entombment*
Aschaffenburg Gallery	*The Raising of Lazarus*
Philadelphia—Johnson Collection	*The Raising of Lazarus*

When Lastman went to Italy in 1604 he was accompanied by two brothers, Jacob and Jan Pynas, who also became pupils of Elsheimer. There is some confusion between the personalities of these two brothers. An old tradition has it that Rembrandt worked with Jacob. Hardly any pictures by this artist are known; the signed *Paul and Barnabas* in the Amsterdam Museum is probably his only certain painting; and Sir Robert Witt has a clearly signed and dated drawing *The Sacrifice of Isaac*, which should be studied in connexion with Rembrandt's pictures of the same subject in Leningrad and Munich. Rembrandt certainly knew both brothers, who established themselves in Amsterdam on their return from Rome; but modern scholars agree that it was Jan and not Jacob, with whom he worked when he left Lastman at the end of 1623.

Of the life of Jan Pynas, apart from his study with Elsheimer, scarcely anything is known. Six or eight of his pictures survive. From these it is clear that he learned as much from Elsheimer as Lastman did (though he selected other aspects of the German-Roman's art) and that he greatly influenced Rembrandt.

'Pynas,' says Sir Charles Holmes, 'deserves to be remembered as a painter upon whom Rembrandt really founded his own style in imaginative composition. The rich warm tone and dramatic massing of light and shade which we find in so many early works by Rembrandt had been used by Pynas twenty years earlier.' But Rembrandt got from Pynas something more than Elsheimer-Lastman motifs in composition. Pynas had perceived that one aspect of Elsheimer's originality was his treatment of the religious subjects without rhetorical emphasis of gesture. This treatment we find in the *Entombment* (Pl. 36) by Pynas, and in his *Raising of Lazarus* (Pl. 37) in the Johnson Collection, Philadelphia. Both pictures reveal an artist whose concept of a religious scene was simple and profound. As a psychological illustration the *Raising of Lazarus* almost rivals in realization and moving simplicity the finest concept by Rembrandt himself. The *Entombment*, moreover, is an ancestor in spirit of Rembrandt's Dresden *Entombment* (Pl. 38), just as Lastman's *Raising of Lazarus* (Pl. 29) is an ancestor of its composition.

It is also interesting to observe that in the year before Pynas died Rembrandt painted the *Raising of Lazarus*, Yerkes Collection, New York. Here we have a circle of figures based on the *Raising of Lazarus* by Pynas; the same compositional motif occurs in Rembrandt's etching of the subject dated twelve years later; and Rembrandt in his great 1654 etching of the *Entombment* retains the simple pathetic attitude of Mary in the Pynas *Entombment*. In Rembrandt's large etching of the *Raising of Lazarus*, however, which dates from 1631, the year Pynas died, there is more of Lastman's rhetoric than of the psychological concept of Pynas—for, as I shall point out later, it was not till his maturity that Rembrandt finally worked through the influences of Dutch Romanism and the Italian 'Grand Manner'.

The reader who has compared my reproductions of pictures by the Dutch-Romanists, by Elsheimer, and by the Elsheimer pupils who were Rembrandt's direct masters, with the reproductions of works by Rembrandt himself, will approach the study of Rembrandt's compositions with what I believe to be an essential preparation. But Rembrandt was not only a painter of imaginative compositions. He was also a portrait painter; and the study of his portraits cannot be approached without a previous appreciation of the great portrait painter who was more than twenty years his senior—Frans Hals.

Part II
FRANS HALS AND HIS SCHOOL

(a) FRANS HALS
Born Antwerp 1580–4, died Haarlem 1666

CHARACTERISTIC PICTURES

London—National Gallery	*Portrait of a Man*
London—National Gallery	*Portrait of a Stout Woman*
Cambridge—Fitzwilliam Museum	*Portrait of a Man*
Haarlem Gallery	*Archers of St. George* (1616)
Haarlem Gallery	*Archers of St. George* (1627)
Haarlem Gallery	*Archers of St. Adrian* (1627)
Haarlem Gallery	*Archers of St. Adrian* (1633)
Haarlem Gallery	*Archers of St. George* (1639)
Haarlem Hallery	*Guardians of St. Elizabeth Hospital*
Haarlem Gallery	*Women Guardians of the Old Men's Almshouses*
Haarlem Gallery	*Men Guardians of the Old Men's Almshouses*
The Hague—Mauritshuis	*Portraits of J. P. Olycan and his Wife Aletta Hanemans*
Amsterdam—Rijks Museum	*The Reael and Blaeuw Company*
Paris—Louvre	*La Bohémienne*
Paris—Louvre	*Portrait of Descartes*
Paris—Louvre	*Woman Standing*
Brussels Gallery	*Portrait of Jan Hoornebeek*
Berlin—Kaiser-Friedrich Museum	*Nurse and Child*
Berlin—Kaiser-Friedrich Museum	*Hille Bobbe*
U.S.A.—Taft Collection	*Man holding a bat*
South Africa (formerly Lane Collection)	*Young Woman*

The terrible siege of Haarlem by Alva's son Don Frederic began in December, 1572. Don Frederic expected to enter in a week; but the city, defended by women fighting side by side with men, held out for six months, and only surrendered after the starving inhabitants had devoured cats, dogs, and rats and the hides of horses and oxen. The Spaniards celebrated this victory by executing two thousand of the survivors and making an effigy of William of Orange which they carried in procession, broke upon the wheel and burned. When egress was again permitted, a burgher named Hals fled with his wife to start afresh in Antwerp.

But Antwerp, then still one of the richest and most magnificent cities of Europe, was about to suffer horrors as great as those of Haarlem. In 1576 the mutinous Spanish army sacked the city and plundered and murdered the citizens in the hideous orgy known as the 'Spanish Fury'. Hals's parents were there when this occurred; they were doubtless there also in 1583 when Antwerp suffered the 'French Fury' of the Duke of Anjou, and they were probably there in 1585 when the Duke of Parma besieged the city and conquered it in spite of the fireships which Gianibelli had made for the defenders, and which he was to make again three years later for the English in the fight with the Spanish Armada; and Frans Hals was born there at some date between the beginning of 1580 and the end of 1584.

Parma's conquest of Antwerp was a real one. From that date it was clear Antwerp would remain 'obedient', Catholic, and outside the new independent and Protestant Holland; and it was also clear that the city was ruined, since the Dutch were to boycott and destroy its trade. In the next ten or fifteen years there was a general exodus of Antwerp's most useful citizens to Amsterdam and the other Dutch cities which were now daily increasing in importance, and in that exodus Frans Hals's parents returned to their own Haarlem with their son.

The exact year of this return is uncertain. All we know is that in 1611 Frans Hals registered the birth of a son of his own in Haarlem, and that in 1616 he was already painting his first military group. A tradition has it that he was a pupil of Carel van Mander in Haarlem; another that he was a fellow-pupil with Rubens in the Antwerp studio of Adam van Noort. Both traditions are probably founded on fact, and the second explains that contact with the art of Rubens which appears in Hals's painting. Rubens was born in Westphalia in 1577 and came to Antwerp with his mother at the age of ten; at about sixteen he entered van Noort's studio, and at nineteen he left it to work with Otto van Veen who was then decorating churches and public buildings in Antwerp for the Spanish ruling circles and was about to design the triumphal arches for the entrance of the Archduke Albert and Philip's daughter Isabella. If Hals was born in 1580 and entered van Noort's studio when he was about fifteen, he would have found Rubens still at work there and it is reasonable to suppose that Rubens's talents would have made on him a deep impression; and he may have kept up the acquaintance when Rubens became assistant to van Veen. Rubens went to Italy in 1600, and it was probably shortly before 1600 that Hals returned with his parents to Haarlem, where he may have obtained work as a pupil and assistant of van

Mander according to the tradition. In Haarlem Hals remained for the rest of his life; and it is to Haarlem that the student must go to-day to form an adequate impression of his art.

Haarlem before the siege had been one of the largest and most prosperous towns in Holland. Nearly all the Dutch 'primitive' artists (whom we assimilate historically with the Flemish 'primitives') were associated with the town. Dirck Bouts, Ouwater, Geertgen tot Sint Jans, and their many associates all lived there at various times; in the first half of the sixteenth century it was the home of Jan Mostaert, and for some years of Jan Scorel. Martin Heemskerk, who worked there under Scorel, painted his *St. Luke painting the Virgin and Child* for the Guild's chapel in Haarlem Cathedral in 1532; after his voyage to Rome, where he was supplied so generously with liquor,[1] he was working there again when the siege threatened; being a poltroon, as various anecdotes testify, he slipped away, and while other Haarlemers were fighting and starving he was comfortably lodged in Amsterdam with a wealthy amateur pupil named Jacob Rauwaerts; and after the siege he returned to Haarlem where he died. Cornelis, as already noted, was in Haarlem during the siege; he went to France afterwards and returned in 1583. Carel van Mander fled from the persecutions at Courtrai in 1578, and took refuge at Haarlem; and after a visit to Flanders he returned there in 1583 and remained till 1603. Goltzius the engraver established himself at Haarlem in 1576, returned there after his travels in 1583, and lived there till he died in 1616.

At the beginning of the seventeenth century Haarlem grew steadily in wealth as its linen and mixed stuff trades and its tulip trade developed; it also profited by the draining of the Haarlem Lake—a feat providing about 15,000 acres of new arable land; and even before 1600 the town had recovered from the siege and was already prosperous enough to induce important artists to settle there.

I have already referred to the art academy founded in Haarlem by Cornelis, Goltzius and Carel van Mander in 1583. It was with the artistic theories of this academy that Hals had contact, either as a pupil or assistant-professor; and it is one of the oddities of art history that in his '*œuvre*', as we know it, there are no pictures reflecting this contact at an impressionable stage in his career. His first picture that we know of, a portrait of Johannes Bogaert (which survives only in an engraving), is dated 1614. If between 1598, or thereabouts, and 1614 he painted pictures influenced by the

[1] *Cf.* p. 36.

van Mander academy, they have all been lost or are ascribed to other hands.

It is often suggested that Hals with one kick of his topboot sent all foreign influences in Dutch art flying; but this, as I have already tried to indicate, is an error. The Dutch Romanists pursued their paths undeterred by his staggering performances, and the burghers of Haarlem continued to admire the works by Cornelis, who lived till Hals was fifty-six. Even as a portrait painter, though successful to a point, Hals was never really popular; he was never able to amass wealth by portrait painting as was done by Mierevelt and Ravesteyn, or to demand high prices like van der Helst.

When Hals appears on the scene of art history with his first Civic Guard Group, *Archers of St. George*, in 1616, Rembrandt was ten years old and Mierevelt and Ravesteyn were the leading portrait painters in Holland. Mierevelt (1567–1641), the favourite painter of the House of Orange, lived at Delft and painted sometimes also at The Hague. With the aid of his many pupils and assistants he produced an enormous number of portraits, the delicate character of which can be judged by his portraits of Dutch ladies in the Wallace Collection and the National Gallery. He painted all the most prominent Remonstrants. Like Reynolds, he kept careful records of his portrait commissions, and it is distressing to note therein that Sir Dudley Carleton, the British Ambassador who had commissioned a portrait of an English lady, left the country without paying for it. Ravesteyn (1572–1657) painted smooth and sober portraits of Dutch officers and notabilities; he worked at The Hague, and in 1616 and 1618 he painted groups of The Hague Civic Guards. These artists continued their careers undisturbed by competition from Hals, who never appears to have been invited to paint portraits either in Delft or The Hague, and who only painted one important group in Amsterdam.

Hals's most important works are the portrait groups of the Haarlem Civic Guards. Every town in Holland had Civic Guards, which were companies of amateur archers who met in the 'Doelen' to practise archery. From the end of the sixteenth century the Dutch armies which fought against Spain were composed of professional soldiers and hired adventurers; and the officers of the Civic Guards who foregathered in the 'Doelen' were scarcely more military than special constables or competitors at Bisley, and they were mainly concerned with shooting competitions, feasting, drinking, and swaggering about in handsome uniforms. In the reception-rooms attached to the 'Doelen' it had been the custom from the beginning of the sixteenth century to hang portrait groups of the officers of these Civic Guards of Archers, in much the same way that athletic clubs hang photographs of teams at the present day in England. The earliest Civic Guard picture preserved is, I believe, a group of heads and hands painted by Dirck Jacobsz in 1529 and now in the Amsterdam Rijks Museum. The same museum has a group of full-length archers painted by Cornelis Ketel in 1588; and when Hals received the commission for his first group in 1616 he had before him not only a number of early groups but also two recent groups painted in 1583 and 1599 respectively by Cornelis of Haarlem himself.

If we compare Hals's first group, *A Banquet of Officers of the Civic Guard of Archers of St. George*, with the 1583 group by Cornelis, we see that Hals invented nothing in the general conception of his picture. But there is a new vigour and style in the attack, derived, I think, from the artist's contact with Rubens, and there is a Flemish elegance in the figure of the standard-bearer which would not disgrace Van Dyck. Unfortunately this picture has been so deplorably restored that it is now impossible to imagine its original condition. Perhaps the heavy flesh tones, the smudgy hair, the shiny, toneless blacks and the lifeless landscape through the window were so when Hals signed the picture. Perhaps, on the other hand, Hals was already as magnificent a craftsman when he painted this work as he was when he painted his great group, *A Banquet of the Officers of the Civic Guard of Archers of St. Adrian*, in 1627. Which is the truth we shall now never know.[1]

Sir William Brereton, who travelled in Holland about 1630, describes a town when the Civic Guard were having a feast. Their flags, he says, were hung out in the street, and when they emerged from the banqueting-hall he could find 'scarce one sober man amongst them'; 'nor', he adds, 'was it safe for a sober man to trust himself among them; for they did shout, sing, roar, skip, leap, &c.' We know just how these men looked, and how Sir William felt, when we stand before the two superb groups which Hals painted in 1627; and it is interesting to remember that the Twelve Years' Truce between Holland and Spain ended in 1621, and that while Hals's swashbucklers were feasting, the Dutch had a number of serious

---

[1] There can be, of course, no valid objection in principle to the cleaning and restoring of old pictures. The National Gallery 'conditioning' proves how greatly the Louvre pictures stand in need of similar treatment. But the particular process adopted for the cleaning of the Hals pictures at Haarlem seems to me to have been disastrous. More of the Haarlem pictures may have been cleaned (and better cleaned) since I was there.

reverses. Thus in 1625 Justinus de Nassau surrendered Breda to the Marquis de Spinola, and Velasquez recorded the episode in the handsome pageant picture in the Prado.

The *St. Adrian Guard* group of 1627 had not been recently restored when I saw it, and unless it has been restored since, it is substantially, I imagine, as Hals painted it. The officers who compose the group have been for some time round the table; the glasses they finger have been filled and re-filled; the oysters in the dish are from the third hundred that have been opened; chairs have been pushed back, talk is waxing loud, there is much casual toasting, coarse jesting and loud laughter; soon man after man will begin to 'shout, sing, roar, skip and leap', and they will all reel forth in a body on the square. It would be with difficulty, one imagines, that a flash-light photographer could keep these feasters still for the instant required for his operation, but by some miracle Hals has achieved this business in a painted picture. And what a picture. How superbly painted. How magnificently pageant art has been converted to a new use in depicting gay silks, glittering glass, starched linen, sombrero hats, feathers, and healthy human flesh. Hals in this group, and others like it, provides the link between the pageant art of Rubens and the descriptive paintings that were about to swarm over Holland.

In the *St. George Guard* group (Pl. 39), painted in the same year, we have Hals at the very height of his powers. Nowhere has he, or any other artist, painted with more consummate virtuosity or 'shown off' with more astonishing success. Observe the glass turned down by the man in the foreground—the forerunner of thousands of such glasses painted later by the vast tribe of Dutch genre painters. Observe how, through the glass, we see part of the plate of oysters on to which another man is squeezing a lemon. Observe how bold and how delicate the painter's hand is; and if you are a painter, when you have once seen this passage you will never be able to forget it.

Observe, too, in this picture how Hals possessed the secret of baroque tactility; how he transports the spectator to within four feet of these half-drunk and gluttonous swashbucklers; how we have only to stretch out our hands to touch the yellow silk scarves, and the white collars, to feel the impact of these massive men and smell the food and drink. The Jesuit baroque artists set out to force the spectator by the tactile sense into a mood of horror and to project his mind into a condition of pain. Hals used his resources to force the spectator by the same means into a mood of gaiety and to project his mind into sympathy with animal heartiness and insensitive good cheer. No painter, not even Ribera in his flayed saints, or

Velasquez in *Los Borrachos* (which was painted in 1629), has ever excelled Hals in baroque tactility. This quality—which is often so revolting in the Jesuit painters who achieved it by a brutal impasto, and which is merely tedious when achieved as by Caravaggio and Honthorst with forced light and shade—is tolerable in Hals, because he combined great dash in handling with delicacy of observation and the power to orchestrate colour and light.

Hals's fourth picture in Haarlem, a *St. Adrian Guard* group, painted in 1633, seemed to me to have been ruined by restoration. His fifth, *Officers and Subalterns of the Civic Guard of St. George*, painted in 1639, had not been restored when I saw it, and it was in need of proper cleaning and revarnishing; but it was still possible to realize what a grand arrangement of colour it must have been when the salmon, yellow, and blue scarves across the black and buff uniforms sparkled and shimmered in their original brightness; and in *The Company of Captain Reael and Lieutenant Blaeuw*, one of the very few pictures which he was called upon to paint outside Haarlem, there are again some figures that are admirable in the same range of colour. Hals's pupil, Pieter Codde, is said to have collaborated in this picture. But only Hals could have painted the two standing figures on the left (Pl. 40). These are the qualities that make the Hals groups attractive to painters, although their architectural structure is casual and confused.

Hals's great period was from 1625 to 1640, from his forty-fifth to his sixtieth year; and it is to this period that most of his single portraits, and most of his studies of laughing children and of types from Haarlem low-life, belong. In his prime he seems to have had a good number of portrait commissions from the upper middle-class families of the neighbourhood, but his touch was too vigorous and his characterization too pronounced for material success in this field. His method might be acceptable to the swashbuckling archers, but it was too insistent for the archers' fathers who had all the pomposity of civic notabilities in a provincial town and who wished to be portrayed like 'potent, grave and reverend signiors' in the smooth style of Mierevelt or Ravesteyn with a dash of van Dyck; and when young Van der Helst of their town began to provide them with a version of Hals's art tempered with these ingredients, they made such a fuss of him that his head became turned and he went off to Amsterdam, where he soon became one of the most highly paid portrait painters of the day.[1]

[1] Van der Helst was born about 1612 in Haarlem and died in Amsterdam in 1670. His two most famous pictures, both in the Rijks Museum, are *The Meeting*

Plate 33. REMBRANDT: 'Abraham dismissing Hagar'
(Cf. Plates 65 and 99)

Plate 34. PIETER LASTMAN: 'The Baptism of the Moor'

Plate 35. REMBRANDT: 'Susanna and the Elders'

(*Cf. Plates 22 and 31*)

Paris—*Louvre*

Plate 36. JAN PYNAS: 'The Entombment'

(*Cf.* Plate 38)

Plate 37. JAN PYNAS: 'The Raising of Lazarus'

Plate 38. REMBRANDT: 'The Entombment'
(*Cf. Plate* 36)

Plate 39. FRANS HALS: 'A Banquet of Officers of the Civic
Guard of Archers of St. George' (*detail*)

Plate 40. F R A N S H A L S : 'The Reael and Blaeuw Company' (*details*)

Plate 41. FRANS HALS: 'La Bohémienne'

Plate 42. FRANS HALS: 'Woman Standing'

Plate 43. FRANS HALS: 'Hille Bobbe'

Plate 44. F RANS H ALS: 'Women Guardians of the Old Men's Almshouses'

Plate 45. FRANS HALS: 'Men Guardians of the Old Men's Almshouses'

Plate 46. JUDITH LEYSTER: 'Serenade'

Plate 47. JUDITH LEYSTER: 'The Merry Toper'

Plate 48. JUDITH LEYSTER: 'The Offer Refused'

FRANS HALS AND HIS SCHOOL

After about 1640 Hals seems to have had few commissions, and it was probably in that year that Van Dyck on his last journey to England called on him and vainly urged him to try his luck here. By 1652 Hals was bankrupt and his last years were spent in an almshouse where he painted his last two pictures, *Women Guardians of the Old Men's Almshouses* and *Men Guardians of the Old Men's Almshouses*.

The taste of the Haarlem burghers was not the only reason for Hals's lack of material success in later life. It seems certain that he was a heavy drinker. He was a member of the Haarlem Civic Guard of St. George, and took part in the riotous banquets he depicted, and between the banquets he spent a good deal of time in the taverns. All travellers in Holland at this time commented on the drunkenness prevailing in all classes. The poor drank to drive away care; the middle classes drank, in a damp climate with a long dark winter, to drive away rheumatism and to escape from homes where women who never washed their faces or bodies, cleaned and polished their houses till they were quite uninhabitable by any normal male; and the rich drank, as a fashionable gesture, to acquire energy for pleasure, and to dissipate superfluous cash. Even in this environment Hals seems to have been an exceptionally heavy drinker. When Van Dyck came to see him and sent word that a gentleman from Antwerp was in his studio and wished to have his portrait painted, tradition has it that he had to send three times before Hals could be induced to leave the tavern where he was drinking. In his youth and middle age Hals was able both to carry his liquor and to 'carry off' his habits, though these included such exceptionally severe beating of his wife that she had to summon him before the magistrate. But as old age approached there is no doubt that the victory was with the bottle, and it was not till his final period in the almshouse, where he was certainly rationed, that he was again able to do his gifts full justice.

In his portraits and 'types' painted between 1640 and 1660 there is thus a notable falling off. His touch becomes heavy and his colour becomes blackish or brown in the shadows. In his best period he constructs his figures with characteristic angular strokes applied with a square-tipped full brush and his touch suggests the action

of the Companies of Captain Bicker and Lieutenant Blaeuw before the Haan Brewery in 1643 and *The Archers' Banquet to celebrate the Peace of Munster* in 1648. Both are enormous and very able pictures. Of the latter Reynolds wrote: 'Perhaps this is the first picture of portraits in the world.' We may assume that van der Helst made visits to his native town to paint portraits after his translation to Amsterdam and that rich Haarlem burghers also went there to sit to him.

of a modeller cutting clay with a sharp tool. Later this touch becomes harsher and coarser and is almost a parody of the old incisive attack. The difference can be well seen if *La Bohémienne* (Pl. 41), the strong but subtle painting which dates from the middle period, be compared with the painting of the crazy woman with the owl called *Hille Bobbe* (Pl. 43), a later work where everything is harsh and coarse. This is one of the reasons why Hals cannot be judged until the great groups have been examined in Haarlem; for it is there that Hals the great colourist is seen; nor can Hals be finally assessed until his last two groups in Haarlem have also been studied.

For these two groups are extraordinary. Hals was over eighty when he painted them, using only white, yellow ochre, one red, charcoal black and perhaps a little blue or green—the only colours with which, tradition has it, the almshouse supplied him. Gone now is the full palette that yielded the delicious yellows, salmon pinks and azure blues for the archers' scarves. Gone, too, is the fire of youth in the artist. But the pictures nevertheless are intensely fascinating and among the artist's most important works.

The *Women Guardians of the Old Men's Almshouses* (Pl. 44) is the first of these two pictures. It has been suggested that this painting reveals the agony of an old artist whose hand will no longer obey his mind and eye; and it has been suggested, on the other hand, that the picture reveals a new sensitiveness in Hals's attitude. I cannot wholly agree with either view. As painting, the work is practically a monochrome. It is less vigorous than the works of the great period or even than the heavier paintings after 1640. The virtuosity, it is true, has gone; but it has been replaced by a sober handling that leaves nothing in itself to be desired. As for the 'new' sensitiveness, we must realize that the atmosphere of this picture is entirely different from that of the groups of Civic Guards; the old women's pathetic character is pathetically seen and painted; in seizing the atmosphere Hals was only doing what he had done before in his Guards groups, when he seized the atmosphere of the festive scenes before him—the oysters were as sensitively seen as the old women's hands, and the tired, desiccated faces of the old women are not more sensitively set down than the full-blooded faces of the feasters. The *Women Guardians* is an echo of his earlier art, but it is not in any sense a different song.

The *Men Guardians* group (Pl. 45) is an equally astonishing performance—though the blacks seem to me to have been ruined by restoration. Hals never painted a more expressive head than the drunken-eyed man in the crooked hat, and he never exhibited his delight in the handling of oil-paint more perfectly than in the painting of the inkstand and book, and in the stocking of the man in the right-hand corner—the last, an entrancing flash of red. Both groups in fact reveal the aged Hals as a man still able to respond to actuality and to express that response in paint.

There is a marked difference of handling between these last two pictures. The old women's heads and hands were underpainted with, probably, white and a little red; the upper surface was then painted by the direct method in a light key, and the heads were finished with a light glaze of black when the final black glazes were applied to the rest of the canvas. But the men's heads and hands were painted directly without underpainting, as though the artist knew that he might not live to complete the work if he carried it out in stages; and, as far as handling goes, it might be the masterpiece of Whistler's *œuvre*; for Hals at eighty-six forestalls the most precious of modern manipulators of oil paint.

In the later years of the last century, when the Impressionists and direct painters of the school of Manet were seeking for precedents, they habitually claimed Hals and Velasquez as their artistic antecedents. I have pointed out in *The Modern Movement in Art* that neither painter is properly so claimed. For Velasquez only used the direct method of painting *à premier coup* by the tone values in the large sketch known as *Las Meninas* (Pl. 127) and in a few smaller sketches; he never used it in any finished pictures. Hals, likewise, except in his very last picture, always underpainted with thick colour, as can be seen even in a spontaneous work like *La Bohémienne*, where the head was slashed in at one sitting with white mixed with a little red or yellow, and the final surface was applied later in thin, transparent paint. In the groups and portraits of the middle period Hals's overpainting, though thin, was frequently opaque, and for that reason it was mistaken by the Impressionists for *peinture à premier coup*.

It is customary to write Hals down as a superficial descriptive artist who copied the externals only and rendered nothing of his sitter's 'soul'.

But was Hals really superficial? It is true that he did not stress and comment on emotive fragments in the nineteenth-century and modern romantic way, and that he did not substitute a mental image for the image before him and use chiaroscuro to suggest mystery in the manner of Rembrandt. But he could realize the character of an atmosphere and the character of the sitter before him; and his records of externals are therefore records of atmosphere and character as well. When I sit before a man's portrait by Hals

I know as much about the man as I should know if I sat facing him for the same time in a train. Has any portrait painter ever recorded more 'fact' than this about a sitter?

Hals, in a word, was the great Dutch painter of actuality between Rembrandt the great Dutch romantic and Vermeer the Dutch master of architectural style.

(b) THE FRANS HALS PUPILS

Frans Hals's first wife, the one he thrashed so vigorously, died soon after the chastisement, and Hals then married a second wife, by whom he had, among other children, seven sons, who were all painters, and who must be reckoned among his pupils, although hardly any of their works are known. He also had a younger brother, Dirck Hals, who was probably at one time his pupil and who became the founder of the school of Dutch gay life popular painters which I shall discuss later.

When he was painting his Amsterdam group *The Reael and Blaeuw Company* (Pl. 40) he had Pieter Codde as his assistant; but Codde developed rather on the lines of his brother. The most distinguished of his pupils were Adriaen Brouwer, Adriaen van Ostade, H. G. Pot, and Jan Miense Molenaer, who all developed into individual artists whose works will be discussed. Hals also had a woman pupil named Judith Leyster, who was Jan Molenaer's wife, and who is now said to have been Rembrandt's mistress; and her place in art history as assigned by various scholars must be examined at this point.

(c) JUDITH LEYSTER

Born Haarlem or Zaandam 1600, died Heemstede 1660

CHARACTERISTIC PICTURES

The Hague—Mauritshuis	*The Offer Refused*
Amsterdam—Rijks Museum	*The Merry Toper*
Amsterdam—Rijks Museum	*The Serenade*

Judith Leyster's birthplace is uncertain. It is assumed that she was a pupil in Frans Hals's studio about 1630. She was received as a member of the St. Luke's painters' guild in Haarlem in 1633; in that year or in 1636 she married Jan Molenaer. In 1637 she was in Amsterdam; and in 1648 she moved from Amsterdam with her husband to Heemstede, where she died twelve years later.

The three pictures detailed above are signed with her monogram,

84

a joined J and L and a little star—a pun on her name which means 'pole-star'. This is all that is really known about her.

The Merry Toper (Pl. 47) and *The Serenade* (Pl. 46) show Judith Leyster as an imitator of Frans Hals. They stand to Hals's work in much the same relation that Berthe Morisot's work stands to Manet's. De Groot, indeed, held the opinion that Judith Leyster was a clever *pasticheuse* of Frans Hals and that a number of pictures ascribed doubtfully to Hals are really by her hand. It is, of course, also probable that she imitated her husband Molenaer and that some paintings ascribed to him are her work.

The following pictures among others have also been assigned to Judith Leyster by various students:

Hampton Court	*A Laughing Boy*
Dublin Gallery	*A Dutch Interior*
Lille Museum	*Woman Examining her Child's Hair*
Haarlem Museum	*Portrait of Vincent Laurens van der Vinne*
Carlsruhe Gallery	*A Laughing Youth with a Glass*
	(formerly ascribed to Honthorst)
Berlin—Kaiser-Friedrich Museum	*The Merry Toper*
	(formerly ascribed to Hals)
Stockholm Gallery	*The Serenade*

These attempts to reconstruct an *œuvre* for Judith from the lesser works of Hals and the works of Molenaer and other artists do not go far enough for Dr. Robert Dangers, who tells us that Molenaer was intolerably unfaithful, that he frequented low taverns and brothels, and that his wife, who had probably been in Amsterdam before her marriage, sought and found consolation in the society of Rembrandt, whom she helped with his pictures and by whom she became the mother of the boy represented in the picture known as *Titus as a Child* (Pl. 50) in the Cook Collection at Richmond.[1]

Such a relationship (says Dr. Dangers), a spiritual choice on both sides, would more than have compensated Rembrandt for the material misfortunes of his life. It can further be assumed that Rembrandt would have married Judith Leyster if she had not been married to Jan Molenaer a short while before or had not already been definitely engaged to him, just as Rembrandt, most probably, had plighted his troth, a short while before he met Judith Leyster, to Saskia.[2]

---

[1] *Die Rembrandt-Fälschungen.* Robert Dangers. (Goedel, Hanover.) 1928.

[2] Es wird für beide eine geistige Wahlverwandtschaft gewesen sein die Rembrandts äussere Missgeschicke des Lebens mehr als aufwog und ausglich. Es ist weiterhin anzunehmen, dass Rembrandt sich mit Judith Leyster vermählt hatte, wenn diese nicht kurz vorher sich mit Jan Molenaer verheiratet hatte oder

Dr. Dangers suggests on this hypothesis that the famous *Rembrandt and Saskia* (Pl. 49) was painted by Judith and that Rembrandt is toasting the painter ('trinkt seiner schönen Maler-Partnerin zu') while Saskia forces a smile to hide her jealousy.

Dr. Dangers further suggests that Judith collaborated with Rembrandt in, or painted entirely, the following (and twenty-two other) pictures in the Rembrandt *œuvre*:

The Hague—Mauritshuis	*Anatomy of Dr. Tulp*
Cassel Gallery	*Portrait of Rembrandt*
Cassel Gallery	*Landscape with Ruins*
Berlin—Kaiser-Friedrich Museum	*Susanna and the Elders* (Pl. 35)
Berlin—Kaiser-Friedrich Museum	*Tobias and the Angel*
Berlin—Kaiser-Friedrich Museum	*Portrait of Rembrandt*
Dresden Gallery	*The Rape of Ganymede*
Brunswick Gallery	*Portrait of Rembrandt*
Brunswick Gallery	*Family Group*
Hamburg Gallery	*Portrait of Maurits Huygens*

In all these cases, and many others, Dr. Dangers states that he has found traces of the Leyster monogram or found passages of repainting in the exact spots in the picture where Judith characteristically signed. These places include the background behind the head, the beard, and the hair on the forehead. In respect of the Cook picture of the little boy, whom he presumes to have been the fruit of Judith's relations with Rembrandt, he finds the monogram in the centre of the hair as it grows from the forehead, where 'the mother placed it for a sign upon his brow'.[1]

Dr. Dangers also finds traces of Judith's characteristic monogram in pictures by various other artists which he assigns to her. These include:

BY FRANS HALS

Cassel Gallery	*Two Singing Boys with a Mandoline*
Cassel Gallery	*The Jolly Toper*
Cassel Gallery	*Portraits of a Patrician and His Wife*
Berlin Gallery	*Boy Singing*
Berlin Gallery	*Portrait of a Young Woman*

BY DOU

Cassel Gallery	*Rembrandt's Father*
Cassel Gallery	*Rembrandt's Mother*
Berlin—Kaiser-Friedrich Museum	*Rembrandt's Mother*
Hanover Gallery	*A Negro*

BY VERMEER OF DELFT

Brunswick Gallery	*The Glass of Wine*

ihm nicht schon fest versprochen war, wie Rembrandt sich hochstwahrscheinlich, kurz vor dem Kennenlernen der Judith Leyster, an Saskia versprochen hätte.

[1] 'Die Mutter legte ihrem Sohne ihren Namen wie einen Segen auf die Stirne.'

Part III
REMBRANDT VAN RYN

Born Leyden 1606, *died Amsterdam* 1669

CHARACTERISTIC PICTURES

London—National Gallery	*Head of an Old Woman*
London—National Gallery	*Portrait of a Man with a Lace Collar*
London—National Gallery	*Self-Portrait at the age of Thirty-four*
London—National Gallery	*Christ before Pilate*
London—National Gallery	*Woman Bathing* (Pl. B)
London—National Gallery	*A Jewish Merchant*
London—National Gallery	*Self-Portrait at the age of fifty-four*
	(*Rembrandt as an old man*)
London—Ken Wood Gallery	*Self-Portrait at the age of fifty-seven*
	(*Rembrandt as an old man*)
London—Wallace Collection	*Jean Pellicorne and son*
London—Wallace Collection	*Wife of Pellicorne and daughter*
London—Wallace Collection	*The Artist's son Titus*
London—Crawford Collection	*Titus as a Schoolboy*
Paris—Louvre	*The Supper at Emmaus*
Paris—Louvre	*Bathsheba*
Paris—Louvre	*Flayed Ox*
The Hague—Mauritshuis	*The Anatomy Lesson of Professor Tulp*
The Hague—Mauritshuis	*Rembrandt's Brother*
The Hague—Mauritshuis	*Two Negroes*
The Hague—Mauritshuis	*David before Saul*
The Hague—Mauritshuis	*Homer*
Amsterdam—Six Collection	*Portrait of Jan Six*
Amsterdam—Rijks Museum	*The Night Watch*
Amsterdam—Rijks Museum	*Syndics of the Cloth Hall*
Amsterdam—Rijks Museum	*The Jewish Bride*
Berlin—Kaiser-Friedrich Museum	*Susanna and the Elders*
Berlin—Kaiser-Friedrich Museum	*Hendrickje Stoffels*
Dresden Gallery	*Saskia with the Red Flower*
Dresden Gallery	*The Entombment*
Leningrad—Hermitage	*The Return of the Prodigal*

i. The Rembrandt Œuvre

Hofstede de Groot gives Rembrandt six hundred and fifty pictures (his catalogue describes a thousand), three hundred etchings and two thousand drawings. To this he adds some seventy pictures (mentioned in old documents) which have disappeared, and another two thousand drawings which also have disappeared. Bode, Bredius and other Rembrandt students accept between six hundred and a thousand pictures; Mr. A. M. Hind's catalogue of Rembrandt's etchings accepts three hundred.

This output, though very considerable, was not a physical impossibility. Rembrandt lived to the age of sixty-three and some of the surviving works were painted when he was twenty or younger. In early and middle life he certainly worked hard and continuously, and even in his last period when, judging by his later self-portraits, he was drinking heavily, he probably painted and drew a great deal. It is, however, unlikely that the six hundred and fifty pictures ascribed to him were all painted entirely by his hand, (a) because he had no less than seventy known pupils whose works, while they were with him, were sold from his studio as 'Rembrandts' in accordance with the common practice in the period; (b) because these pupils in many cases painted in the Rembrandt manner all their lives, and their works are therefore often genuinely confused with those of the master; and (c) because, from Rembrandt's days to our own, dealers of low standing have often eliminated the signatures on works of Rembrandt's pupils and put that of Rembrandt in their place.

Professor J. van Dyke,[1] an American student who has examined what he calls the Rembrandt snowball, ascribes to Rembrandt himself something less than fifty paintings. All the rest he has divided among the pupils and followers, Maes, Bol, Backer, Barent Fabritius, Drost, Flinck, Eeckhout, Aert de Gelder, Salomon Koninck, van der Pluym, Horst, Lievens and so forth. He also suggests that the so-called self-portraits of Rembrandt—of which no less than sixty-four exist in galleries and private collections—are probably not portraits of Rembrandt at all, but portraits of his studio servant and favourite model, who posed for his pupils over a number of years, or alternatively that Rembrandt himself posed for his pupils[2]; and that the so-called 'Rembrandt's Father', 'Rembrandt's Mother', 'Rembrandt's Sister', 'Saskia' and the other alleged mem-

[1] *Rembrandt and His School*, by Professor John C. van Dyke. Charles Scribner's Sons, New York, 1923.

[2] The National Gallery has recently acquired a portrait of Rembrandt by his pupil Flinck. It has been cleaned and restored. Fifty or a hundred years ago this picture would not have been cleaned but revarnished with brown varnish, and with or without a forged signature it would have passed as a self-portrait by Rembrandt.

bers of Rembrandt's family who appear in dozens of pictures ascribed to Rembrandt, and also in pictures signed by his pupils, were also professional models who posed in the Rembrandt school.

In making his attributions Professor van Dyke shows a decided tendency to remove from the Rembrandt *œuvre* all the dramatic and rhetorical compositions, and the figure which emerges after this drastic procedure is undeniably one of singular dignity and simplicity. It is a Rembrandt whose work is purged of all bombast, romantic vagueness and Wardour Street frippery and melodrama, a Rembrandt who painted rather carefully in an even light and grey colour in his early years, and more richly and freely with much thumbing of the paint and elaborate treatment of light and shade in the later; a Rembrandt who was a great portrait painter, and an imaginative illustrator of the Bible, excelling in pathos and simplicity. Is Professor van Dyke's figure the real Rembrandt?

European Rembrandt students have refused to accept it. They admit that the American student has done much useful work and made perhaps a score of attributions which are probably correct. But yielding a picture here and there, they stand by the Rembrandt *œuvre* of six hundred or more pictures. For my own part, without pretending to special Rembrandt scholarship, I think that Professor van Dyke is substantially wrong and that de Groot, Bredius, and the others are substantially right, and this for a very simple reason—the existence in Amsterdam of *The Night Watch* (Pl. 51).

The pedigree of *The Night Watch* is known from the artist's studio; it was originally in the Kloveniers Doelen, and later in the Town Hall; and no one, not even Professor van Dyke himself, can doubt or dispute its authorship. This picture contains within itself all the qualities and defects, the complexities, the contradictions and the inequalities which occur all over the pictures which Professor van Dyke has been at such pains to remove. If we accept *The Night Watch*, as accept it we must, then there is no general case against the six hundred and fifty other pictures taken as a whole, though individual pictures, and perhaps many of them, will doubtless be assigned to various pupils from time to time, just as new pictures from time to time may be added to the *œuvre*; and the Rembrandt who stands before us is then not the simple figure created by Professor van Dyke, but the man who at the age of thirty-six painted *The Night Watch*, and only worked completely through its rhetoric in his middle age and final years.

The adjustment and readjustment of attributions within the larger Rembrandt *œuvre* is a matter of importance to dealers and collectors, because, as all the world knows, pictures confidently ascribed to Rembrandt himself are now enormously expensive, far more expensive than pictures by any of his pupils or followers. But outside these circles these adjustments of attribution are much less important. It matters little to the general student whether a dull or a weak picture in the Rembrandt *œuvre* was painted by Rembrandt when he was working beneath his higher levels or whether it was painted by a pupil; it would hardly matter even if a picture of the finest quality, a picture pre-eminently characteristic of the master's mind and hand, were to be proved the work of another man, because there are enough pedigree pictures to make it certain that the original achievement which we understand by the words 'the art of Rembrandt' was really his. That others may have compassed the same thing or something extremely like it under the master's influence does not make the master himself less notable or interesting, nor need it destroy the integrity of our conception of his art. The Rembrandt *œuvre* of approximately six hundred and fifty pictures, three hundred etchings and two thousand drawings—subdivide it as you will into periods and styles of the master, or into groups of works by various pupils—remains the record of Rembrandt's contribution to art; and that, taken as a whole, is what the general student wants to understand and appreciate.

ii. Rembrandt's Life

Rembrandt's father, a miller, sent him to the Latin School in the Leyden University in 1620 when he was fourteen years old. There Rembrandt learned about Andromeda, Flora, Diana, Sophonisba and so forth. But he did not pursue his studies in mythology and history very far. After a year or two he left and became the pupil of an artist named Jacob Isaacsz Van Swanenburgh—an obscure Dutch Italianist who painted views of buildings. After that he went to Amsterdam and became successively the pupil and assistant of Pieter Lastman and Jan Pynas, both pupils of Elsheimer. In 1626 he was back in Leyden, where he remained till 1631.

During this period in Leyden, Gerard Dou, who was his junior by seven years, worked with him as pupil and assistant from 1628, when Rembrandt was twenty-two and Dou fifteen, to 1631 when Rembrandt went to Amsterdam. The National Gallery has a picture which represents Rembrandt's style at this time—*Tobit and his Wife*, in which Dou is said to have collaborated. Other works ascribed to this period include a number of head studies of the models known as 'Rembrandt's Father' and 'Rembrandt's Mother', and some 'Philosophers' at work in their studies. Dou, a man of mean spirit and no brains, acquired a technical training in naturalistic painting and a grasp of the mechanical aspect of chiaroscuro effects from Rembrandt in these years; he painted studies of the same models, 'Rembrandt's Father' and 'Rembrandt's Mother', and then left to develop on this foundation a miniature art of his own, from which he made a fortune.

From 1631 Rembrandt lived in Amsterdam till he died. He probably visited other Dutch cities from time to time and he is said to have been in England about 1661.[1] When he was twenty-eight he married Saskia van Uylenburch, a bourgeoise from Friesland, who brought him a dowry of 40,000 gulden. Saskia was the mother of Titus, and she died the year following his birth, which was ten years after her marriage.

From his arrival in Amsterdam at the age of twenty-five to the death of Saskia in 1641, Rembrandt's fame steadily increased. In these years he had many commissions for portraits—though he was never so much sought after in this field as van der Helst or Santvoort. He also painted subject pictures which were admired and collected, and made etchings and drawings. Also he had many pupils at this time and his house was divided into rooms and compartments allotted to their use.

The *Jean Pellicorne and his son Gaspar* and the companion piece of Pellicorne's wife, both now in the Wallace Collection, are good examples of his portraits of this period. *The Anatomy Lesson of Professor Tulp* in The Hague was painted the year after his arrival in Amsterdam. The painting of groups of professors and surgeons— like the painting of the groups of the Civic Guards—was already a tradition in Holland. Mierevelt had painted a famous *Anatomy Lesson* for the hospital at Delft in 1617, and the Tulp picture was thus Rembrandt's first attempt at a life-size portrait group of a recognized kind. All critics, from Fromentin to the present day, agree that, compared with his later works, Rembrandt's *Anatomy Lesson of Professor Tulp* is a failure. In Mierevelt's picture all the doctors are grouped round the corpse, but they are frankly posing for their portraits. In Rembrandt's, two out of the seven doctors who listen to the

---

[1] This tradition rests on the uncorroborated statement of Marcellus Laroon (born The Hague, died Richmond 1702) to Vertue, quoted by Walpole, that Rembrandt was in Yorkshire, and lived sixteen or eighteen months at Hull, 'where he drew several gentlemen and seafaring persons', and that the painter Dahl had one of these pictures.

Professor's exposition look intently at the corpse, but the others and the Professor himself are posing, and there is thus a lack of unity in the concept at the start, because the picture is partly a portrait group and partly an illustration. The actual handling of the paint, moreover, in this picture is timid. Without Rembrandt's name it would hardly attract a second glance from the student familiar with the motif in other Dutch painters' works. But as the heads were doubtless recognizable likenesses, the picture at the time was a success, and to it Rembrandt possibly owed his introduction to Jan Six, because Professor Tulp was acquainted with the Six family and Jan Six later married his daughter.

Rembrandt himself was, probably, conscious of the mediocrity of this picture, and he doubtless regarded the Pellicorne portraits as works in which—since they were commissions—he had been too cautious to do himself justice. In *The Head of an Old Woman* and *The Head of a Man with a Lace Collar* (Philips Lucasz) in the National Gallery, both probably painted from people whom he had invited to sit, we see him pushing his study of the form of a human head much farther than he does in his commissions. The *Head of an Old Woman*, in particular, is relentlessly modelled; no picture that I know by Rembrandt has more actuality and baroque tactility; it is one of the most 'solid' oil paintings in existence. But it is mainly remarkable as a technical exercise; it contains scarcely any of the elements of Rembrandt's personal contribution to art.

The pictures painted at this time include subjects from the Old and New Testaments and the Apocrypha. *Samson's Wedding Feast* (Pl. 28), *Abraham dismissing Hagar* (Pl. 33), *The Angel leaving Tobias*, in the Louvre, and the Dresden *Entombment* (Pl. 38), show their general character.

Rembrandt had etched from the very beginning of his career. The plates ascribed to the Leyden period are mainly self-portraits and head-studies of his 'Father' and 'Mother' and other models; and the first Amsterdam period includes *The Descent from the Cross, Joseph's Coat brought to Jacob, Christ and the Woman of Samaria, The Stoning of Stephen, Christ Mocked* (Pl. 68), *The Return of the Prodigal, Abraham dismissing Hagar, The Death of the Virgin, The Presentation in the Temple* and the *Self-portrait* corresponding to the 1640 portrait in the National Gallery.

In 1641 Rembrandt painted *Saskia with a Red Flower*, the double portrait group *Anslo, the Preacher of the Mennonites, with his wife*, and *Anna Wymer*, the mother of Jan Six. The next year he painted *The Night Watch*, which marked the turn in his fortunes.

The Night Watch (Pl. 51), which was so called in derision after
the picture was delivered, was a Civic Guard group commissioned
by the Company of Captain Frans Banninck Cocq, and it was to be
paid for by the officers depicted. Rembrandt's first effort at a typical
Dutch social portrait group *The Anatomy Lesson of Professor Tulp*,
though it was not remarkable as a picture, had brought him material
success. His second, though remarkable as a picture, was a complete
failure with the sitters. Those who were depicted in shadow were
discontented, many were reluctant to pay their share, and one and
all found the picture confused, bewildering, and much too dark.
Frans Hals, though he had been too vigorous and truthful in depicting
the swashbuckling archers for older and more sober Dutch taste,
had delighted his sitters who were men of his own generation and
his own outlook on life. Rembrandt, with his romantic and dramatic
composition, made demands on the sitters' forbearance and imagination with which they were unable to comply.

After the material failure of *The Night Watch* Rembrandt seems
to have been in growing financial difficulties all his life. In Saskia's
day he made money fast and easily by his pictures, his portraits, and
his etchings, and also by his art school because his pupils paid him
a high rate for their apprenticeship. In those days he was extravagant.
He bought a house, jewels for Saskia and studio properties of all
kinds; and he collected pictures and engravings. After Saskia's
death (which took place in 1641 just before *The Night Watch* was
painted) he seems gradually to have lost touch with the moneyed
bourgeois world from which he had derived his commissions for
portraits—though his friendship with Jan Six, who was some years
his junior, continued all his life. Engrossed in his art, he became
ever more casual in material affairs, ever more at home in humble
company, and ever more and more in debt because he continued to
buy prints and bric-à-brac and pictures and was also drawn into the
prevailing habit of speculation. Saskia had left him her money in
trust for Titus, half to go to Titus if Rembrandt re-married. By
1647 Saskia's relations began to make official inquiries into Rembrandt's administration of the trust. In 1649 his housekeeper, Geertje
Dircz, a trumpeter's widow, whom he had engaged to look after
Titus, brought an action for breach of promise against him which
was unsuccessful. Her place in his house was taken by another
young woman of the people, Hendrickje Stoffels, who lived with him
till her death (about 1662), and who did her best to help him in his
financial difficulties in later years by establishing, with the aid of
Titus, a regular depot for the sale of his etchings. In 1656 another

guardian was officially appointed for Titus, and in the same year Rembrandt, who was then fifty, was declared bankrupt and all his collections and property were dispersed in a forced sale.

The general character of Rembrandt's work from the death of Saskia to the arrival of Hendrickje can be seen in the Munich *Adoration of the Shepherds*, and the same subject in the National Gallery, in *Susanna and the Elders* (Pl. 35), *The Supper at Emmaus*, *Rembrandt's Brother* (Pl. 56), and the *Jewish Merchant* in the National Gallery. The landscape called *The Mill*, now in the Widener Collection, Philadelphia, was also produced at this time.

A number of landscapes, including the *Three Trees*, occur in the etchings of this period, which also include *The Angel leaving Tobias*, the *Self-portrait by the Window, Jan Six by the Window, Anslo the Mennonite, Jan Asselyn*, the small *Raising of Lazarus* and the *Christ receiving Little Children*, known as the Hundred Guilder print.

When Hendrickje came to live in Rembrandt's house she sat to him for the nude *Bathsheba* in the Louvre and the *Woman Bathing* (Pl. B); and Rembrandt painted two portraits of her, the half-length in the Louvre, where she is wearing some of Saskia's jewels, and the half-length in Berlin (Pl. 52). Just before the bankruptcy Jan Six stepped in and commissioned him to paint the celebrated *Portrait of Jan Six*, and just after this Rembrandt painted *The Rabbi* in the National Gallery.

The etchings of this period include *Christ Preaching*, known as *La petite tombe*, the sketch portrait *Titus in a Cap*, the *Flight into Egypt, The Three Crosses, Christ presented to the People, Circumcision in the Stable*, the small *Holy Family crossing a Brook*, the *Christ between His Parents returning from the Temple*, also the 'dark manner' prints, the *Presentation in the Temple*, the *Descent from the Cross*, the *Entombment*, and the portraits *Jacob Haaring, Arnold Tholinx* and *Jan Lutma*, and a self-portrait *The Artist Etching*.

With the year 1659 we enter into Rembrandt's last period—the ten years before his death. It is a period both of triumph and degeneration. After his house was sold he lived in various humble quarters and became more and more of a recluse. He was always a singularly spare eater in a land of gluttons, but I am convinced, though there is no external evidence, that he drank heavily in the last years.

There is a notable difference in his appearance at this time from that in the earlier periods of his life. His self-portraits (paintings and etchings) depict him as a youth, slim, broad-nosed, small-eyed and curly-haired, and as a well-groomed man of early middle age in the period of his success. A self-portrait in Vienna painted about the time of his bankruptcy shows a man of fifty who has put on flesh, but whose face is temporarily drawn with anxiety, though he still holds his head up, still has a certain vanity in his clothes, and still fronts the world with searching eyes. The National Gallery portrait known as *Rembrandt as an Old Man*, painted when he was about fifty-four, shows a man who, as the phrase goes, has 'broken up' and gone physically to pieces. The nose has become bulbous, large pockets have formed beneath the eyes; the eyelids have begun to droop and the cheeks are no longer drawn, but fat, pendulous and swollen, and an old skull-cap replaces the stylish hat in the earlier works. In the Bridgwater House self-portrait we have once more the bulbous nose and here the forehead is terribly and deeply lined. In the Louvre portrait of 1660 the skull-cap has become a night-cap; in the Iveagh portrait at Ken Wood, painted when he was fifty-seven, the night-cap has become an old napkin tied round to keep out the draught; in the Uffizi portrait, painted the next year, the artist has clearly lost all his teeth, and in the last portrait of all, in the Carstanjen Collection in Berlin—a mask painted at one sitting—he leers and laughs in premature senility.

In the works of the last period there are no more etchings—mind and eyes can no longer concentrate on the minute handling of the needle; and there are scarcely any subject pictures, though the master's imagination, which is nearly spent, can still rise for a moment to a height in *The Return of the Prodigal* (Pl. 53). The main works of the period are self-portraits referred to above, the portrait of Hendrickje and one of their children known as *Venus and Amor*, in the Louvre, which shows that his faithful mistress had also put on flesh, the study of an old man known as *Homer* and the sketch of the *Two Negroes* (Pl. 54). All these pictures were painted in the studio; they involved no contact with the outside world. The same applies to the superb work known as *The Jewish Bride* (Plate 55) depicting some friend and his young wife in 1668, and to the last picture of all, the portrait group in the Brunswick Gallery, which also probably depicts some friend with his wife and children, and was presumably left unfinished at his death. In the last years Rembrandt must have lived almost entirely by the sale of prints from his etchings, for once only did he receive an important commission in these years—the 1661 commission, which Jan Six doubtless procured for him, to paint *The Syndics of the Cloth Hall* in Amsterdam.

When the end came, it was thus recorded in the Doelboek of the Westerkerk: 'Tuesday October 8th 1669, Rembrandt van Rijn, painter, on the Rozengracht opposite the Doolhof. Leaves two children.'

REMBRANDT VAN RYN

I have two images of Rembrandt in my mind.

In the first I see him in the days of his prosperity, well dressed, assured, standing in his reception-studio hung with Italian pictures and littered with carpets, helmets, jewels and bric-à-brac of all sorts; his most recent portraits are disposed on easels: pictures painted by his own hand, and others painted by his pupils from his designs and under his direction and signed with his name are also on view. Portfolios of etchings stand about on chairs. Rembrandt adjusts a picture more favourably to the light and rubs some oil on a dull spot on another. The bell rings; an Amsterdam merchant or civic dignitary comes in; he inquires the price for a portrait and I hear Rembrandt bargaining—for Descamps, quoting the old biographers, describes him as notoriously avaricious. The visitor asks why the subject pictures are so gloomy and Rembrandt makes some fantastic and cynical reply that is in no sense an answer; the burgher offers to buy a picture with a certain alteration but Rembrandt haughtily refuses the offer—for, unlike Rubens and Titian, who were both willing to make modifications, he was always proud.

In the second image I see him in premature old age and poverty at fifty-four. It is the familiar figure of the later self-portraits— a night-cap on his head, old and filthy clothes and a smock covered with thick dabs of paint. The studio is still littered, but now only with torn stuffs and tools of trade. One picture only stands upon the easel. The bell rings. Rembrandt turns the picture to the wall. Jan Six comes in. He is now forty-two. He speaks of his own successes, tries to interest the artist in matters of the world. He treats him as a great master and a cherished friend, inquires about his health, longs to ask if he stands in need of money, but knows that it will be useless, begs finally to be allowed to see some pictures. But Rembrandt is rude to him and will show him nothing. Instead he repeats a coarse anecdote and his lips part with the leer seen in the Carstanjen portrait. Jan Six leaves him with a sigh. When he has gone the master sits on a low stool and wipes a palette-knife slowly on his smock. A mirror hangs before him on the wall. He notes how the light breaks across his well-known features. The palette-knife is still. The light fails. The studio is a cave of gloom where nothing appears but Rembrandt's face and its reflection on the wall. And then Hendrickje bustles in with a candle to say that she has put some onions in the soup.

Plate 49. REMBRANDT: 'Rembrandt and Saskia'
Ascribed by Dr. Dangers to Judith Leyster

Richmond-Cook Collection

Plate 50. REMBRANDT: 'Titus as a Child'

Plate 51. REMBRANDT: 'The Night Watch'

Plate 52. REMBRANDT: 'Hendrickje Stoffels'

Plate 53. REMBRANDT: 'The Return of the Prodigal'

Plate 54. REMBRANDT: 'Two Negroes'

Plate 55. REMBRANDT: 'The Jewish Bride

Plate 56. REMBRANDT: 'Rembrandt's Brother'

iii. Rembrandt's Art

'A master capable of nothing but vulgar and prosaic subjects . . . who merely achieved an effect of rottenness.'—GERARD DE LAIRESSE[1] (1669, the year of Rembrandt's death).

'It must not be imagined that because Rembrandt was never in Rome he was ignorant of the Italian Masters. He had ample material at hand which should have changed his manner or at least have corrected it. But he admired everything and profited from nothing. The Italian genius and his own had nothing in common. . . . His was a fiery genius, quite devoid of nobility and ignorant of the resources which Poetry provides.'—J. B. DESCAMPS (1763).

'Perhaps we shall one day find that Rembrandt is a greater painter than Raphael. I write down this blasphemy which will cause the hair of the schoolmen to stand on end without taking sides.'—EUGÈNE DELACROIX (early nineteenth century).

'He accosts with his dark lantern the world of the marvellous, of conscience and the ideal. He has no equal in the power of showing the invisible.'—FROMENTIN (mid-nineteenth century).

'Vulgarity, dulness or impiety will indeed always express themselves through art in brown and greys as in Rembrandt.'—RUSKIN, *Modern Painters III* (1856).

'The light is not Rembrandtesque on the current or banks of a river; but it is on those of a drain. Colour is not Rembrandtesque usually in a clean house; but is presently obtainable of that quality in a dirty one. And without denying the pleasantness of the mode of progression which Mr. Hazlitt describes as obtainable in a background of Rembrandt—"you stagger from one abyss of obscurity to another" —I cannot feel it an entirely glorious speciality to be distinguished, as Rembrandt was, from other great painters, chiefly by the liveliness of his darkness and the dulness of his light. Glorious or inglorious the speciality itself is easily and accurately definable. It is the aim of the best painters to paint the noblest things they can see by sunlight. It was the aim of Rembrandt to paint the foulest things he could see— by rushlight.'—RUSKIN, *Cestus of Aglaia* (1864).[2]

'A mysticism entirely peculiar to himself speaks to us from the

---

[1] *Cf.* pp. 121–123 and Pl. 64.

[2] For comments on Ruskin's attitude to Rembrandt's chiaroscuro (which resulted from a special phobia) see my *John Ruskin*. (Faber.)

great Dutchman's pictures, as well as from his sketches whether with pencil or the etcher's needle.'—DR. BODE (1909).

'Except in a few of his later works Rembrandt's sense of form and design is utterly lost in a mess of rhetoric, romance and chiaroscuro.' —CLIVE BELL (1914).

'Rembrandt . . . the most profound interpreter of the human soul who ever handled brush.'—SIR CHARLES HOLMES (1925).

In the earlier sections of this book I have shown Rembrandt's historical background as an artist, and if we consider his work as the culmination of Dutch Romanism, of the art of Elsheimer and his Dutch pupils, and of the art of Hals, we have the first clue to the strange contradictions which occur in it—the alterations, the very blending even, of rhetoric and simplicity, of actuality and vagueness, of romantic illustration and of Italian baroque style.

Rembrandt set out in the beginning to paint pictures 'like the Old Masters'. He studied engravings after the Italian painters and such originals as he could find. In the days of his success and his extravagance, when he bought pictures and prints, he owned paintings ascribed to Raphael, Palma Vecchio, Bassano and Michelangelo, engravings by or after Mantegna, Marc Antonio, Dürer, Cranach and Holbein, and engravings and woodcuts after Pieter Brueghel, Rubens, Van Dyck, Jordaens, Michelangelo, Titian, the Carracci, Guido Reni and others. He absorbed Italian Renaissance and Baroque art as far as this could be done without living in Italy; and he also absorbed the art of the Dutch Romanists, of Elsheimer and his pupils, and of other Dutch artists like Brouwer and Seghers.

Thus it comes that the sources of his art have given rise to almost as much research as the sources of Shakespeare's. But as in the case of Shakespeare, so in the case of Rembrandt, the more the sources of details are collected, the more original the master himself appears. A small man uses another man's work to make good his own creative inability. A great man uses another man's work as a jumping-off point for an enlargement of his own experience. From the science of the Italian Renaissance, the eclectic technique and the drama of Italian Baroque, from the Romanism of Goltzius and Cornelis, the naturalism of Bloemaert and Hals, the torch-light tricks of Honthorst, the rhetoric of Lastman before he knew Elsheimer's art and after he had forgotten it, Rembrandt set out in his youth to evolve a pictorial architecture of his own. But his interest in pictorial architecture, as conceived by these men, was only half-hearted. The art of Elsheimer as he knew it from Lastman and Pynas was much nearer to the art which he felt an urge to create. For years he preserved contact with the whole of his historical background; and *The Night Watch* (Pl. 51) is an attempt to use it all as a foundation. But eventually he achieved his own synthesis, he shed the Romanism, the actuality and the rhetoric, and at the end, out of the whole historical background, only the contributions made by Elsheimer and Pynas remained.

If we examine Rembrandt's compositions we find that they were never excuses for the display of natural facility or acquired tricks, or the enlargement of purely architectural experience. No work by Rembrandt is primarily architectural art like the classical works by Raphael or Vermeer or Poussin or the modern Cubists and their successors. With the classical artists the form of the picture is the real subject and the nominal subject is incidental. With Rembrandt the form of the picture comes after his concept of the subject as human drama and derives from it. Motifs from twenty sources may be exploited in a Rembrandt composition at different stages, but the first stage—as we see it in his drawings or in the first states of his etchings—is Rembrandt's concept of a dramatic subject which has aroused his sympathy and interest and which he has set out to illustrate. With Rembrandt the form is the expression of his attitude to his subject, and to the universe as a whole.

Rembrandt's compositions have no relation to the descriptive illustrations in popular art where the artist's concept is limited by his familiar experience of everyday life and where his aim is contact with the familiar experience of spectators. Rembrandt was not concerned in his compositions with the little everyday appearances of the Dutch life around him, or with little national characteristics like the Dutch popular painters whose works I shall discuss later. His concepts were the opposite of popular, that is to say, they were essentially original; they were not descriptive but imaginative; and Rembrandt's imagination was of the romantic kind.

In *The Modern Movement in Art* I referred to Rembrandt as the herald of the nineteenth century Romantic Movement. As I pointed out there the artists of that movement substituted the recording of unusual emotive fragments for the attempt to create a formal harmony and unity symbolizing a formal harmony and unity in the universe, which is and always has been the classical architectural idea of art; the nineteenth-century romantics also entertained the notion that fragments remote in time or space were more emotive than those near at hand; and the foundation of their procedure was the stressing of the aspect of their subject to which they had emotionally reacted, and the form of their pictures was dictated by that stress.

At the same time in discussing the typical classical-architectural artist's activity, I described it as deriving from an instinct towards order, and I described the typical work of classical-architectural art as a finite ordering of architectural experience in a form comprehensible to the human mind. To achieve this synthesis a man must conceive the universe as a finite entity in space, with bounds and a definite shape (a cube for example or a sphere), and functioning within its boundaries as an organization in accordance with a system of laws which man as such, and the formal artist in particular, is instinctively impelled to attempt to discover.

Such a concept of the universe was entirely foreign to the mind of Rembrandt, and it was because it had also been foreign to the mind of Elsheimer (as already noted) that Elsheimer's pictures meant so much to him. For Rembrandt the universe was essentially boundless, not only in space but in time. He could not contemplate the use of geometric symbols to synthesize what he divined as infinite. For him the universe was not a miraculously functioning geometric organization, but a boundless and eternal mystery, and the fragments in it were emotive in relation to that mystery.

It is this attitude of mind which explains the difference between Rembrandt's dramatic illustrations and those by his historical antecedents. If we realize the attitude, we understand his reluctance to define physical forms, we understand his reaction to the remote in place—the turbans, the parasols and other exotic frippery which must seem otherwise no more than the Wardour Street 'Orientalism' of the nineteenth-century Romantic Movement; we understand the crazy buildings of no time, place or recognizable style taken from the Elsheimer tradition which derive from his reaction to the remote in time; and we understand, too, those backgrounds in which we not only 'stagger from one abyss of obscurity to another' to the delight of Hazlitt and the horror of Ruskin, but in which we can also travel freely from undefined light to undefined darkness, and from undefined darkness to undefined light, in a universe without bounds or geometric shape.

The form of Rembrandt's pictures, in a word, is the logical expression of his attitude of mind. By the process of rejecting pictorial architecture as he knew it from his studies, he arrived at the creation of a new architecture of his own which was based on Elsheimer's; and though this architecture is not the subject of his

Plate B. REMBRANDT: 'Woman Bathing'

works or his main preoccupation, it is none the less an essential part of them. In works where his hand failed him or in works ascribed to him but really by one of his pupils, this becomes an affair of a theatrical spot-light scarcely more impressive than a spot-light effect by Honthorst. But in the works where his hand obeyed him his whole attitude is expressed in the relations of massed light and shade which have poise and balance though none can say where the light begins or the shadow ends.

It is this attitude also which explains his treatment of religious subjects. Once he had worked through the rhetoric of a plate like the large *Raising of Lazarus* which he etched at the age of twenty-six, to the small plate of the same subject done the year after Saskia died, his religious paintings, etchings and drawings developed the character of the religious paintings by Elsheimer. They are not religious art in the sense of art called forth by the service of the Church. They are so palpably unecclesiastic that he is believed by some to have been a Jew or of Jewish extraction, though nominally a member of the Protestant Faith.[1] But these works can be explained without this hypothesis. To the conventional mind religion is dogma which satisfies because it claims to provide a finite explanation of the universe. To the original mind, on the other hand, religion stands for the unknown; its function is to keep the unknown continually in human consciousness. The architectural religious mind conceives one definite after-life for good men and another definite after-life for bad men. The romantic religious mind conceives a disembodied spirit disappearing after death into infinite space and infinite time. To Rembrandt's romantic mind Christianity was not the Roman Church or the Protestant Church or Christian dogma; it was not even a symbol of a divine order; it was a symbol of the mystery of life. To Rembrandt the life of Jesus was the life of man and the life of every man was the life of Jesus. In the same spirit he conceived the figures in the Old Testament and the Apocrypha. He is generally said to have thought of the Bible stories in terms of daily life. But it is more accurate to say that he thought of life in terms of the Bible; for he conceived the simplest aspects of the life around him in relation to a boundless past and a boundless future and the Bible stories as symbols of that relation.

[1] Arguments for this theory are (1) the Jewish appearance of Rembrandt in the National Gallery portrait by Flinck, (2) the Jewish appearance of the man known as his father, (3) the number of portraits he painted of Jews, (4) the undogmatic character of his religious pictures, (5) the prevalence of Old Testament subjects in his *œuvre*.

REMBRANDT VAN RYN

Is Rembrandt's romantic attitude the best foundation for an artist? Does not a painter, engaged in an art of form, start with a certain handicap if he conceives the universe as formless and seeks the indefinite in time and space?

The answer to the first question I am certain is not for, but against, Rembrandt. The romantic attitude is extremely dangerous for an artist. I have pointed out the dangers in *The Modern Movement in Art*, and described how the romantics of the nineteenth century succumbed to them. Rembrandt succeeded not because of his romantic attitude of mind but in spite of it. His success must be measured by quite other values.

The answer to the second question is also against the master. For a maker of pictures Rembrandt's attitude was anything but advantageous. The creation of artistic form from such an attitude was only achieved by the force of his personality, by the intensity of his negation of the conventional outlook. Here again the nineteenth-century romantics reveal the dangers of the attitude to which they themselves succumbed, when, for Rembrandt's area of focus which melts so magically into the area of the undefined, they substituted the stress of the emotive fragment surrounded by a background of dark slush. Rembrandt generally escapes these dangers in his imaginative illustrations. But he succumbs to them often in his portraits. But there again he is great by reason of another quality which permeates the finest examples of his art.

This other quality is his human sympathy which was wide and deep. Without this quality much of his work would be 'the effect of rottenness' that it appeared to Gerard de Lairesse, the 'vulgarity, dulness and impiety' that it appeared to Ruskin, and the 'mess of rhetoric, romance and chiaroscuro' referred to by a modern critic. On the strength of it Rembrandt triumphs over the rhetoric of his historical artistic background, over the handicap of his romantic attitude, and over an artistic language which dissolves form to the point where it escapes the formless by a miracle and reduces colour to a point where it is always without gaiety and often almost without life. When we look at Rembrandt's paintings of the character of the *Entombment* (Pl. 38) and *The Return of the Prodigal* (Pl. 53), at a sketch like *The Two Negroes* (Pl. 54), at etchings like *The Angel Departing from the Family of Tobias*, the small *Raising of Lazarus*, *Christ carried to the Tomb*, *The Adoration of the Shepherds*, and hundreds of the moving drawings, we know that the greatness of his art lies in the fact that he was not only a great artist but also, and still more, a great interpreter of man's spirit.

Rembrandt is often called a naturalist or a realist; in fact he was neither, as appears at once if we compare his works with those by Hals. For Hals in his Civic Guard groups used baroque tactility to secure a gay clear actuality. Rembrandt in his romantic-psychological illustrations used it in a manner more akin to the Jesuit ideal, except that while the typical Jesuit artists were concerned with exciting pity and terror in the spectator, Rembrandt was not concerned with the spectator at all, and used baroque impasto to express a sentient ideal of his own. The impasto in *Susanna and the Elders* (Pl. 35), for example, or in The Hague study for the picture, differs not only from the voluptuous impasto of Titian, but also from the exciting impasto of Ribera. It is an impasto that *repels* touch by its sentience. In his portraits—once he has passed the early, smooth painting of the *Anatomy Lesson of Professor Tulp* and the art school illusionist impasto of the *Head of an Old Woman* in the National Gallery—he uses impasto in much the same way as in his romantic illustrations; and in the late middle and last periods he presses it with a palette knife, scratches it with a brush handle, and rubs and dents it with his thumb till it becomes a sentient substance symbolizing the sentience of flesh and bone. Tactility in Hals's painting is a jovial illusion. In the later works by Rembrandt it performs an opposite function; it is there to prevent illusion, to lift the painting from an eye-and-hand transcription of appearance to a symbol of life.

This transformation of illusion into tactile symbolism which is the secret of the original style in Rembrandt's later portraits, is one element rendering them non-naturalistic and non-realistic as compared with portraits by Hals. Another is the simple fact that Rembrandt was not really concerned with recording the shapes of mouths and noses. He is concerned in the main, and by reason of his sympathy, with discovering the secrets of expression, the human meaning of the faces before him. His portraits are not categoric transcripts from nature, but they are also not the smudged impressions of the over-exposed plates in artistic 'Rembrandtesque' photographs. They are records of emotive fragments in relation to boundless and mysterious space and time; and they are also records of Rembrandt's reverence for humanity as such.

When Rembrandt looked in his glass and painted his own head again and again he was not designing an architectural picture, he was not producing a trick effect of light and shade, he was not painting a 'lifelike' portrait, he was not indulging in self-praise or self-vilification; he was saying without irony what Portia said in fun from exuberance of spirits: 'God made him, and therefore let him pass for a man.'[1]

[1] Elsewhere I have contrasted Rembrandt's *Self-Portrait as an old Man* (National Gallery) with Poussin's *Self-Portrait* (Louvre) which shows Poussin, his French contemporary, at about the same age; and I have suggested that Poussin's picture might be titled 'Portrait of a rationalist' with the legend:

> Sure he that made us with such large discourse
> Looking before and after, gave us not
> That capability, that God-like reason
> To fust in us unused.

For Poussin and Rembrandt are indeed type figures—the one a supreme intellectual-rationalist and the other a supreme romantic. (*Cf.* my *French Painting*. Medici. 1931 and 1949 editions.)

ADDENDUM (1946)

I have just come across a comment by Horace Walpole on Rembrandt which deserves a place between the comments by Descamps and Delacroix quoted above (p. 97). It reads as follows: "Rembrandt, whose peculiarity of style and facility of glory, acquired rather by a bold trick of chiaroscuro than by genius, captivated the young painter and tempted him to pursue that manner." (*Anecdotes*, Notice on J. Griffier, 1786 edition.)

Part IV
MORE FOREIGN INFLUENCES

i. Picturesque Art

Eighteenth-century amateurs used the word 'beautiful' for effects which reminded them of classical pictures by Renaissance masters like Raphael; they used the word 'sublime' for effects which reminded them of the romantic art which originated with Elsheimer and Rembrandt; and they used the word 'picturesque' for effects which reminded them of paintings by Claude Lorrain and his school. It is accordingly the word 'picturesque' that I use to describe the Dutch seventeenth-century landscape painters who were influenced by Claude and his circle in Rome.

Mathys Bril and his more celebrated brother Paul Bril (1554–1626) were the founders of picturesque landscape as such. Paul Bril was born in Antwerp and arrived in Rome about 1574, where Mathys, his elder brother, was already working. There is a tradition that he was influenced by the landscapes in Titian's pictures, and it may be that he visited Venice and saw not only Titian's works and those of Giorgione, but also Carpaccio's St. Ursula series which was painted in 1490. Bril's *Seaport* (Pl. 58), for example, may be influenced by Carpaccio's *Departure of St. Ursula*, and it is thus Carpaccio whom we must regard as the real founder of the tradition of the picturesque port scene which was developed by Bril, Tassi and Claude in the seventeenth century in Rome, continued by Joseph Vernet in France and by Richard Wilson in England in the eighteenth century, and which has been transformed and regenerated in our own day by artists like André Lhote in Paris and Edward Wadsworth in London.[1]

[1] The influence of Carpaccio's pictures on art has not, as my knowledge goes, been sufficiently investigated. It can, I am certain, be assumed that all Italian artists, foreign artists resident in Italy and artistic dilettanti, who could afford it, went at one time or another to Venice, in the same manner and for much the same reasons that every one who can afford it now goes at one time or another to Paris. I have suggested elsewhere (*Italian Painting* by P. G. Konody and R. H. Wilenski) that Raphael himself must certainly have made the journey and that the Pintoricchio frescoes in the Library of Siena Cathedral are based on drawings by Raphael from Carpaccio's 'St. Ursula' series.

Bril had great success in Rome, where he painted a series of large frescoes for Popes Gregory XIII, Urban VII, Gregory XIV, Clement VIII and others. In the Sala Clementina in the Vatican he painted a seventy-foot landscape with small figures and he was also employed on works for the sacristies of Sta. Cecilia and Sta. Maria Maggiore. No Italian artist before this may have made the landscape the main content of his work. But Bril had precedents in the works of his own countrymen, Patinir, Pieter Brueghel, and others who had depicted outdoor scenes peopled with small figures as opposed to the tradition of large figures with a landscape background treated as part of an architectural design. There was also a certain amount of precedent in Venetian pictures like Giorgione's *The Tempest* and his *Judgement of Solomon* and *Trial of Moses* and Titian's *Landscape with Sheep and Shepherd* at Buckingham Palace, and so forth.

I have already referred to a contact between Bril and Elsheimer who arrived in Rome about twenty years later, and to Elsheimer's apparent use of Brueghel's *St. John preaching in the Wilderness* (Pl. 10) to which he was possibly introduced by Bril; and it is also possible that Elsheimer's visit to Venice was suggested by Bril from his admiration for Carpaccio, Titian and Giorgione. But Elsheimer developed, as noted, into the father of romantic landscape, while Bril—though he was in close touch with the baroque developments of the Carracci—(Annibale Carracci actually painted figures in some of his pictures)—kept Carpaccio in his mind and escaped the temptations both of baroque naturalism and of the new romantic outlook of Elsheimer.

One of Bril's pupils and assistants was Agostino Tassi (1565–1644), who was acquiring a considerable reputation for works in the style of his master when, for some offence, the nature of which is unrecorded, he was sent to the galleys at Leghorn. After his release he resumed his work as an artist, and painted picturesque landscapes and also marine subjects, for which he became especially well known. Tradition has it that his marines were painted from drawings made at Leghorn, which is possible, since, as Bril was interested in port scenes, his pupil had learned to regard them as material suitable for art. Tassi was the master of Claude Lorrain (1600–1682), by whose hands the classical-picturesque style of landscape was given its most famous and characteristic form.

Claude arrived in Rome in 1613, and for nine years he was attached to Tassi, first as studio boy, then as pupil and assistant. Tassi was much employed in decorating apartments in private houses, and Claude thus commenced as a decorator in the Carpaccio-

Bril-Tassi tradition. After leaving Tassi he went to Venice, Munich and Nancy; he returned to Rome in 1627, where he took a place in the foreign circle and met Nicholas Poussin (1594–1665), who was already one of its recognized leaders.

Claude's mind was of the classical architectural type and his characteristic achievement was to subject landscape to the artistic laws which he had observed in the classical compositions of the Italian Renaissance masters. He had no sense of boundless space nor boundless time as they were understood by Rembrandt, who was his exact contemporary. He conceived the universe as finite and his picture space as a section of a cube. His concept of time also was finite. He took over from Elsheimer and Bril the ruined towers of a dateless past, but he used them merely as pictorial motifs and 'properties' in the same way that he used titles like *The Embarkation of the Queen of Sheba*, *The Departure of St. Ursula* and so forth. The past for Claude was a limited, not an unlimited, extension of the present, and space was a limited, not an unlimited, recession from the front plane of the picture.

This classical-architectural foundation of Claude's picturesque style becomes evident if we compare his *Queen of Sheba* in the National Gallery with Turner's *Dido building Carthage* which Turner directed in his will should be hung near it. Claude, thinking of the picture space as a cube, gives us a foreground of terra firma running right across the picture and a building on the left running up to what we may call the picture's ceiling. Turner, who was a romantic, with a sense of infinity and little architectural feeling for the picture space, gives us no solid foreground and no indication of a top plane, but takes us along a path of light in the centre of the picture right up to the horizon and beyond it into boundless light. Claude's sky is not a suggestion of boundless space or boundless light, but a luminous backcloth which illumines the defined architectural space of the picture, but illumines it *towards* the spectator and is thus in fact a new version of the *closing* background of the old Italian tradition. Claude is often referred to as a painter of light; but light in his hands was an architectural factor and the sky that rises from his horizons, however luminous, is always in the nature, architecturally speaking, of a backcloth or a closing wall.[1]

Claude's landscapes, like those by Bril, and those by the artists

[1] The student should compare Claude's *Abraham dismissing Hagar* in the Munich Gallery with the pictures of the same subject by Rembrandt (Pl. 33), Jan Steen (Pl. 99), and Van der Werff (Pl. 65). Claude as usual is not concerned with the little figures which constitute the illustrative content; without the title, **Hagar**

of the Claude school, were never painted from nature. All the artists in his circle in Rome went out daily into the country and made drawings and sketches, but it would never have occurred to any of them to pass off a study for a picture, or, like the Dutch topographical popular painters, to be satisfied with a mere eye-and-hand copying of a landscape. Sandrart, a German artist and art historian in the Claude-Poussin circle in Rome, wrote in astonishment that Claude, when he was out in the Campagna, sometimes *painted* his sketches instead of merely drawing or tinting them; but Claude, in fact, rarely went even to this length, as we can see from the admirable pen and wash drawings from his hand which survive. But though Claude never painted his pictures from nature, he used his perception of nature, as recorded in his drawings, for the constituent parts of his pictorial inventions; and in so doing he was pointing the way not only to Vermeer of Delft, but also to modern Cubist and post-Cubist art.

It will be recalled that Claude's works were violently attacked as untrue to nature by Ruskin, who had no notion of what Claude was after. 'There are,' wrote Ruskin of the *Embarkation of the Queen of Sheba*, 'many inlets of the Italian seas where sweet gardens and regular terraces descend to the water's edge; but these are not the spots where merchants' vessels anchor, or where bales are disembarked. On the other hand, there are many busy quays and noisy arsenals upon the shores of Italy; but queens' palaces are not built upon the quays nor are the docks in any wise adorned with conservatories or ruins. It was reserved for the genius of Claude to combine the luxurious with the lucrative and rise to a commercial ideal, in which cables are fastened to temple pillars and light-houses adorned with rows of bean-pots.' Apart from the obvious retort that Claude was a classical architectural artist and not a descriptive popular illustrator, it must be observed that Ruskin here is blind to Claude's fundamental attitude to his subject. Claude had no romantic interest in the past; living in Rome and hearing much talk of antiquity, he naturally assumed that a classical 'subject' and an occasional toga and chiton were essential ingredients of a picture, but he cared so little for the past that he sets out again and again to dress his figures in the costumes of antiquity and before the picture is finished half are dressed in Italian costumes of his time, and his buildings, even

and Abraham would never occur to the spectator, who is confronted with a typical Claude box-picture with a building on one side running up to the ceiling, a terra firma floor, a bridge at right-angles to the building, and a radiant backcloth throwing the light forward.

when he inserts ruined towers in his landscapes, are always painted from drawings of actual Italian buildings or ruins, and their form is clearly and architecturally defined. Claude did not indulge in exotic Wardour Street costuming like Rembrandt or insert the crazy buildings we find in works by Rembrandt or Turner, because he did not react romantically to ideas of remoteness in time and space. For the same reason, Claude's world is not made up of the 'abysses of obscurity' that we find in Rembrandt's, but is a world of defined shape, where everything is limpid and serene. Ruskin's attacks on Claude on the ground that he is untrue to nature are fundamentally untenable, because *all* architectural art, being a symbol for man's concern with universal order, is true to nature if true to itself; and they are also untenable because when Ruskin spoke of nature he meant here neither universal order nor infinity, but nature as depicted in Turner's pictures; and when he wrote that Claude's pictures lacked 'Nature's breaking lights on shattered stones, vague shadows from waving vegetation, irregular stains of time and weather, mouldering hollows, sparkling casements', and the 'little shadows and sparkles and scratches making a transparent palpitating various infinity', he was merely complaining that Claude's *Embarkation of the Queen of Sheba* was a classical-architectural picturesque work, and not a romantic pseudo-classical picturesque work like Turner's *Dido building Carthage*.[1]

Claude's pictures were bought by owners of elegant apartments, not only in Italy and France, but also in Denmark, the Netherlands, and above all, in England. In the year 1644 he had nineteen commissions for pictures from English collectors. Engravings after his pictures were also widely disseminated. It was, therefore, only natural that his Dutch followers, when they returned from Rome to Holland, were welcomed by the wealthy Dutch merchants and speculators who were then building themselves handsome mansions and wanted graceful decorations for their walls; and thus, whereas the pictures by the Dutch Romanist precursors of Rembrandt and of Rembrandt himself were bought or commissioned by civic bodies and a few collectors, and (as I shall point out in Part V) the pictures by the Dutch popular painters were bought and sold in the marketplace, the picturesque paintings by the Dutch followers of Claude were the standard decorations in the apartments of the Dutch upper classes till the later years of the seventeenth century, when they gave

[1] Since this was written, I have spent much time in study of Ruskin and his work. The curious will find the result in my *John Ruskin* (Faber).

place to pictures by Dutch followers of Poussin and other artists admired by the Court of Louis XIV.

The Dutch painters of the picturesque were numerous, and many were extremely famous in their day not only in Holland, but elsewhere as well. I select Both, Poelenburgh, Berchem and Pynacker as among the most famous and more interesting figures.

(a) JAN BOTH

Born Utrecht 1610, died Utrecht 1652

CHARACTERISTIC PICTURES

London—National Gallery	*Landscape—Morning*
London—National Gallery	*Landscape with Cattle and Figures*
London—National Gallery	*The Judgement of Paris* (Figures by Poelenburgh)
London—Royal Collection	*Baptism of the Moor*
Dulwich Gallery	*Italian Landscape*
Paris—Louvre	*Landscape with Figures*
The Hague—Mauritshuis	*Landscape with Travellers*
Amsterdam—Rijks Museum	*Italian Landscape with Artists Sketching*
Amsterdam—Rijks Museum	*Landscape with a Ferry*
Amsterdam—Rijks Museum	*Peasant Scene in Rome*
Dresden Gallery	*Ruins by the Seashore*

Jan Both was the son of a glass painter and was apprenticed as a boy to Bloemaert, whose position as the most celebrated artist in Utrecht I have referred to in Part I. About 1630 he went to Rome with his brother Andreis and joined Claude's circle. He remained in Italy for about ten or twelve years, during which time he went with his brother to Venice where Andreis—it is said after a supper party—fell out of a gondola and was drowned.

Both painted picturesque landscapes influenced mainly by Claude, though it is possible to detect in them also Venetian influences; also in pictures like the *Peasant Scene in Rome* in Amsterdam and the *Ruins by the Seashore* in Dresden there seems also an influence from Bamboche. He returned to Utrecht about 1640 after his brother's death, and his work in its turn influenced Berchem and Pynacker and also, I suspect, Turner.

Both is, in fact, a figure of consequence in art history. He was one of the earliest of the Dutch painters of the picturesque, and thus a link not only between Claude and Berchem, who probably never went to Italy, but also a link between the landscapes by Bril and the Dutch naturalists. He evolved a pleasant formula for painting trees (cf. Pl. 57), but he does not rank high as an individual artist, because he neither grasped Claude's principle of architectural composition on the one hand, nor on the other, the sense of infinity in the works of Elsheimer and his school.

(b) CORNELIS VAN POELENBURGH

Born Utrecht 1586, died Utrecht 1667

CHARACTERISTIC PICTURES

London—Royal Collection	*Italian Landscapes with Ruins, Cattle and Peasants*
England—Halifax Collection	*Diana and her Nymphs*
Paris—Louvre	*Women Bathing*
Paris—Louvre	*Nymph and Satyr*
Amsterdam—Rijks Museum	*Men Bathing in a River*
Amsterdam—Rijks Museum	*Diana and Her Nymphs Surprised*
Vienna Gallery	*Women Bathing*
Florence—Uffizi	*Moses striking the Rock*
Munich—Alte Pinakothek	*Diana and Callisto*
Munich—Alte Pinakothek	*Lot and his Daughters*
Madrid—Prado	*Diana and her Nymphs Surprised*
Dresden Gallery	*Rest on the Flight*
Leningrad—Hermitage	*Rest on the Flight*
Augsburg Gallery	*Cascades at Tivoli*
Cassel Gallery	*Cattle splashing in a Stream* (with Berchem)

Cornelis van Poelenburgh was a much more interesting artist. Some twenty-four years older than Both, he was a student in Bloemaert's school some twenty years earlier, and he was in Rome some five years before Both was born. When he joined the circle of foreign artists in Rome, Claude was still a child and Elsheimer's influence was paramount, and he was soon attached to the German master as pupil and assistant.

Poelenburgh's first commissions seem to have been for religious subjects. The Dresden Gallery has a picturesque *Rest on the Flight* from his brush, where the Holy Family is seen in the foreground of a campagna landscape with ruins; and there is a *Moses striking the Rock* in the Uffizi, Florence, with an Oriental procession of camels and so on in the middle distance and a landscape recalling the Elsheimer *Daedalus and Icarus* series in Naples. Later he developed a style of mythological picturesque painting, in which elements derived from both Elsheimer and Albani were welded into a personal concept of a picture, the roots of which are already apparent in the works in Dresden and Florence. Leaving Rome, he worked for some time for the Court in Florence. He returned to Utrecht in 1627, where he was visited by Rubens, who had known him in Rome, and who bought several of his pictures, and where the Estates paid him 575 gulden for a picture to be included in the wedding gift of pictures to Amalie de Solms (which also included, as already noted, two pictures by Moreelse). In 1637 Charles I, probably on the recommendation of Rubens, invited him to London, and the collections of both Charles I and James II contained examples of his work. Returning to Utrecht, he founded the usual art school, and produced a large number of pictures to meet the continual demands for his work. A Rotterdam merchant named Jacob Meyers, for example, had a gallery of his paintings in the same way that later, the picture dealer Johan de Bye of Leyden had a gallery of works by Dou. Foreign collectors also acquired his pictures. In the eighteenth century there were many examples in the Orléans and other French collections, and the Elector Palatine at Düsseldorf had, at that time, the group of the children of Frederick I of Bohemia in a fine, spacious landscape, which is now in the gallery at Budapest. Poelenburgh died a rich man in 1667, two years before the death of Rembrandt. He usually painted on copper or wood and rarely used canvas.

Poelenburgh's art was based in the first place on that of Elsheimer, but like Elsheimer himself, he was also influenced by Albani. But accepting Albani's notion of a picture and Elsheimer's conception of boundless three-dimensional space, Poelenburgh gave the art of Albani more intellectual significance and he clarified the concepts of Elsheimer. He evolved, moreover, eventually a highly interesting and quite individual solution of the problem of pictorial construction, and his pictures are worth the student's attention not only from this point of view, but also because of his individual and interesting treatment of the nude figure.

His *Diana and Callisto* (Pl. 60) is an excellent composition. The spectator's eye travels from the light drapery and the figure of Callisto to the figure of Diana, and it is carried thence to the cow in the middle distance, thence again to the woman on the hillock and thence to the light on the horizon and back through the clump of trees to the starting-point of this rhythmic circle. The figures are exactly the right size to seem appropriate in this particular statement of space; and the finer aspects of Dutch descriptive landscape painting are contained in the wide, broad expanse of earth and sky.

Poelenburgh's *Diana and her Nymphs Surprised* in the Amsterdam Rijks Museum is an equally interesting, though not perhaps quite

Plate 57. JAN BOTH: 'The Baptism of the Moor'
(*Reproduced by gracious permission of Her Majesty the Queen*)

London—Buckingham Palace

Florence—Uffizi

Plate 58. PAUL BRIL: 'A Seaport'

Plate 59. POELENBURGH: 'Women Bathing'

Plate 60. POELENBURGH: 'Diana and Callisto'

Plate 61. BERCHEM: 'Italian Landscape'

Plate 62. ADAM PYNACKER: 'Landscape with Shepherd'

Plate 63. ADAM PYNACKER: 'Landscape near Tivoli'

Plate 64. Gerard de Lairesse: 'Parnassus' (detail)

Plate 65. ADRIAEN VAN DER WERFF: 'Abraham dismissing Hagar'
(*Cf. Plates 33 and* 99)

Plate 66. ADRIAEN VAN DER WERFF: 'Christ Mocked'
(*Cf. Plate* 68)

Plate 67. ADRIAEN VAN DER WERFF: 'Portrait Group'

Plate 68. REMBRANDT: 'Christ Mocked'
Hind Catalogue, No. 143

Plate 69. P. VAN LAER (BAMBOCHE): 'Playing Bowls'
(Cf. Plate 72)

Plate 70. P. VAN LAER (BAMBOCHE): 'The Quack Doctor'

(*Cf. Plates 93 and 97*)

Plate 71. PHILIPS WOUWERMAN: 'Halt of a Hunting Party'

Plate 72. PHILIPS WOUWERMAN: 'Courtyard with Farrier'

(*Cf. Plate* 69)

so attractive a picture. Here the group of female nudes starts from the right-hand foreground, and runs diagonally across the canvas to figures in the middle distance, and thence to a mountain landscape and horizon, while an opposing diagonal from the men or satyrs approaching from the foreground on the left joins the middle distance at the same point.

In *Women Bathing* (Pl. 59) the recession is achieved by a circle of light starting from the seated figure in the foreground and running round the ruin to a point of a light in the sky immediately above the foreground figure; and the rhythm started by this figure's arms and leg is completed by the diving girl who terminates the ingenious foreground arabesque. No student of modern art will fail to compare the seated figure in this picture with the figure in a similar attitude (reversed) in Renoir's 1885 *Baigneuses* in the Tyson Collection, Philadelphia, which inaugurated his classical manner after his Italian voyage of 1880 and his five years' study of the old Masters.[1] Poelenburgh in Rome was acquainted not only with the works of his contemporaries but also with the works of Raphael, and there is something of Raphael's large sense of form in Poelenburgh's conception of this nude figure which is absent from the final version of Renoir's *Baigneuses*, though it appears in several of Renoir's numerous preliminary studies for the picture and also, of course, in the majestic figures in his last 'red' period, when he continually recalled his first rapture at the massive arms of Raphael's Venus in the Farnese.

Eighteenth-century critics, admiring the Praxitelean grace of nudes by Van der Werff and Boucher, reproached Poelenburgh with the heaviness of his figures. But we, who are accustomed to-day to the staggering weight of the figures produced by contemporary painters concentrating on 'volumes' and to the monumental figures of Picasso's classical manner, are not likely to quarrel on this ground with Poelenburgh's convention for the female form. We recognize that his figures have neither the boudoir grace of the eighteenth century nor the voluptuous grace of the nudes by Titian; compared with those by Van der Werff or Boucher, Poelenburgh's figures are admittedly squat and stumpy; and his Callisto is gauche indeed compared with Titian's Callisto in Bridgwater House or the still more graceful Callisto in the Madrid copy. But this very gaucherie imposes itself upon the unprejudiced spectator because it is consistent, because it arises from a purely plastic concept of form, and because it is expressed in a personal language which has admitted no formulae borrowed without adaptation from elsewhere.

[1] Reproduced as Plate 19B in my *Modern French Painters* (Faber).

The gaucherie in Poelenburgh's figures may lead some spectators to regard him as a naturalist. But we have only to compare his figures with the Mars and Venus in Bloemaert's *Marriage of Peleus and Thetis* (Pl. 18) to see how he escaped from the terre-à-terre naturalism of his first master who was so dependent on the model on the studio throne. Poelenburgh was under no such fatal bondage. He painted, obviously, not from models but from drawings or from memory and from architectural imagination. Thence the unity that pervades his pictures and the classical character of his nudes.

It is for this reason also that whereas Bloemaert's figures are merely naked, Poelenburgh's are properly called 'nudes'. The various developments of the nude in art are significant accompaniments of the development of human mind, knowledge and civilization. Thus Titian's nudes derive from the Renaissance ideas of physical desirability, but they nearly always escape nakedness, because they were not painted from nature. The Jesuit encouragement of tactility in painting was an important factor contributing to the introduction of the naked in art. From this the painters of the picturesque escaped; and Poelenburgh, without attaining to the purely intellectual treatment of Raphael or Poussin, has given us nudes which are not only interesting forms, but which we can also accept as denizens of that 'Golden Age' which all the seventeenth-century painters of the picturesque ostensibly set out to portray.

Students of Poelenburgh's works will find them strangely unequal. The reason is that many pictures ascribed to him are not really by his hand. In the days when his pictures were sought after, and were highly paid for, numerous works by his pupils and imitators were sold as Poelenburgh's, sometimes with or sometimes without the addition of false signatures. Jan van Hansbergen, Jan van der Lys, Daniel Vertangen, Francis Willaerts, Warmard van Rysen, and Abraham van Cuylenborch, were among the Poelenburgh *pasticheurs* whose works were exploited in this way.

PICTURESQUE ART

(c) NICOLAS BERCHEM

Born Haarlem 1620, *died Amsterdam* 1683

CHARACTERISTIC PICTURES

London—National Gallery	*Crossing the Ford*
London—Wallace Collection	*The Old Port of Genoa*
London—Wallace Collection	*Jupiter with the Nymphs on Mount Ida*
London—Wallace Collection	*Halt at an Inn*
London—Wallace Collection	*The Musical Shepherdess*
London—Royal Collection	*Italian Landscape with Cattle*
London—Duke of Devonshire	*Italian Landscape*
London—Bridgwater House	*Landscape with Nymphs, Satyr and Cattle*
Paris—Louvre	*Landscape with Cattle*
The Hague—Mauritshuis	*Convoy attacked in a Ravine*
The Hague—Mauritshuis	*The Wild Boar Hunt*
The Hague—Mauritshuis	*An Italian Ford*
Amsterdam—Rijks Museum	*Winter Landscape*
Amsterdam—Rijks Museum	*Allegory of Amsterdam's Growth*
Amsterdam—Rijks Museum	*Italian Landscape*
Leningrad—Hermitage	*Rape of Europa*
Leningrad—Hermitage	*The Seamstress*
Dresden Gallery	*The Annunciation to the Shepherds*
Dresden Gallery	*Shepherds in a Landscape with a Château in the Background*

Nicolas Berchem was another excellent and most famous painter of the picturesque. Collectors commissioned his pictures and bought them from his easel; one offered him a retaining fee of ten gulden a day in return for the first refusal of all his pictures, but the artist found the arrangement did not pay him and he abandoned it. Pictures by Berchem are in all the galleries and collections of Europe. There are six, for example, at Buckingham Palace, five at Bridgwater House, six in the National Gallery, seven in the Wallace Collection, six at Dulwich, nine in the Louvre, four in the Mauritshuis, thirteen in Amsterdam, thirteen in Dresden, and the Hermitage in Leningrad used to have a 'Salle Berchem' which contained about twenty. In his lifetime Berchem received high prices for his pictures, and in the eighteenth century and a hundred years ago collectors had to pay from £300 to £1,200 to secure one. In the later years of the nineteenth century and the opening years of our own, while high prices were being paid for pictures by the Dutch descriptive-naturalists, Berchem's pastorals fell to the region of £20, and the echo of this attitude can still be seen in the relative neglect of his works by the general public and in the poor places accorded to them

115

in galleries where many are now frequently kept in cellars or private rooms to make room for pictures more generally admired.

Berchem was born at Haarlem fourteen years after Rembrandt. His father, Pieter Claes of Haarlem, was one of the earliest Dutch still-life painters. Pieter Claes painted still-life for itself, and he was followed by a long series of Dutch painters, whose works, executed with incredible patience and microscopic vision, constitute an aspect of Dutch seventeenth-century production in themselves.

Berchem worked as pupil and assistant with various masters, including Jan van Goyen (1596–1656), one of the founders of the Dutch naturalistic landscape, and with the picturesque landscape painters, J. B. Weenix (1617–1660) and Jan Wils (1610?–before 1680), whose daughter he married. It is always assumed, from the Italian character of the landscapes in Berchem's pictures, that he went to Italy and came into personal touch with the picturesque painters in Rome. But I see no reason to assume this journey, which is not recorded by any contemporary biographer. The Dutch picturesque pictures were always put together from drawings, engravings and other paintings and even not infrequently by several hands. It is known that Berchem painted figures in landscapes by Wils; and even Poelenburgh himself, deeply interested though he was in the principles of composition, did not disdain to paint the figures into landscapes by other hands—witness *The Judgement of Paris* in the National Gallery, where he painted the figures in a landscape by Jan Both. Berchem had pictures and drawings by Both, Weenix, and other artists who had been to Italy, to draw upon for his landscapes; he also had engravings after Claude and other artists, since it is recorded that he had a passion for buying prints and a very large collection. He may, of course, have visited Italy, but his work, given the circumstances of its production, is not impossible without the assumption.

All biographers depict Berchem as an amiable man henpecked by his wife. Descamps, writing in the eighteenth century and summarizing Houbraken and other earlier writers, says:

'His wife was extremely avaricious. Her husband never left his studio from morning till night; but this did not content her, for she was only satisfied if he worked without ceasing. When she could not be actually in the studio she took up her position in the room immediately beneath, and if she could not hear him moving about or singing, in fear that he might waste a moment or take a nap, she would knock on the ceiling to stir him up. She carried this avarice so far that she appropriated her husband's earnings and left him no money at all; and on more than one occasion he had to borrow money from his pupils to buy the drawings or prints which he coveted.'

For the sake of other henpecked husbands and of artists who hold their wives responsible for their production of 'pot-boilers', I should like to be able to record that as a result Berchem soon degenerated and produced ever more and more hurried and inferior pictures. But scarcely any of his pictures that I know in the original or in photographs show signs of hurry or degeneration. On the contrary, all are admirable in technique and all are in excellent condition without cracks or undue blackness—unless they have been varnished and revarnished without cleaning—to this day. Also, though dozens of Berchem's pictures are the same in character, they are all different in composition and individual constituents. The explanation is to be found in Descamps' note that his wife became suspicious if she failed to hear him *singing*. Houbraken obtained the detail that Berchem habitually sang at his work from Justus van Huysum, one of Berchem's pupils (and incidentally the father of the famous still-life painter of flower pieces) who recorded it. Berchem, in a word, cared nothing for his wife's persecution. He was perfectly happy at his easel. He generally had no desire to use the money he made for any purpose except to buy engravings, and, when he wanted money for any other purpose, Houbraken tells us, he contrived to deceive his wife about the price agreed for a picture, and to pocket the difference between the real and the nominal sums.

In 1661, eight years before the death of Rembrandt and the year in which he painted the *Syndics of the Cloth Hall*, Berchem was commissioned by the Amsterdam authorities to paint an *Allegory of the Growth of the City*. In this work (Pl. 4), which is one of the very rare pageant pictures in Dutch seventeenth-century art, Berchem obviously drew freely on his collection of prints after Italian pictures, and the work is a link between the traditions of pageant painting and the art of Boucher. Perhaps, as Berchem doubtless received a considerable fee for this picture and painted it entirely from his portfolios, he was able at last to convince his wife that purchase of the engravings had not been entirely a waste of money.

In his picturesque pastorals Berchem can be said to have perfected a type of furniture picture that was personal, classical and admirably carried out (*cf.* Pl. 61). A feature of these works is that the figures are often represented advancing along a road with their backs to the spectator. This motif occurs in Titian's *Landscape with Sheep and*

Shepherd in Buckingham Palace, and it was used by Berchem as a means of achieving recession into the picture space. Berchem was, in fact, an extremely intelligent artist who grasped not only the principles of Claude's architectural concept of space, but also the significance of Elsheimer's unlimited recession; and, without departing from the fundamentally architectural nature of his own concept of space, he often successfully introduced a romantic quality into his closing backcloth by means of clouds breaking over mountain tops and such devices.

For the details of his pictures Berchem borrowed right and left from pictures by his Dutch contemporaries and from engravings of all kinds. In this respect he was, in fact, as eclectic as Rembrandt. Thus his *Winter Landscape* in Amsterdam shows the influence of the Dutch descriptive landscape painters; his *Seamstress with a Pricked Finger* in Leningrad shows the influence of Metsu or Terborch; his *Attack on a Convoy* in The Hague shows the influence of Wouwerman; and there is a landscape at Buckingham Palace which shows the influence of Rembrandt's pupil, Philips Koninck. Other pictures recalled Bamboche, and we have to go back to Bloemaert's 'history' compositions to understand the source of his *Othello and Desdemona*, which was sold recently from the Six Collection in Amsterdam and which was the forerunner of the Shakespearian illustrations produced more than a century later by English artists working for Alderman Boydell.

A curious picture of yet another kind is *The Old Port of Genoa*, now hung in a second-floor gallery in the Wallace Collection. Here we see a negro servant holding a round parasol over a lady's head. It would seem to have been a Genoese fashion for negro boys thus to hold parasols over their mistresses' heads when they walked abroad, and it became a favourite motif in art. It occurs, for example, in Van Dyck's celebrated portrait *The Marquesa Cattaneo* in the National Gallery in Washington; and round parasols are found in Both's *Baptism of the Moor* (Pl. 57), in Lastman's *Baptism of the Moor* in Carlsruhe, in Rembrandt's *Narcissus* in Amsterdam and some other of Rembrandt's pictures, and later, of course, in French decorative art and in the tapestries by Goya.

If Berchem borrowed he also gave. Cuyp, Paul Potter, Carel du Jardin and hundreds of other artists took individual elements from his compositions and exploited them; and his numerous pupils included Jacob Ochtervelt and probably Pieter de Hooch.

In 1677 he moved from Haarlem to Amsterdam, and he died there in 1683, twenty years after Rembrandt's death and twenty before Boucher, who learned so much from him, was born in Paris.

(d) ADAM PYNACKER

Born Pynacker 1622, died Delft 1673

CHARACTERISTIC PICTURES

London—Wallace Collection	*Landscape with Animals*
London—Wallace Collection	*Landscape with Shepherd*
Dulwich Gallery	*Landscape with Sportsmen*
Richmond—Cook Collection	*Building on a Lake*
England—Wantage Collection	*River Scene with Bridge and Boats*
England—Crawford Collection	*The Bridge at Francheville*
The Hague—Mauritshuis	*The Torrent*
Amsterdam—Rijks Museum	*Landscape with Cattle*
Amsterdam—Rijks Museum	*River Landscape with Boat*
(formerly Six Collection)	
Augsburg Gallery	*Italian Landscape*
Munich—Alte Pinakothek	*Landscape with Ships*
Leningrad—Hermitage	*Lake Scene with Boat*
Vienna—Kunsthist: Museum	*Landscape near Tivoli*

Adam Pynacker was another distinguished painter of the picturesque. He took his name from the village where he was born, which is near Delft, and he went at an early age to Rome, where he was influenced by Jan Both and Claude. Either on his journey out or his journey back he evidently made a drawing of the bridge at Francheville near Lyons, from which he painted the picture with that title in the Crawford Collection (for Francheville was on the route taken by the Dutch and Flemish artists travelling to Italy in those days). When he returned to Amsterdam he became at once a favourite painter of the rich Amsterdam burghers, and there was a time when to have a series of decorative pictures by Pynacker let into panels round the walls was the height of fashion. Pynacker reaped the fruits of this vogue, which lasted till his death, and he painted relatively few easel pictures. But after his death painted panels went out of fashion, and his works were relegated to store-rooms and attics. When Descamps wrote in the middle of the eighteenth century scarcely any rooms in Amsterdam retained their Pynacker panels, and in 1820 the house of one Umgrove in Amsterdam was remarked on as a curiosity because it had retained a salon with all the Pynacker pictures undisturbed. Nevertheless, both in the eighteenth century and in the early nineteenth, Pynacker's easel pictures were sought after by collectors, and as late as 1872 Sir Richard Wallace paid £400 for the *Landscape with Animals,* which can now only be seen by the curious in a second-floor gallery at Hertford House.

Students of Dutch art should examine both this picture and the *Landscape with Shepherd* (Pl. 62) by Pynacker which is hung in a main gallery in the Wallace Collection. For in Pynacker we have an artist with the architectural sense, with a real power of reducing order out of the apparent chaos of the minor forms in landscape, and with quite admirable skill of hand. He borrowed motifs like all the picturesque painters from other painters. We find in his works the round towers, the ruins, the ships in calm waters, the sheep and cattle, the shepherds and all the stock material of the picturesque landscape (cf. Pl. 63). But he arranged his material with intelligent discretion, he never attempted to palm off a sketch or study as a picture, and to the motifs which he borrowed he contributed others which we can find in his brilliant, nervous, and elegantly stylized drawings.

ii. *French Influences*

By the middle of the seventeenth century Holland was the central point of interest in north-western Europe; she was not only the richest country in the region, but she held also a leading place in culture, in learning, in taste, and to a large extent in fashion. By 1640 Dutch enterprise and navigation had carried the fame of Holland to the four corners of the world, and wealth flowed back to Holland from all quarters. At home Dutch industry furnished jewels, silver and golden ornaments, tiles and textiles and flowers to all lands; the Dutch painters of the types I have been discussing were famous all over western Europe; Dutch domestic architecture was the basis of the charming style in which London was rebuilt after the Great Fire, a rebuilding to which we owe Clifford's Inn, New Square Lincoln's Inn, King's Bench Walk, Berkeley Square and so forth; Dutch universities attracted students of the quality of Descartes; and the social life of the Dutch upper classes attracted young men with money even from Paris. Rome remained, of course, Rome—the unquestioned central foyer of the arts, just as Paris has been Paris for the last hundred years. But Holland was regarded in much the same way that we now regard the United States of America—as a country which had broken away from tradition and had acquired wealth and a new civilization in what seemed the twinkling of an eye; and travellers from all parts marvelled at

Rotterdam and Amsterdam, which seemed to be re-living the history of Venice; at the verdure of the Dutch lanes, the traffic on the Dutch canals, the Dutch systems of pasture and agriculture, the domestic gardens, the civil institutions, and the extravagance of the upper classes who built themselves magnificent mansions on the Heerengracht and Keizergracht in Amsterdam, filled with rich furniture and silver, and drove portentous equipages in the streets.

But after 1661, when Louis XIV assumed the reins of government in Paris and made the French Court the model for all courts and the arbiter of all fashions, Holland ceased to be a centre of focus, and the Dutch upper classes, like the rest of Europe, modelled their taste, culture, and fashion on the taste and standards of Paris—indeed they out-Parisianed the Parisians, and rich Dutchmen were conspicuous in Paris by their over-elaborate clothes bedecked with lace and ribbons.

From this time onwards the rich and cultivated classes in Holland were not only admirers of Claude and the Dutch artists who followed him, but they took also an enthusiastic interest in Nicholas Poussin, whom the French recognized as a master, and in other French painters of classical subjects like Charles Lebrun, the art dictator at the court of Louis XIV.

Poussin, like Claude, had a real grasp of classical-architectural art; Lebrun's grasp was only superficial; but to the eyes of the Dutch amateurs, with the tradition of Dutch Romanism behind them, both masters were equally impressive; and they were equally impressive also in the eyes of Gerard de Lairesse, who took Amsterdam by storm soon after his arrival in 1665.

(a) GERARD DE LAIRESSE

Born Liége 1641, died Amsterdam 1711

CHARACTERISTIC PICTURES

Dulwich Gallery	*Apollo and Daphne*
Dulwich Gallery	*Pan and Syrinx*
England—Methuen Collection	*The Judgement of Paris*
Paris—Louvre	*Cleopatra at Tarsis*
Paris—Louvre	*Hercules between Vice and Virtue*
The Hague—Mauritshuis	*Achilles and the daughters of Lycomedes*
Amsterdam—Rijks Museum	*Seleucus renouncing Stratonice to Antiochus*
Amsterdam—Rijks Museum	*Antony and Cleopatra*
Brunswick Gallery	*Achilles and the daughters of Lycomedes*
Dresden Gallery	*Parnassus*

Cassel Gallery   *Achilles dragging Hector's Body round the Walls of Troy*
Cassel Gallery   *Bacchanale*
Vienna Gallery   *Cybele receiving Neptune*

Gerard de Lairesse, whose judgement on Rembrandt has already been quoted,[1] was one of the most spectacular figures in art history. He was born in Belgium, but as he established himself in Holland before he was twenty-five and lived and worked there, exercising great influence till he died at the age of sixty-nine, he cannot be omitted from the story of Dutch art.

Gerard de Lairesse had what we now call a classical education in Liége from his father, who was an artist and man of letters, and from one Bertholet Flémalle, a canon in that city, who was an artist and a man of parts. Lairesse showed precocious talents for painting and music and a passionate industry in reading the Greek and Latin authors and in studying archæology and the art of the Italian masters in engravings. He was soon established as an artist and painting pictures for various churches in Liége and historical compositions for the Electors of Cologne and Brandenburg.

Lairesse started life with the physical disadvantage of extreme ugliness—the ugliness that results from a nose with a depressed bridge and the accompanying abnormal length of upper lip. But being a man of great energy and ambition he set out to triumph not only in the realms of the Muses, but in the realms of Venus as well. Tradition relates that he became embroiled with two girls of Maestricht, and that in a violent quarrel he stabbed one with a dagger and had to take refuge with the Dominicans until he managed to escape to Hertogenbosch with a devoted girl cousin named Marie Salme, whom he then married.

From Hertogenbosch Lairesse went to Utrecht, where his facility as a painter was exploited by a dealer named Uylenbourg, and about 1665 he removed to Amsterdam, where he obtained the right of citizenship, and where he remained.

When Lairesse arrived in Amsterdam, Rembrandt was sixty and living in obscurity. Lairesse with his erudition, his passion for the classics, and his facility in painting mythological compositions, was just the man to create a sensation among those who had remained faithful all through the century to the Dutch Romanist traditions, who had welcomed the classical picturesque works by Poelenburgh, Berchem and Pynacker, and who were now admiring Poussin and Lebrun. With these patrons he soon won success; he received

[1] *Cf.* p. 97.

commissions for compositions of mythological and classical subjects for many of the new houses; he executed decorations for the Loesdyck Palace; and in the house of one rich patron, Philippe de Flines, he painted a series of allegorical panels in grisaille depicting *Poetry and Painting*, *Athene and the Liberal Arts*, *The Path to Immortality* and so forth; he also painted ceilings and easel pictures and produced engravings and etchings after his own work. He had a large art school where he instructed his pupils in the principles of architecture and of classical composition, as he understood it, and where he continually preached against the naturalism of Dutch popular art.

As Lairesse never went to Italy, his knowledge of Italian art was mainly derived from engravings, and of these he made continual use; and he also made use of the pictures by the Dutch Romanists who had preceded him. The composition of his *Antony and Cleopatra* in Amsterdam recalls the work of Bloemaert and of Lastman in his more academic manner, and there are echoes of Lastman, too, in his *Achilles dragging Hector's Body round the Walls of Troy* in Cassel, where we see piebald horses taken from Guercino's horses in the *Chariot of Aurora* on the ceiling of the Villa Ludovisi in Rome. He must, moreover, have been familiar with originals by Lebrun and Poussin, and it was those masters that he especially sought to rival. He is perhaps seen at his best in *Parnassus* (Pl. 64) in the Dresden Gallery, where the relation of the central group to Poussin's *Dance to the Music of Time* in the Wallace Collection is obvious; and in Lord Methuen's *The Judgement of Paris*.

In Amsterdam and The Hague in the days of his success Lairesse was a well-known and flamboyant figure. He was always elegantly and extravagantly dressed, and he used to stencil designs on his clothes and adopt other means of making his costumes conspicuous. He was engaged in continual gallant adventures and also in debauch. Charles Blanc says 'il eut des amours obscures et des passions qu'on n'avoue point', and it seems certain that he contracted syphilis.[1] As a result, at the age of fifty he became totally blind; but such was his energy and his enthusiasm for his theories of pictorial art that he continued to lecture to his pupils, and he succeeded in dictating a book called the *Groot Schilderboeck*, in which he elaborated his principles and convictions. He lived for twenty years after his blindness and was held in esteem by artists and men of letters to the end.

[1] This characteristic is seen in a half-length picture which belongs or belonged to Herr Leopold Koppel of Berlin and which both Dr. Hofstede de Groot and Dr. Schmidt-Degener ascribe to Rembrandt and believe to be a portrait of Lairesse.

(b) ADRIAEN VAN DER WERFF

Born Kralingen 1659, died Rotterdam 1722

CHARACTERISTIC PICTURES

London—National Gallery	*The Repose in Egypt*
London—Wallace Collection	*Venus and Cupid*
London—Wallace Collection	*Shepherd and Shepherdess*
Dulwich Gallery	*The Judgement of Paris*
Paris—Louvre	*The Magdalene in the Desert*
Paris—Louvre	*The Annunciation to the Shepherds*
Amsterdam—Rijks Museum	*The Dancing Lesson*
Amsterdam—Rijks Museum	*Venus and Cupid*
Schleissheim Gallery	*The Judgement of Solomon*
Dresden Gallery	*Abraham dismissing Hagar*
Dresden Gallery	*Lot and His Daughters*
Munich—Alte Pinakothek	*Christ before Pilate*

At the end of the seventeenth century no Dutch painter received such high prices for his pictures as Adriaen van der Werff, none was more highly esteemed by his contemporaries, and if it was the privilege of the rich to decorate their mansions with panels by Pynacker and compositions by Lairesse, it was almost the privilege of princes to own pictures by Van der Werff.

This extremely successful and, in his way, most able artist was born at a village near Rotterdam; and he was a pupil in Rotterdam of Eglon Hendrik van der Neer (1635–1703), later a Court painter to the Elector Palatine Johann Wilhelm. Van der Neer, a son of the landscape painter Aert van der Neer (1603–1677) who painted effects by moonlight, was influenced by Frans van Mieris the Elder (1635–1681), a pupil of Gerard Dou, who painted *Tableaux de modes* (*cf.* Pl. C and p. 29) and also mythological subjects in the Albani style carried out with Dou's smooth surface and elaborate 'finish'.

Van der Werff thus began in the Dou tradition and this can be seen in the *Portrait Group* (Pl. 67) where elements from Dou are used in a classical-picturesque composition. By the age of seventeen he had already attracted attention by his talents, and he made the acquaintance in Amsterdam of the rich amateur Flinck (a son of Rembrandt's pupil of that name), who had a large collection of engravings after the Italian masters and antique statues, and who was a friend and admirer of Gerard de Lairesse. This amateur with his prints had a great influence on Van der Werff, who based his art on the classical theories of Lairesse and the grace of Praxiteles, and who eventually married a relation of his friend and patron.

When Van der Werff was just over forty the Elector Palatine, on a visit to Holland, came to see his pictures and commissioned him to paint the *Judgement of Solomon* which is now in the Schleissheim Gallery. The Elector was a zealous patron of the arts, and his Court painters at Düsseldorf included Eglon van der Neer, Godfried Schalcken (a Dou pupil) and Jan Weenix (1640–1719) who painted the series of game pieces and hunting scenes now at Munich, Schleissheim and Augsburg. The Elector had a decided preference for painting with a smooth enamel finish, and the handling and surface of Van der Werff's pictures were exquisite from this stand-point—witness the Child and the flower in his *Rest on the Flight* in the National Gallery. When Van der Werff went to Düsseldorf the next year with the completed *Judgement of Solomon* the Elector was charmed with his work and invited him to join the group of his Court painters. Van der Werff was not willing to put his whole faith in one prince, but compromised with an arrangement whereby he agreed to work six months in the year exclusively on pictures for the Elector which he would send from Rotterdam. This arrangement was carried out till some years later when the Elector insisted in increasing the six months to nine and conferred on him at the same time the title of Chevalier.

There was much competition among rich Dutch amateurs for works produced in Van der Werff's 'free' months, and when Augustus King of Poland was in Rotterdam in 1710 he was unable to obtain a picture, and had to apply to the Elector who presented him with two; and in these circumstances the artist naturally became extremely rich.

Van der Werff also practised as an architect. He designed a number of façades for mansions and made the plans for the Rotterdam 'Bourse'. He had the usual art school and a large number of pupils.

The modern student will find the enamel finish of Van der Werff's pictures less tiresome than that in the works of Dou, because it is one thing to put together an artificial furniture picture with exquisite craftsmanship and another to imitate with pointless minuteness the litter and bric-à-brac of a studio. There is some Praxitelean grace in many of Van der Werff's female figures such as the Hagar in *Abraham dismissing Hagar* (Pl. 65), the mother in the *Judgement of Solomon*, the Venus in *The Judgement of Paris* and so forth; and it may be that no artist has ever achieved his purpose more exactly.

But if we consider that purpose it cannot be denied that Van der Werff's mind was distressingly confused. He tried to paint Praxitelean figures in compositions in which he made use of Rembrandt's light and shade; and in each case he achieved the letter of his law, but entirely missed its significance and spirit. His conception of a picture was not architectural enough to achieve a true classical result, and considered as a romantic or a descriptive artist he fails obviously to convince. The student will find it of interest to compare his *Abraham dismissing Hagar* (Pl. 65) with Rembrandt's picture (Pl. 33) in the Victoria and Albert Museum, with Rembrandt's etching of the same subject, where Hagar is blowing her nose as she leaves in tears and Sarah grins in triumph from the window, and with Jan Steen's version (Pl. 99) in Dresden. Such a comparison reveals Van der Werff's mind more completely than is possible in a verbal description, particularly as he has followed the main lines of Rembrandt's etching for his composition. Another comparison which will be useful is between Van der Werff's *Christ Mocked* (Pl. 66) and Rembrandt's etching of the subject (Pl. 68); here Van der Werff has followed Rembrandt's composition even more closely, and the student will not fail to note the steps which he has taken in order to improve on what seemed to him Rembrandt's muddled picture with its crazy buildings and its neglect of 'beauty'.[1]

iii. Picturesque Genre

There was yet another type of picturesque picture in Dutch Art all through the seventeenth century—picturesque genre.

This art was essentially hybrid, since the artists retained in their minds the classical concept of the painter's function as the designing of pictures with definite pictorial form, and they flirted at the same time with the descriptive popular attitude which regards the painter's function as the recording of familiar experience of everyday life.

A similar duality of concept marked certain works by Caravaggio

---

[1] Rembrandt's oil sketch *Christ before Pilate* in the National Gallery is the composition from which the etching is reversed. Mr. Roger Fry has chosen this sketch in his 'Transformations' as a supreme example of the co-operation of dramatic and psychological illustration with plastic form in a single picture. Professor Van Dyke ascribes the picture to Salomon Koninck. The comparison between the composition and Van der Werff's picture is, of course, equally interesting and valuable, whether the painting is by Rembrandt or by an able pupil and follower like Koninck.

126

and Bassano, and we find it also in Gerard Honthorst's *The Dentist* (Pl. 27). But whereas Honthorst grafted motifs from popular wood-cuts and engravings on to baroque 'historical' composition, the picturesque genre painters grafted the same motifs on to picturesque compositions by the Elsheimer-Claude circle in Rome.

Picturesque-genre art thus joins hands with the classical-picturesque works by Both, Berchem and Pynacker, and with the vast Dutch popular production, some aspects of which I shall discuss in Part V.

The pioneer artist of this school was Pieter van Laer (Bamboche) who may be said to have invented this type of picture in Rome at the beginning of the century. He was followed by Philips Wou-werman, who stressed the picturesque strain and died in 1668; and Wouwerman's style was continued by his brothers, his sons, his pupils and imitators right into the eighteenth century. Like the art of the Dutch-Romanists, the art of Rembrandt, the classical-picturesque landscape art, and the art of Lairesse and Van der Werff, it went its way unperturbed by the Dutch popular art which flooded the country from the time of the Twelve Years' Truce onwards; and the artists were continuously favoured by persons of wealth, education and taste, not only in Holland but in other lands as well.

(*a*) PIETER VAN LAER (BAMBOCHE)

Born at Laer or Haarlem before 1595, died Haarlem before 1660

CHARACTERISTIC PICTURES

Paris—Louvre	*The Departure from the Inn*
Paris—Louvre	*Milking Goats*
Florence—Uffizi	*Peasants and Soldiers before an Inn*
Cassel Gallery	*The Quack Doctor*
Cassel Gallery	*Peasants dancing under a Bridge*
Dresden Gallery	*Peasants playing Bowls*
Brunswick Gallery	*Halt before an Inn*

Pieter van Laer seems to have come from a well-to-do family of the neighbourhood of Haarlem, and he may be presumed to have had his first art lessons in the Goltzius-van-Mander-Cornelis Academy. Before 1610 he went to Rome where he was received into the circles of foreign artists and was at first a pupil of Elsheimer.

A contemporary in Rome, the historian Passeri relates that it was the custom in Rome in the cafés frequented by the foreign artists for a new-comer to have to 'stand' a bean-feast. '*Questa recreazione,*' says Passeri, '*durava almeno 24 ore continue senza mai levarsi di tavola nella quali facevano portare il vino a barili intieri'*; and he adds that a beanfeast of this kind was called a *Festa del Battesimo,* because the newcomer always received thereat a nickname and that the name given to van Laer by his colleagues at his *Festa* was 'Bamboccio'.

This nickname, of which 'Punch' is the nearest equivalent in English, had reference to the unusual appearance and character of the new arrival, who had abnormally long legs, an abnormally short torso and no neck, and who carried off these physical disadvantages by a lively disposition and a bristling upturned moustache. In Italy van Laer was accordingly known as Bamboccio, and elsewhere he was, and is, generally referred to as 'Bamboche'.

The only picture by Bamboche that I am aware of which shows the influence of Elsheimer is one called *The Night Robbery,* of which I have seen an engraving by Cornelis Vischer. As the picture's name implies, it is a night-scene, and the moon, which looks down so serenely on the *Flight in Egypt* in Elsheimer's Munich picture, here surveys an incident of robbery and violence in which the figures in the foreground are illumined in the Elsheimer manner by artificial light.

This exploitation of Elsheimer's art for another purpose was typical of Bamboche. For later he attached himself to the Poussin-Claude circle, and exploited the classical-picturesque world in Claude's pictures as a *décor* for his own observation of daily life in the streets of Rome and in the Roman Campagna. In these pictures, which were known as 'bambocciate' or 'bambochades', we see Italian peasants playing at bowls, dancing or travelling from inn to inn with horses or cattle, soldiers calling at smithies, and so forth. To Italian baroque eyes these pictures were insufferably vulgar and a profanation of art. Passeri says *'il suo genio nella pittura fi solo di dipingere bambocciate, e introdusse quelli suggetti vili di baronate e di bassi spezzi che rendono tanto diletto alla plebe'.* But Passeri had not seen the descriptive pictures of Dutch popular art—still nearer and dearer *'alla plebe'*—or he would have realized, as we do, that, compared with the gay-life and low-life popular painters whose works I shall discuss in Part V, the pictures by Bamboche are still relatively classical productions.

The German artist and historian Sandrart, who was a member of the Claude-Poussin circle, relates that Bamboche often accompanied them when they went out sketching in the Campagna, and that he painted his pictures in his studio usually without models or notes but entirely from memory; and there can be no doubt that Bamboche was not a mere eye-and-hand copyist of peasant and soldier models posing in his studio, but an extremely clever and

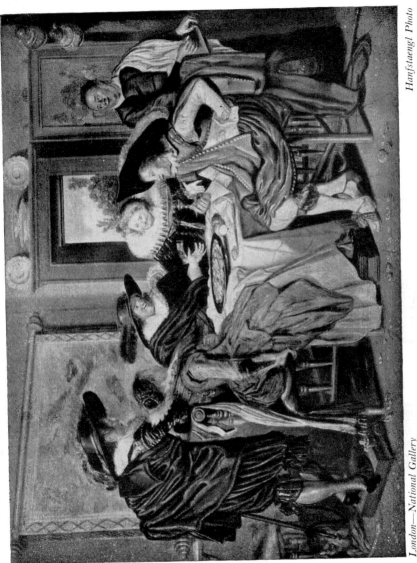

Plate 73. DIRCK HALS: 'The Prodigal Son', known as 'Merry Party'

(*Cf. Plates* 13, 24, 28, 75, 77, 78 *and* 79)

Brunswick Gallery

Plate 74A. BUYTEWECH: 'A Fop'

Drawing

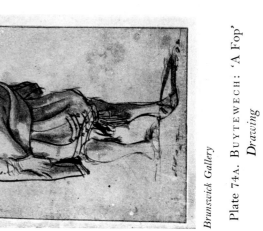

Bremen Gallery

Plate 74B. BUYTEWECH: 'A Fop'

Drawing

Budapest Gallery

Plate 75. BUYTEWECH: 'The Prodigal Son'
(*Cf. Plate* 73)

Paris—Louvre

Levy et Neurdein Reunis Photo

Plate 76. H. G. Pot: 'Charles I'

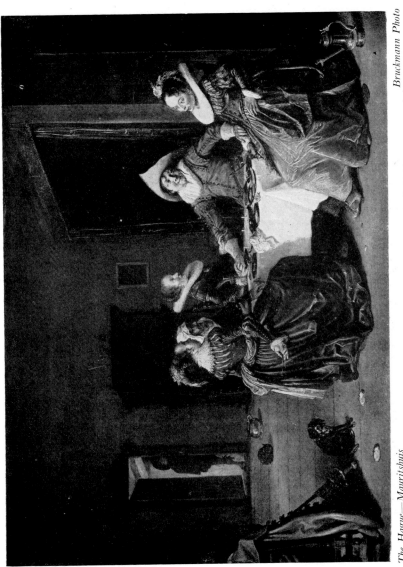

Plate 77. H. G. Pot: 'The Prodigal Son', known as 'Merry Company'

(*Cf. Plate 73*)

Plate 78. JAN STEEN: 'The Prodigal Son' ('Bad Company')

Plate 79. JAN STEEN: 'The Prodigal Father' ('Bad Company')

Plate 80. A. PALAMEDES STEVENS: 'Guard Room'

Plate 81. A. PALAMEDES STEVENS: 'Portrait of a Boy'

Plate 82. W. C. Duyster: 'The Young Officer'

Plate 83. W. C. DUYSTER: 'Soldiers quarrelling over Booty'

Plate 84. JACOB DUCK: 'The Stable'

Plate 85. TERBORCH: 'The Despatch'
(*Cf. Plates* 80, 82, 83, 84, 104 *and* 105)

Plate 86. BROUWER: 'Interior of a Tobacco Den'
(*Cf. Plates* 87, 88 *and* 89)

London—Wallace Collection

Plate 87. BROUWER: 'The Pipe Drunkard' ('Boor asleep')
(*Cf. Plates* 86, 88 *and* 89)

Plate 88. JACOB DUCK: 'The Pipe-drunk Woman'
(*Cf. Plates* 86, 87 *and* 89)

original designer of picturesque furniture pictures, which he put together in the classical tradition from drawings, and enlivened with details stored in his mind from constant and intelligent observation of everyday life.

The liveliness of Bamboche's observation, though not appreciated by the intellectual Italian artists, made an inevitable appeal to the lay public, and his pictures were a great success in Rome, where they were regarded as a new form of popular production. Bamboche enjoyed this success for some fifteen or sixteen years, and then about 1639 he returned to Holland, where examples of his work and engravings after them had preceded him and where he continued his success.

Bamboche's influence on Dutch art was considerable. I have already noted his influence on Berchem, and the student should compare Bamboche's *The Quack Doctor* (Pl. 70) with Jan Steen's picture of the same subject (Pl. 97), and also (if he cares to see the continuation of this tradition) with the picture called *Parade* in the National Gallery, painted by the French artist Gabriel Jacques de Saint Aubin in the middle of the eighteenth century. Speaking generally, Bamboche may be said to have opened the door to the whole school of Dutch gay-life and low-life popular painting; he may have influenced Hogarth, and the picturesque aspect of his art was especially imitated and developed by Wouwerman.

Bamboche died in Haarlem about the age of sixty. According to an old tradition he committed suicide from chagrin at Wouwerman's rise to fame and fortune.

(b) PHILIPS WOUWERMAN

Born Haarlem 1619, *died Haarlem* 1668

CHARACTERISTIC PICTURES

London—National Gallery	*Interior of a Stable*
London—National Gallery	*Halt of Officers*
London—National Gallery	*Landscape with Beggars*
London—National Gallery	*The Stag Hunt*
London—Wallace Collection	*The Horse Fair*
London—Wallace Collection	*Shoeing a Horse*
Dulwich Gallery	*Courtyard with Farrier*
Dulwich Gallery	*Coast near Scheveningen*
Dulwich Gallery	*Halt of a Hunting Party*
Dulwich Gallery	*Return from Hawking*
Paris—Louvre	*Leaving for the Chase*

I

MORE FOREIGN INFLUENCES

Paris—Louvre	*Interior of a Stable*
The Hague—Mauritshuis	*Leaving the Inn*
The Hague—Mauritshuis	*Battle Scene*
The Hague—Mauritshuis	*Camp Scene*
Amsterdam—Rijks Museum	*White Horse and Groom*

Philips Wouwerman was the son of an obscure painter who was his first master, and he afterwards studied with Jan Wynants (1625–82), a landscape painter by whom Gainsborough was influenced. In early youth Wouwerman, who was a Protestant, eloped with a young Catholic girl to Hamburg. There he married the girl and worked with an artist named Evert Decker, of whom nothing is known. By 1639, the year when Bamboche returned to Haarlem, Wouwerman had also returned there, and he made Haarlem his headquarters till he died at the age of forty-nine.

Wouwerman's working period was thus from 1640 to 1668, and in that time he is said to have produced over a thousand pictures. Dr. Hofstede de Groot's catalogue describes over twelve hundred and fifty pictures ascribed to him, and De Groot has himself examined and accepted over six hundred. All the galleries of Europe and many private collections have examples of his work. The Dresden Gallery has sixty pictures ascribed to him, the Hermitage at Petrograd as many, the Louvre and the Rijks Museum each has fifteen examples, and the National Gallery has eleven. The pictures include scenes of military and social life in the open air, hunting parties, travellers arriving and leaving inns, and so forth. Sometimes Wouwerman painted landscapes without figures, at other times his landscapes contain two or three figures, and at others again as many as fifty or more. He was fond of introducing a white horse into his compositions, and this is often referred to as a hall-mark of his pictures, but Dr. Hofstede de Groot has pointed out that in the *œuvre* of the gay-life painter Isaack van Ostade (1621–49), a brother of Adriaen van Ostade, a white horse occurs in an even higher proportion of pictures.

Wouwerman's pictures, like all picturesque landscapes with figures, were put together from drawings and engravings; and if we compare his *Courtyard with Farrier* (Pl. 72) with Bamboche's *Playing Bowls* (Pl. 69), we see that there is no reason to question the old tradition that Wouwerman made use of sketches and drawings by Bamboche and engravings after his pictures; and there is an echo of Jan Both, in the *Halt of a Hunting Party* (Pl. 71). At the same time there is no doubt that Wouwerman himself made many drawings and sketches, and it must be recognized that he amplified and developed the Bamboche tradition and gave it a pleasing gaiety of his own.

The pronounced French accent in many of his pictures had led some to assume, and probably quite rightly, that he must have gone to France and perhaps stayed there for some period. But it is also possible—given the conditions of production of the picturesque school—that the French accent arrived from the use of drawings and engravings by French painters. In any case, this French accent stood him in good stead in view of the appreciation of French taste which began among the Dutch upper classes in the middle of the century.

He was able to sell as many of his pictures as he could produce, and was able to dower his daughter with twenty thousand gulden. He died a rich man, and was buried with considerable pomp. He had two brothers and a son, who were artists, and many pupils who were responsible for countless pictures in his style.

As a painter Wouwerman at his best had a light and nervous touch, and his colouring is often a symphony in light, pleasant greys and pale tints. His pictures accord perfectly with French eighteenth-century furniture, and for that reason, and because the subjects of his pictures frequently depict upper-class amusements in the open air, his works were enormously in demand in the eighteenth century, particularly in France, where it was the fashion to hang whole rooms with them.

Part V

DUTCH POPULAR ART

i. Art for the Middle Classes

Dutch popular art at the beginning of the seventeenth century was produced for and bought by the Dutch middle classes. After the Dutch Revolution all classes in Holland—except the lowest—became rich and grew steadily richer as the century advanced. In particular there arose large well-to-do middle classes who prospered in trade, commerce and speculation. The Dutch self-made man in these classes, if exceptionally rich and snobbish, bought the same pictures as the aristocrats and dilettanti—the pictures, that is to say, which I have hitherto discussed. But the average self-made man was of moderate means, and he was also an average Philistine who demanded pictures depicting a world with which he was himself familiar—a world in which he could move at ease and in which he himself and his familiar experience would appear of cardinal importance; and the Dutch portraits of *Mijnheer*, his wife, his house, his meadow and his dog were the response to this demand.

Also, it must be noted, the average Dutch bourgeois wanted his pictures to be cheap. The exceptionally rich merchant might indulge in the luxury of a painting by Poelenburgh, Berchem or Wouwerman, even perhaps by Honthorst, Lastman or Van der Werff; but the average Dutch bourgeois preferred something that made less demands on his imagination, something more directly flattering to his vanity, and also something which cost less money. The old popular art of the woodcut and engraving had always been cheap; and when that art was widely translated into oil paint it was also offered at low prices. It was not, in fact, till the nineteenth century that popular artists anywhere began to demand high prices for their works, and they were only enabled to do this because institutions like the Royal Academy invested them with official honours and thus gave them a status which they had never attained or aspired to before.

The pictures painted in Holland to please the middle classes had thus certain fixed characteristics. They were small, because middle-class houses in town or country, compared with noblemen's mansions, were not large; they were descriptive of some aspect of everyday life, because the middle classes only reacted then—as they only react now—to art depicting life within their own familiar experience; they were naturalistic in technique, because this technique is the record of the automatic vision of the normal human eye, and works painted in this technique can be apprehended by the patron's eye without the exercise of any imagination or other mental activity; and, above all, they were cheap.

As already noted in discussing the development of chiaroscuro painting and baroque tactility, the system of naturalistic painting from the model, which began in the Carracci art school, soon arrived in Holland. Early in the seventeenth century, any Dutch boy could acquire in a few months a considerable degree of efficiency in the new system of copying the lights and shadows on a posed model, which was so much easier than the old system of representation by symbolic line; and the Dutch artists soon discovered that to paint small descriptive pictures of everyday life in the naturalistic technique was a relatively easy and not unpleasant way to make a modest living. Hence the enormous number of these Dutch popular painters of the period.

It is sometimes thought strange that whole families of these Dutchmen for several generations were painters. But this was really no more strange than that whole families for several generations should have been shoemakers or carpenters. The production of the Dutch popular picture was a trade, and one quite quickly learned; and the son who left a trade which had supported his father to run after some other was regarded quite naturally as a fool until he justified his bohemian excursion by results.

At first the demand for this popular art was larger than the supply, but as the production was so easy, over-production soon inevitably arrived. From being cheap, the pictures soon became cheaper, and finally so cheap that all classes, except the very poor, could afford to buy them. In Holland in the middle of the seventeenth century there were oil paintings everywhere—in all the rooms of the houses of the middle classes, in the taverns, in the back rooms of shops, and in cottages. They were hung up everywhere, just as photogravures of *The Sailor's Return* or *The Dancing Dog* were hung up everywhere at the end of the nineteenth century in England. Even so, the production was not absorbed; several Dutch towns passed protectionist measures designed to prevent dealers from other towns 'dumping' pictures upon them to the detriment of the local artists, but the edicts seem to have been evaded or defied, and the artists were forced more and more to dispose of their works wholesale to dealers or to sell them in the open market.

Evelyn travelling in Holland in 1641 says, 'Roterdam . . . where was their annual marte or faire so furnished with pictures (especially landscapes and Drolleries as they call those clownish representations) that I was amaz'd. Some I bought and sent to England.' Brereton, who was there seven years earlier, also bought half a dozen pictures at a market to bring home with him; and as Holland at this time attracted many visitors who were all successfully importuned to buy oil paintings of Dutch popular subjects as souvenirs—in the same way that visitors to Venice are now importuned to buy glass or filigree knick-knacks, or visitors to Nice to buy a paper-knife decorated with a swallow—the over-production was met to some extent by this trade with tourists who bought pictures at prices ranging from two or three to thirty gulden apiece—the equivalent of from six shillings to three pounds in English money of the time.

The painters of popular pictures were thus far from enjoying either the fame or the rewards of the intellectual painters whose works were admired by collectors and the upper classes. They had to adopt any and every means to sell their pictures, even when they were priced in half-crowns rather than in pounds. Many started shops in which they tried to sell their own and other painters' wares; and some combined painting with other methods of earning their living—Jan Steen, for example, the son of a brewer, ran a brewery himself.

Eventually the Guild of St. Luke in Haarlem issued an official protest against the 'lotteries, raffles and all the like kinds of annoying and unwonted ways of selling pictures' to which artists resorted, procedures which were described as 'bound to lead to the disrepute and decay of the arts'. The Guild was unquestionably right in this protest. For 'the disrepute and decay of the arts' was inevitable in such circumstances. A large uneducated demand in any field can never produce anything but a glut of inferior commodity; and sensational methods of disposing of a surplus can never produce respect for the commodities which stand in need of them. The general level of prices for works of art in Holland was undoubtedly brought down by the trade in popular pictures; even works by the pupils of Poelenburgh, Berchem and Rembrandt, when they were not sold under the masters' names, were disposed of for quite nominal sums in the market; and indeed we find such pictures depicted on the walls of taverns in the pictures by Dirck Hals and his school. Many of the more able of the popular painters suffered also from these conditions, because, as they offered their pictures to a public which was only interested in the *subject*, the incidental fact that the pictures by men like Dirck Hals or Buytewech were better painted than those by their pupils and imitators made no difference to their market value. In these conditions, moreover, the better painters were certain to degenerate; and we do, in fact, find that, from the technical standpoint, the Dutch popular painters of gay life, low life and bourgeois life tended to become less attractive as painters as they got older, and that each school as the century advanced tended to become less and less concerned with artistic problems, and more purely concerned with pleasing their patrons by the subject.

Certain popular artists did, of course, attract the attention of rich people and dilettanti, and so escaped from the prevailing depression in their trade. The old-maidish and illusionist finish of Gerard Dou's painting of trivialities appealed to a class of rich collector who felt that he was getting his money's worth in a Dou picture, since it appeared to have taken a long time to produce; and Dou, who was a bachelor, a recluse and a miser, and whose pictures were bought from his easel, died a very rich man; Metsu seems to have been able to get reasonable prices for his *tableaux de modes*; and Terborch, who came of a family of means, was also able to stand apart from the fever and fret of the market. But, apart from such exceptions, it is clear that the vast output of a popular art produced to please a huge untrained middle-class public was disastrous for the material welfare of the painters.

The over-production and the conditions of sale were also disastrous for artistic standards. Dutch popular art was not an emanation of mind like the intellectual Dutch art which I have hitherto discussed. It was more in the nature of a popular recreation bearing the same relation to intellectual art that the cinema of to-day bears to the drama, or that the newspaper or magazine bears to literature. It was not in any sense a new form of art, but only a development of the old popular art of the woodcut and popular engraving. The only new feature was its execution in the permanent material of oil paint—the same material used by artists whose works were an emanation of the mind. But the huge amount of the Dutch popular production, and its use of a permanent and pretentious medium, not unnaturally led people of the time to regard it as on the same plane as the art previously executed in that medium; and this confusion, which was also widespread in the nineteenth century, created false standards which persist in ill-informed circles even to this day.

ii. Painters of Gay Life

The first aspect of Dutch popular art that must be considered is the painting of gay life. I have already referred to the roots of this form of popular art in the tavern scenes labelled 'The Prodigal Son' which crept into Renaissance painting from popular woodcuts; and we have seen degrees in 'sublimation' of the theme in 'Romanist' pictures by Cornelis of Haarlem (Pl. 13) and Moreelse (Pl. 15). We are now concerned with the pictures which museum catalogues generally title 'The Merry Party', but which in Dutch seventeenth-century catalogues were frankly referred to as *bordeeltjes*. There were numerous brothels in Holland at this period, and some of the Dutch painters of gay life depict scenes in them, but more frequently they depict scenes where men are drinking and merry-making with women in establishments equivalent to present-day night clubs, *maisons de rendez-vous*, taverns or cafés.

A contemporary of one of the younger members of the Palamedes family of artists, describing an establishment of this kind, writes as follows (as quoted by Henri Havard):—

'Palamedes logeait à Breda chez un hotelier du nom de Peer van Heusden, baptisé "l'Espagnol" parce qu'il faisait plus de tapage à propos des vertus d'une lame de Tolède que son père avait remassée lors de l'investissement de Breda par le marquis de Spinola, qu'un marchand d'écrevisses ne se donne de mal, dans le mois de mai, pour vanter les vertus peu communes de sa marchandise. Ce Peer van Heusden avait le meilleur vin et les filles les plus avenantes qu'on put trouver dans cette place frontière. C'étaient là deux aimants par lesquels les officiers bardés de fer se laissent volontiers attirer. Aussi dans ce cabaret, surnommé le "Paradis des fous", comparaiss-aient chaque jour les militaires, les notables et les bourgeois qualifiés de Breda. Les uns attirés par le besoin de tremper une croûte dans un verre de vin, les autres pour donner en spectacle leurs beaux habits achetés a credit, ceux-ci pour vanter les mérites secrets de leurs chevaux ou de leurs maîtresses, et quelques-uns pour mas-sacrer leurs ennemis en pleine paix, comme autant de moucherons ou de cousins, et cela avec non moins de dexterité que les bouchers de Breda en mettent, tout en coupant la viande, a écraser les insectes qui voltigent autour d'eux.'

Taverns of this kind were portrayed by the Dutch popular painters of gay life—Dirch Hals, Buytewech, Duck and their followers.

Molenaer and Jan Steen sometimes take us to more disreputable places, and the latter, in two celebrated pictures (Pls. 78 and 79), shows us a young man and an old man being robbed there—a motif which was a favourite in popular prints from Renaissance times onwards and reappears in Hogarth's *The Rake's Progress*.

A certain number of obscene pictures were produced by the Dutch popular painters, and they were offered to tourists just as obscene Italian pictures were offered to the gentlemen who made the grand tour of Italy. But very few of such pictures survive, firstly because this kind of work is generally sooner or later destroyed, and secondly because the Dutch authorities dealt severely with artists who were held to have overstepped the mark. Some obscene subjects were certainly painted, for example, by Jan Torrentius (1589–1644) who also painted *trompe-l'oeil* still-life pieces and was arrested and tortured as a libertin and a Rosicrucian and condemned to twenty years imprisonment in Haarlem. But these offending pictures seem to have been mythologies; the Dutch gay-life pictures, speaking generally, were neither salacious nor obscene, and the vast majority of those that survive are perfectly decorous.

In many of the Dutch gay-life pictures—as indeed in the low-life and bourgeois-life pictures—some members of the company are represented as playing upon musical instruments. In Jacob Duck's *Prodigal Son* in the Hermitage, for example, the central figure plays the violoncello. We may assume that the favourite tunes in the Dutch *bordeeltjes* were quite different from those performed by the little orchestra in Duyster's *Wedding Party of Ploos van Amstel* (Pl. 101), which doubtless played the chamber music of the kind enjoyed by Pepys in his home and by the company in Dirck Hals's *Banquet in a Garden*, or by those other companies whom we see lunching off peacock pies in their parks in the 'respectable' pictures of this school. An inquiry into the music played by performers in the sixteenth and seventeenth centuries might, indeed, prove useful in assessing certain values. Perhaps the difference in character between the pictures by Giorgione and those by Caravaggio or Honthorst would be found confirmed by the difference between the music played in Venetian gardens and that played in the taverns represented by Honthorst or Baburen (Pls. 17, 19 and 24); and the difference between Van Ostade and Jan Steen's attitudes to life might appear in the difference between the dismal dirges ground out by the wandering hurdy-gurdy players in Van Ostade's pictures and the old ditties and ballads sung together by three generations round a table in Jan Steen's tavern and the broad innuendoes of the song sung by Jan Steen himself as

he 'vamped' his own accompaniment in the *Lute Player* (Pl. 94).
Perhaps also some useful facets of the Dutch *tableaux de modes* might
appear were we to hear the wrong notes played by Molenaer's young
lady and gentleman in his *Musical Pastime* in the National Gallery,
and by the young ladies in the famous music lessons by Metsu and
Terborch. Here, however, we need only observe that the Prodigal
Son's entertainments in the seventeenth century in Holland included
the equivalents—according to his purse—of the 'Jazz' orchestra
and the gramophone.[1]

The gay-life painters also painted scenes of military life known
at the time as *cortegaardjes*. As the Dutch wars from the last years
of the sixteenth century were fought by professional troops and
adventurers of all kinds, the military were not very popular either
with the citizens in the towns or with the peasants in the country.
They were welcomed in second-rate establishments of gay life when
they had reserve of pay to dispose of; but their conduct in the
country was too often like that of the soldier in Anatole France's
La Rôtisserie de la Reine Pedauque (who explained war as principally
an affair of stealing chickens from peasants) for their presence to be
very welcome in the villages. Nevertheless there was, of course,
a feeling in the hearts of the people for the glamour and swagger of
the *militaires*; and the mercenaries in the Dutch armies were not
unpopular in the sense that the Spanish soldiery were unpopular in
the old days.

The Dutch gay-life painters, therefore, show us a certain number
of pictures of camp life, a certain number of soldiers spending money
with women in taverns or guard-rooms, and a certain number of
soldiers requisitioning, plundering, and bullying peasants, quarrelling
over booty and so forth; and Terborch in *The Despatch* shows an
officer receiving a message that will cause him to leave the arms of
his mistress (Pl. 85). These popular 'military' pictures are, of course,
different in character from the comments on war produced by Callot
in his engravings of military parade and in his *Misères de la Guerre*;
they are different also from the 'picturesque' military pictures by
Wouwerman; and they are also quite different from the life-size
battle pieces produced later in France and England. They are not,
in fact, war pictures but popular presentments of the ordinary Dutchman's familiar experience of soldiers away from the front; and as
most of them show the soldiers at their recreations they are conveniently ranked with the pictures depicting gay life of other kinds.

[1] Since this was written the subject has been brilliantly explored by Lawrence
Haward in the *Music in Painting* volume of the Faber Gallery series.

PAINTERS OF GAY LIFE

The Dutch popular gay-life pictures were bought for small sums by all the middle classes. The lower middle classes saw in them the only gaiety in life with which they were familiar, and they were glad to have them on their walls; the young men of the middle classes saw in them representations of their own recreations and adventures; and the respectable fathers of families saw in them echoes of their youth and opportunities for a release of inhibitions without risk.

(a) DIRCK HALS

Born Haarlem 1591, died Haarlem 1656

CHARACTERISTIC PICTURES

London—National Gallery	*The Prodigal Son (Merry Party)*
Paris—Louvre	*The Prodigal Son (Le festin champêtre)*
Haarlem Gallery	*Woman playing Flute*
Amsterdam—Rijks Museum	*Banquet in a Garden*
Stockholm Gallery	*Tavern Scene*
Vienna Gallery	*Elegant Company*
Haarlem—Teyler Museum	*Drawing of a Merry Company round a Fire*

Dirck Hals, a younger brother of Frans Hals, was one of the founders of the Dutch School of gay-life painters. Little is known of his life. He is said to have been a pupil of his brother and also of Bloemaert. I see no trace of Bloemaert in his work, and very little of the style of Hals. On the other hand, the influence of Rubens is very evident, and I have no doubt that Dirck Hals visited Antwerp and had contact with his work. The Rubens influence is obvious in the Prodigal Son picture called *Merry Party* (Pl. 73) in the National Gallery. Here we have the light fluid touch, the thin paint, the iridescent colour, the grace and *désinvolture* of Rubens—all so different from the painting by Frans Hals. In this picture moreover Dirck Hals is not only a product of Rubens, but also an ancestor of Watteau—a link, in fact, between the two masters; the young man standing with his back turned, in this picture, and the young woman next to him, might have been painted from a drawing by Watteau, and in this connexion it is not without significance that many of Dirck Hals's pictures show festive gatherings in the open air.

Dirck Hals is in many ways an attractive artist. His most characteristic works fall into three classes: (*a*) indoor pictures of the Prodigal Son motif, (*b*) outdoor pictures of the same motif, and (*c*) indoor and outdoor groups of weddings or other social gatherings.

In the first group Dirck Hals takes us to private rooms in taverns where the young bloods are entertaining their mistresses or women of the town. The rooms are hung with pictures and with the maps which the Dutch, justly proud of their maritime excursions, delighted to hang upon their walls; the table, where oysters, wine and cakes are the general refreshment, is covered with a white cloth; the company sit on three-legged chairs or stools with rush seats covered with cushions. Sometimes the tavern-keeper chalks up the reckoning on a slate—a gesture already noted in the curious Romanist Prodigal Son pictures by Cornelis of Haarlem. Often there are one or more dogs and sometimes one of the company plays a lute or other musical instrument. The oyster party is sometimes varied by a scene in which the company smoke, play at tric-trac or cards and cuddle the girls, or in which the favourite motif of the procuress appears; in a very accomplished and stylish drawing in the Teyler Museum at Haarlem a man and woman sit by the fire which throws its light upon the legs of the woman who has pulled her skirt above her knees —a gesture erotic to the Dutch public of the seventeenth century, though in our own day, when the same effect is visible at all times, it shocks us less than Moreelse's portrait of the Princesse de Rohan with bare breasts; and we have to remember this change also in considering pictures like Jan Steen's *Young Girl at Her Toilet* in Buckingham Palace and his *Morning Toilet* from the Rudolphe Kann Collection, where the attitude depicted was shocking at the time.

In Dirck Hals's outdoor Prodigal Son pictures the meal is generally the central motif, though the artist also pays attention to the landscape, and often he clearly enjoys painting one or more dogs. In his social or wedding groups which rank him a founder of the Dutch school of bourgeois-life painters, he finished more elaborately and more timidly than in his gay-life pictures; presumably these groups were commissions, and he was for that reason both more conscientious and more cautious. The Amsterdam picture, *A Banquet in a Garden*, is a good example of this aspect of his work; it contains about twenty-five figures; one group is seated round a table with the usual oysters, wine and cakes or pies; and another in the foreground contains what I take to be a bride and bridegroom and members of their families, and a group of musicians in which a woman plays the flute and a man the lute; the scene is set in a park adjoining a large house with a terrace; graceful greyhounds, a monkey, and a lap-dog are on the ground, parrots perch on the balustrades of the terrace, and boy attendants take the wine from coolers—as they do in pictures by Tintoretto and Bassano—and bring fresh supplies from the house. All the figures in this as in the other types of Dirck Hals's pictures are fashionably dressed; and this interesting artist must thus also be ranked among the Dutch painters of *tableaux de modes*.

At one time a considerable number of pictures were ascribed to Dirck Hals, and many inferior works by his numerous followers and by the hack gay-life painters who sprang up at this time all over Holland were included in his *œuvre*. Modern students tend to relieve him of works below his technical standard; and to ascribe others to the excellent gay-life painter, W. Buytewech.

(b) W. BUYTEWECH THE ELDER

Born Rotterdam c. 1590, *died Rotterdam c.* 1624

CHARACTERISTIC PICTURES

Amsterdam—Rijks Museum	*The Prodigal Son (Elegant Courtship)*
Berlin—Kaiser-Friedrich Museum	*The Prodigal Son (A Merry Party)*
Budapest Gallery	*The Prodigal Son (A Merry Party)*
Brunswick Gallery	*A Fop* (Drawing)
Bremen Gallery	*A Fop* (Drawing)
Rotterdam Gallery	*Man and Dog* (Drawing)

Even less is known of Willem Buytewech's life than of that of Dirck Hals. It is known that he was born at Rotterdam and died there, and that he lived at one time in Haarlem. It seems very likely that he was at one time a pupil of Dirck Hals. Houbraken, the old Dutch biographer, who describes him as 'Geestige Willem' (William the Gay), names him as master of one Maartensz Zorgh.

In Dirck Hals's pictures, all the figures, as I have pointed out, are fashionably dressed; in Buytewech's pictures they are definitely foppish and have an air of extreme elegance in attitude and attire. This foppishness resided doubtless to some extent in the artist's eye, since he depicted the same young bloods as were depicted by Dirck Hals. The air of elegance in Buytewech's figures is conveyed not only by the clothes, but also by the delicacy of the wrists and ankles, feet and hands, and by the smallness of the heads which gives the figures lightness and height. In looking at his pictures we feel that we are in the presence of the younger sons of an aristocracy who are having a good time and scattering their money. *The Prodigal Son* in Budapest (Pl. 75) is a good example of these characters.

Some of Buytewech's pictures were painted when fashionable young men and women both wore a species of top hat adorned with a wreath or feather round the crown. Censors of the younger generation in

Holland at this time complained that the women borrowed fashions such as this top hat from the men, and that the men wore extravagantly wide breeches trimmed with lace and ribbons, and that they wore long-haired wigs and used scent. This type of hat appears in the two drawings of fops (Pl. 74) which belong to a series of seven drawings by Buytewech for engraved fashion plates; and a companion series of engravings depicts the contemporary fashions of women.

These drawings prove that Buytewech, like Dirck Hals, was an artist who retained the art of stylistic drawing which Dutch popular art was to abandon and destroy; and this stylistic character persists in many of the better gay-life Dutch painters after it had disappeared from the other forms of popular art.

Engravings by or after Buytewech include scenes from the story of Bathsheba and a 'St. Francis in Ecstasy'. But all his pictures and drawings with which I am acquainted show scenes of gay life or of fashion.

(c) H. G. POT

Born Haarlem 1585, *died Amsterdam* 1657

CHARACTERISTIC PICTURES

London—National Gallery	*The Prodigal Son (A Merry Party)*
London—Wallace Collection	*The Prodigal Son (Scene in a Gambling House)*
London—Buckingham Palace	*Charles I, Queen Henrietta Maria and the Prince of Wales*
Hampton Court	*A Startling Introduction*
Paris—Louvre	*Charles I*
Paris—Louvre	*The Family van Beresteyn*
Haarlem Gallery	*Apotheosis of William the Silent*
Haarlem Gallery	*Officers of the Civic Guard*
The Hague—Mauritshuis	*The Prodigal Son (Merry Company)*
Berlin—Kaiser-Friedrich Museum	*The Dispute for the Inheritance*

Hendrick Gerritsz Pot was another painter of gay life. He was born at Haarlem and worked there and at Amsterdam. He is said to have worked with Frans Hals in the studio of Carel van Mander, and certain of his pictures, such as the *Officers of the Civic Guard* at Haarlem, show technical characteristics resembling those of Hals; and the *Family van Beresteyn* in the Louvre, now ascribed to him, was formerly catalogued as by Frans Hals. But most of Pot's gay-life pictures stand much closer to the work of Dirck Hals, and their colour, like that in Dirck Hals's pictures, sometimes recalls the palette of Rubens.

In 1631 Pot came to England and painted the portrait group of *Charles I, Queen Henrietta Maria and the Prince of Wales*. In this singular picture the King and Queen are at opposite corners of the canvas and the Prince, as a baby, is perched on a table between them. On this visit he also painted the small full-length *Charles I* (Pl. 76) in the Louvre, which is said to be an adaptation of the life-size full-length portrait by Daniel Mytens at Buckingham Palace, and which makes a curious contrast with the elegant presentment of the King by Van Dyck. A third picture painted here is at Hampton Court; it is called *A Startling Introduction* and depicts a cavalier introducing himself to a lady into whose apartment he has entered by the chimney. The composition of this picture resembles that of the Royal group, as there is a large table between the two figures; the cavalier stands by the chimney at one end of it and the lady curtsies at the other; and a dog and a monkey play in the background. The exact subject of the work remains a matter for speculation. It is presumably based on some episode or story which had entertained the King.

How did Pot, a relatively obscure portrait and gay-life painter, receive the invitation to the Court of Charles I? It is possible that he owed it to Rubens, who was there the year before; and perhaps he visited Antwerp, as I have also assumed in the case of Dirck Hals. Some contact with originals by Rubens can, I think, be assumed with certainty in the case of this painter, particularly as Pot was one of the exceptional Dutch artists who painted a pageant picture—namely *The Apotheosis of William the Silent* now at Haarlem. In the Haarlem Gallery there is also a picture by his hand called *Flora's Chariot of Fools*—a satire in allegorical form on the rage for speculation in rare tulips in Holland in 1637, when as much as 13,000 gulden (£1,100) was paid for a single bulb called the *Semper Augustus*.

The most attractive of Pot's gay-life pictures that I know is the Prodigal Son picture called *Merry Company* (Pl. 77) in The Hague. Here the Prodigal Son sits at a table holding the hands of two young women. A third young woman is at the table, and the procuress completes the party. The ordinary Dutch cupboard-bed with curtains is in the background, a dog and cat wander about the floor, and a man, perhaps the proprietor of the establishment, listens behind the door. All this is sufficiently sordid. But there is considerable charm about the actual painting of the picture. The young women have flowers in their hair and wear their best clothes. The one next to the young man has a pleasant head, and she wears a yellow skirt and blue over-dress. The woman on the far side of the table is dressed in violet, and the third young woman is dressed in red. The gaiety of the scene, in fact, resides entirely in the colour of the picture; but from this quality—which we also find in works by Dirck Hals—the later gay-life painters departed, as Pot himself departed from the stylistic drawing of Dirck Hals and Buytewech. For, as I have already noted, the production of popular art inevitably leads to artistic degeneration, because the artist tends to neglect artistic considerations when experience has taught him that they count for nothing with a public entirely concerned with the subjects of his pictures.

(d) A. PALAMEDES STEVENS

Born Delft 1601, died Amsterdam 1673

CHARACTERISTIC PICTURES

Paris—Louvre	*Portrait of a Man*
Amsterdam—Rijks Museum	*The Supper Party*
Antwerp Gallery	*The Sportsman Returns (Interior with family group)*
The Hague—Mauritshuis	*Music after Dinner*
Hanover—Provincial Museum	*Guard Room*
Cassel Gallery	*Hunting Company with Dogs*
Vienna—Liechtenstein Gallery	*Guard Room*
Berlin—Kaiser-Friedrich Museum	*Company at a Peacock Feast*
Berlin—Kaiser-Friedrich Museum	*Portrait of a Young Girl*
Berlin—Kaiser-Friedrich Museum	*Portrait of a Boy*

There was at one time a good deal of confusion between the works of several Dutch artists of the family called Palamedes, and even now sale catalogues on this point are often vague. It would seem, however, to be established that there was (*a*) Palamedes Stevens or Stevaerts who was an 'agate carver' and was born in England; (*b*) his son Anthony Palamedes Stevens; (*c*) Anthony's brother Palamedes Palamedes, who painted camp and battle scenes; and (*d*) Palamedes Palamedes II, Anthony's son, who also painted battle scenes.

The most considerable of these artists was Anthony, who was born in Delft in 1601 and probably worked with Mierevelt and with H. G. Pot. He painted gay-life, camp and guard-room scenes, portraits and bourgeois parties. He was long supposed to have painted the figures in the singular picture by Dirck van Deelen in The Hague Mauritshuis which represents the States-General Assembly in the Binnenhof in 1651, and has a large flap over the

Plate 89. JAN STEEN: 'After the Carouse'

(Cf. Plates 86, 87 and 88)

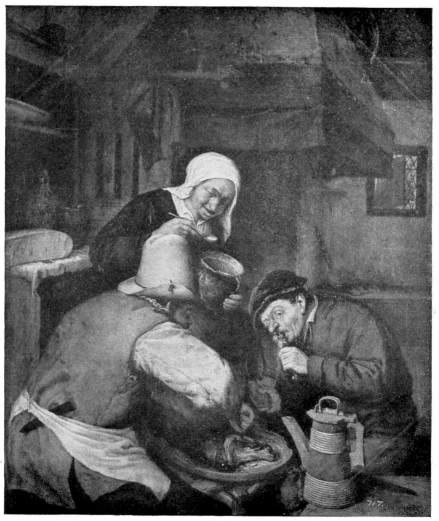

Plate 90. ADRIAEN VAN OSTADE: 'Peasants Eating'

Plate 91. ADRIAEN VAN OSTADE: 'Peasants at an Inn Table'

Plate 92. ADRIAEN VAN OSTADE: 'The Cobbler'

Plate 93. JAN MOLENAER: 'The Dentist'
(Cf. Plates 27, 70 and 97)

Lugano, Baron Thyssen Collection

Plate 94. JAN STEEN: 'The Lute Player'
(*Self-Portrait*)

Cassel Gallery

Hanfstaengl Photo

Plate 95. JAN STEEN: 'Twelfth Night'

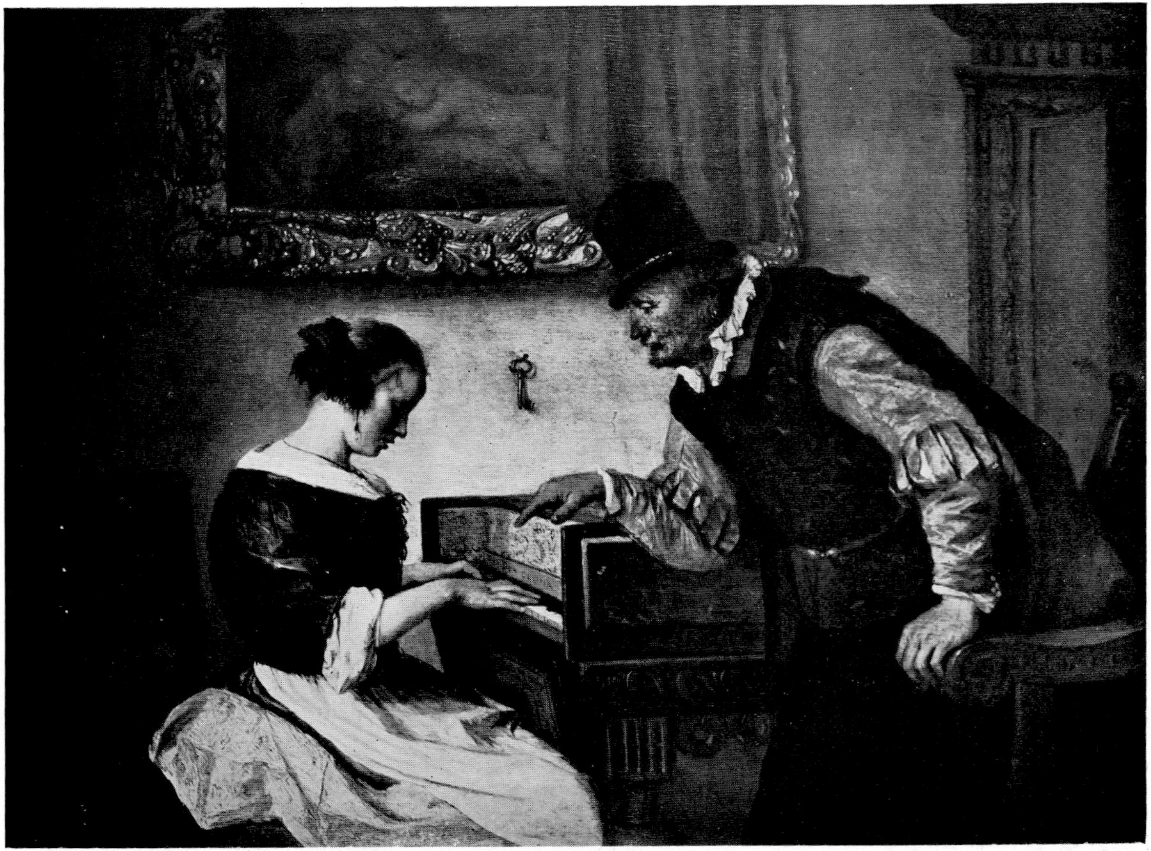

London—Wallace Collection *Mansell Photo*

Plate 96. Jan Steen: 'The Harpsichord Lesson'

Plate 97. JAN STEEN: 'The Quack Doctor'

(*Cf. Plate* 70)

Plate 98. JAN STEEN: 'The Happy Family'

Plate 99. JAN STEEN: 'Abraham dismissing Hagar'
(*Cf.Plates* 33 *and* 65)

Plate 100. JAN STEEN: 'Merry Company'

Plate 101. W. C. DUYSTER: 'Wedding Party of Ploos van Amstel'

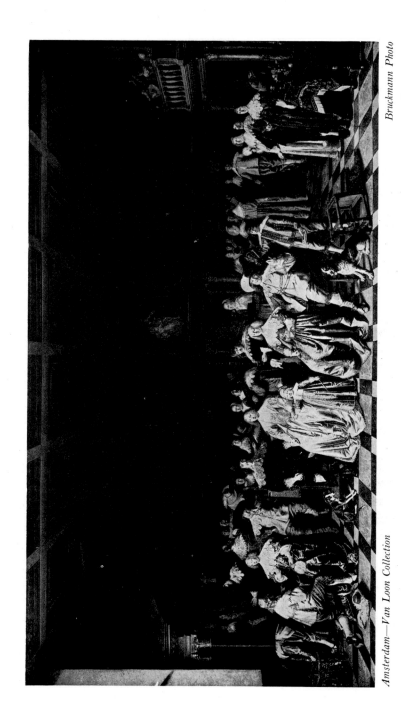

Plate 102. MOLENAER: 'Family Feast'

Plate 103. MOLENAER: 'Family Feast' (*detail*)

Plate 104. TERBORCH: 'Portrait of a Gentleman'

lower half which, when lifted, converts the scene into an ante-room of the Binnenhof decorated with tapestries, and peopled only with a few citizens and peasants, one or two dogs and so forth; but Van Deelen is now given credit for the whole work.

Palamedes in his military gay-life scenes paints with a lighter touch than Pot and the arrangement of his *Guard Room* (Pl. 80) in the Hanover Museum is agreeable. Like Pot he often makes his figures rather stumpy, and this appears also in his portrait groups of bourgeois parties like the *Peacock Feast* in Berlin, where an expensively dressed company is about to eat a peacock pie from a table set in a park. He was happiest as a portrait painter of heads. In this field he was very good indeed. The drawing of the face in the *Portrait of a Man* in the Louvre is extremely subtle and the same quality appears in the *Portrait of a Boy* (Pl. 81).

(e) W. C. DUYSTER

Born Amsterdam 1599 or 1600, died Amsterdam 1635

CHARACTERISTIC PICTURES

London—National Gallery	*Soldiers quarrelling over Booty*
London—National Gallery	*Tric-Trac Players*
England—Wellington Collection	*A Musical Party*
The Hague—Mauritshuis	*The Young Officer*
Amsterdam—Rijks Museum	*Wedding Party of A. Ploos van Amstel*
Leningrad—Hermitage	*Guard-room with Soldiers by a Fireplace*
Basle Gallery	*Soldiers and Women*

Willem Cornelisz Duyster, who died at the age of thirty-five, holds an exceptional place among the Dutch gay-life painters. Many inferior pictures of guard-rooms, requisitioning scenes and so forth were formerly ascribed to him; but now that students have relieved his reputation of these works and ascribed them to minor painters of the school, he stands out as a military gay-life painter linking the craftsmanship of the picturesque art of Berchem and Bamboche with that of Terborch, Metsu and Vermeer himself.

Duyster is generally assumed—without apparently any evidence —to have been a pupil of Pieter Codde, whom I have mentioned as having completed the *The Reael and Blaeuw Company* (Pl. 40) by Frans Hals. But I suspect that he was also a pupil of Berchem or Bamboche. It was, I feel, from Berchem or Bamboche that he learned his technical procedures—the sharp crisp light and shade on the figures, the Italian simplification, and the feeling for an enamel surface which in the case of his pictures has generally, as in the case of Berchem's, lasted without cracks or damage to this day.

It was also certainly from the standpoint of some picturesque painter that Duyster approached his work. His attitude to his subject is completely artificial. The soldiers are incredibly clean and tidy; they have long delicate hands and shapely ankles and they stand in elegant refined attitudes, witness *The Young Officer* (Pl. 82). Even when they are shown in a brawl as in the *Soldiers quarrelling over Booty* (Pl. 83), they are more like a group of young men by Buytewech engaged in a charade than anything approaching real mercenaries inflamed by greed and rage; moreover, no dust rises from the fracas in this picture; the silk clothes, the arms and accessories glitter like the clothes and accessories in the later *tableaux de modes*; and every fold of silk or satin has its high light as in the white satin skirts of the ladies by Terborch (who—as Dr. Hofstede de Groot and Dr. Bode agree—was probably his pupil).

Duyster was famous in his lifetime for his painting of stuffs—indeed his skill in this field was especially praised in the *Lof der Schilderkonst* published by Philips Angel in 1641, six years after the artist's death; and it must be recognized that in taking over the craft of painting textures from Berchem or some other picturesque artist (who had used it as part of an architectural scheme) and adapting the craft to the purpose of popular description, Duyster indicated the way to the eye-and-hand texture painting of the Dutch *tableaux de modes*. His influence in that sense was unfortunate; for imitation of textures for an illusionist purpose is the least significant form of baroque tactility; Reynolds, it will be remembered, continually exhorted his students to avoid it, and in this case, *mirabile dictu*, he practised what he preached and always avoided it himself.

The most attractive pictures by Duyster that I know are *The Young Officer* (Pl. 82) which has considerable dignity, and *The Wedding Party of Adriaen Ploos van Amstel* (Pl. 101). Duyster was certainly at his best in the wedding picture. His elongation of the figures and the hands, and his glittering rendering of stuffs, seem in place in this small picture, which contains passages of delightful craftsmanship, like the head and ruff of the red-haired woman reading the letter and the transparency of the collar and head-dress of the woman with her back turned on the right; and there is a pleasant descriptive incident at the back, where a boy and girl kiss at the foot of the stairs while the graver members of the company are engaged in sitting for their portraits. This episode and the informal grouping of the figures give an air of spontaneity to an elaborately-worked picture which is a minor triumph in its way.

(f) JACOB DUCK

Born Utrecht about 1600, *died The Hague about* 1660

CHARACTERISTIC PICTURES

Amsterdam—Rijks Museum	*The Stable*
Munich—Alte Pinakothek	*The Pipe-drunk Woman*
Munich—Alte Pinakothek	*Officers Playing Cards*
Munich—Alte Pinakothek	*Camp Scene*
Berlin—Kaiser-Friedrich Museum	*Soldiers Foraging*
Stuttgart Gallery	*Soldiers and Pipe-drunk Woman*
Leningrad—Hermitage	*A Gaming House*
Leningrad—Hermitage	*The Prodigal Son (A Merry Company)*

Jacob Duck was formerly confused with Jan le Ducq, a pupil of Carel du Jardin and so a descendant of Berchem. Duck presumably was a pupil of Duyster, and he may have been a fellow-student with Duyster under Berchem. The pictures now ascribed to him, in addition to those quoted above, include: *Prisoners brought before a Captain* in the Hamburg Museum, *Marauding Soldiers* in the Louvre, where a woman is seen in an attitude of entreaty before an officer while soldiers plunder in the background,[1] *Soldiers and a Woman in a Tavern* in the Rouen Galley, *A Woman picking the Pocket of a Sleeping Soldier* in the Liechtenstein Gallery in Vienna, and *Soldiers showing Booty to a Woman* in the Hermitage at Leningrad.

Duck's painting in *The Stable* (Pl. 84) is clearly related to the Berchem quality in Duyster's pictures. His officer has here a Duyster-esque elegance, but the painting is heavier, the substance more solid, and the feeling for form is more generous. In his *Prodigal Son* in the Hermitage, there is dignity in the figure of a woman with her foot on a foot-warmer; and the arrangement of the curtain and still life on the left in this work suggest that the artist had seen some pictures by Vermeer.

The most striking of Duck's pictures known to me is *The Pipe-drunk Woman* (Pl. 88). I shall refer to the subject of this picture when discussing Brouwer and the tobacco vice and to the woman's attitude in connexion with figures in Jan Steen's *Twelfth Night* and the *Allegory of the New Testament* by Vermeer. But here I would

---

[1] Dr. Bredius and M. Emile Michel attribute this picture to Terborch.

point out the majesty of this figure of the pipe-drunk woman and the architectural structure of the whole picture. The man who painted it must assuredly be regarded as one of the most distinguished artists of his school.

iii. Painters of Low Life

Paintings of low life are a well-known feature of Dutch popular art. Holland produced not only hundreds of painters of gay life in the manner of Dirck Hals, Duyster, Palamedes and so forth, but also hundreds of painters of peasants in their homes, in low taverns, or gathered together in the open air. Of these painters I have selected Brouwer, Van Ostade, Jan Steen and Molenaer for discussion, because each was a *chef d'école* and was so widely imitated that all the Dutch low-life pictures may be said, roughly speaking, to be founded on these four men's several styles.

Brouwer was an exceptional figure in Dutch Art, who depicted exceptional peasants, and his works appealed mainly in his lifetime to artists and dilettanti as they do to-day. But Van Ostade, Jan Steen and Molenaer depicted normal peasants and small tradesmen, and their works made a much more general appeal.

The Dutch low-life pictures were sold as a rule in the open market for small sums to members of the class depicted. They were also bought by travellers as curiosities and by the Dutch middle classes for the same reason that the English middle classes in the nineteenth century bought pictures of ragged beggars and low-life scenes. The Dutch bourgeois contemplating pictures by Van Ostade could indulge in the pleasures of condescending pity and self-satisfaction. He could contrast the dirt and gloom with the cleanliness and cheerfulness of his own apartments; the poor interiors and their litter of battered and broken accessories with his own shining brass, his own painted clavichord, and his own carpets and curtains; the peasant's rags with his own simple but expensive clothes and his wife's silks and furs; and the sad pygmies with himself and his wife, large, well fed, and well behaved; and he could reflect that if these pygmies had had his own sterling qualities—his industry, honesty, morality, and relative sobriety—they would doubtless have attained to conditions like his own.

In contemplating the pictures by Jan Steen, the Dutch bourgeois was in a different position. Jan Steen depicted the life of the small tradesman and his family who were well above the submerged line; and his world was gay with a gaiety less likely to arouse the pity of the bourgeois or give him cause for congratulation than to arouse his jealousy—since the idea of happiness without a substantial balance at the bank always arouses jealous resentment in the bourgeois mind. For this reason Jan Steen could only sell his pictures to the class depicted in them, and to a few dilettanti who admired his handling of oil paint.

Jan Molenaer was a curious eclectic who painted pictures both of low life and bourgeois life in various techniques; and he probably sold his pictures both in the market and to the bourgeoisie.

The majority of the Dutch low-life pictures are of no interest to the modern student of painting. But the artists I have selected all had artistic gifts, and though Van Ostade, Jan Steen and Molenaer eventually degenerated, like all popular artists, into painters of subjects rather than of pictures, they all three produced a number of artistically-interesting pictures both in youth and early middle age.

(a) ADRIAEN BROUWER

Born Oudenarde 1605, died Antwerp 1638

CHARACTERISTIC PICTURES

London—National Gallery	*Three Boors Drinking*
London—Wallace Collection	*The Pipe Drunkard (A Boor Asleep)*
London—Dulwich Gallery	*Interior of a Tobacco Den*
Paris—Louvre	*Interior of a Tobacco Den*
Paris—Louvre	*The Smoker*
Paris—Schloss Collection	*Interior of a Tobacco Den*
Paris—Schloss Collection	*The Operation on the Foot*
Brussels—Gallery	*Scene in grounds of Antwerp Citadel*
The Hague—Mauritshuis	*Self-Portrait*
Amsterdam—Rijks Museum	*Interior of a Tavern with Smokers*
Munich—Alte Pinakothek	*Interior of a Tobacco Den*
Munich—Alte Pinakothek	*Peasants Singing in a Tavern*
Munich—Alte Pinakothek	*The Operation on the Arm*
Munich—Alte Pinakothek	*Peasants Quarrelling*

When Hals was painting his great St. George and Adrian groups in 1627 he had with him as pupil or assistant a young man called Adriaen Brouwer, a bohemian after his own heart, who spent any money that came his way on tobacco and drink, and helped Hals with his pictures and generally about the studio when he was sober.

Hals is said to have treated him badly, and perhaps he did, for eventually Brouwer put his pipe and his brushes in his pocket and went off to Flanders, where he had been born some twenty-eight years before.

Brouwer was a son of the lower middle classes. His father had some appointment as a draughtsman on cartoons in the tapestry factory at Oudenarde, where Adriaen was born in 1605; and his mother sold bonnets and handkerchiefs in what we should call a one-man draper's shop. As a boy he was doubtless taught to use pencil and brushes by his father. At sixteen he ran away from home —probably to Antwerp where, perhaps, he saw works by Pieter Brueghel and by Rubens; and from Antwerp he went to Amsterdam. It was from Amsterdam that he went to Frans Hals at Haarlem, and he remained there for six years; when he returned to Antwerp, he fared not better but worse, for he soon found himself imprisoned, for an offence not recorded, in the Spanish citadel; and some years after his release he was found dead outside a tavern in 1638.

This 'Villon of Holland', as he has been called, was one of the founders of the school of low-life painting which developed in Holland in the seventeenth century. Nearly all the pictures ascribed to him show peasants in low dens; hardly any show peasants in their homes. The Dutch or Flemish peasants in his pictures are poor, stunted creatures, the debris of half a century of war. They wear torn and dirty garments and congregate in conditions of misery and filth. Sometimes they try to overcome the gloom of their surroundings with the stimulant of raw spirits, sometimes they break into a coarse and discordant chorus, but most frequently they have fled to the narcotic of tobacco and we see them completely stupefied or half-way to that state.

It is obvious from Brouwer's pictures that the tobacco in the pipes smoked by these peasants was more like opium than the tobacco that we smoke to-day; and that the smoking of such tobacco was a definite vice practised in especially low taverns or tobacco dens. The stupefying effects of this tobacco were due either to the strong nature of the actual leaf or to admixture, by the vendors, of other narcotic ingredients—hemp, coltsfoot, or belladonna—to make the supplies go further. Brouwer worked in the early days of smoking, when tobacco was expensive; and the flotsam and jetsam shown in his pictures doubtless demanded something adulterated for cheapness and as strong as possible in its effects. Later—perhaps even in Brouwer's time—mild tobacco was obtainable in Holland, and it was mild tobacco that was smoked when the habit became general in Holland. Pipes appear in many of the Dutch gay-life pictures, in low-life pictures by Van Ostade and Jan Steen, and also in some of the scenes of bourgeois interiors by painters of *tableaux de modes*. But Brouwer depicts smokers of another kind. His smokers were anxious to become what was called at the time 'tobacco-drunk' as quickly and as cheaply as possible; and tobacco dens were there to enable them to do so. The strong or doped tobacco supplied to them was cut, rolled, and smoked in the white clay pipes that we see in Brouwer's pictures; and it is clear from those pictures that it was invariably inhaled.

The smokers depicted by Brouwer are thus not the normal Netherlandish peasants of the time, but eccentric degenerates addicted to a special vice. We have it from Brouwer's earliest biographers that he himself was *extrêmement adonné au tabac et à l'eau de vie*, and that he used to work in tobacco dens. He was, thus, addicted to the same vice as his models; he was at home in the dismal haunts he frequented, and the men he depicted were men whose weaknesses he shared.

Brouwer made the drawings for his pictures in these tobacco dens, presumably before the drugs in his own pipe had begun to take effect, and he painted the pictures from the drawings later on. In several of his pictures we see, in fact, one of his drawings— generally a portrait sketch—pinned up on the wall.

In Brouwer's pictures we see 'smoke drunkards' in all stages of their vice. In a picture in the Schloss Collection in Paris they are grouped round a bench; one takes the tobacco from a bowl and is holding it in a scrap of paper, the second is just lighting his pipe, the third is inhaling the first poisonous whiff. In a picture in the Dulwich Gallery we have again the initial stages of the debauch; the scene here would seem to be not a smoking-den but a low tavern where the visitors are drinking as well as smoking, and a peasant is seen with his arm round a woman in the background. In the *Interior of a Tobacco Den* in the Munich Pinakothek (Pl. 86) we see six peasants in the later stages of smoking. Here there is no con- viviality. The smokers sit singly at all angles with their backs to one another, each lost to the world in the pleasures of the drug. The man in the foreground is almost completely drugged; his eyes are closed and he is more than half asleep, but he still holds the little white pipe in his hand; and a seventh peasant jeers at the smoke- drunkards through the open door. The final stage of this kind of smoking is seen in the famous picture called *A Boor Asleep* (Pl. 87), in the Wallace Collection, which really represents a smoker on a stool in the tavern-yard where he has been placed to sleep off the effects.[1]

But Brouwer himself was something more than a drugged and drunken sot. He was an original descriptive artist, with the power to observe intensely and record his observations. He also had great sensibility and an eye for architectural form. He painted in the thin glaze technique of the Flemings, Brueghel and Rubens, combined with tints mixed up on the palette in the new manner of Hals; he drew with style and precision and his colour is varied and subtle. There is undeniably a certain plastic nobility in his work and, as pointed out in the Wallace Collection catalogue, the attitude of *A Boor Asleep* reminds one of the famous 'Barberini Faun'.

The Brouwer we know from the tobacco pictures is thus one of those rare and interesting artists who are at once the victims of a vice and consciously active as strong artists. Toulouse-Lautrec immediately comes to mind as an example in more recent times. Brouwer, addicted to drugged tobacco, was something of a pariah among normal Dutch and Flemish peasants and in his own middle class, though, as we know, mere drunkenness was too general to call for comment. He was only at home among others addicted to his vice, but being truly an artist he carried with him to the tobacco dens the knowledge that, though he had come to feel at home in such surroundings, he was not entirely of that world. In the tobacco dens he was inevitably most consciously the artist and most impelled to justify to himself his presence in such company. In respectable company he was the sot Brouwer who was destined to die in the gutter; in the tobacco dens he was the artist Brouwer who is living to this day. Toulouse-Lautrec, the French aristocrat who died at thirty-seven in 1901, was a cripple and a neurotic—neurosis in his case being caused perhaps by rage that owing to his broken legs he was not as the long line of open-air country gentlemen from whom he sprang had been, and that he was unable to live an active life. In Paris he became fascinated by the underworld and was soon only at home among artists, or at the Moulin Rouge, in bars or in *maisons closes*. In such places he felt himself most essentially both a

[1] Other Dutch artists occasionally depicted tobacco-drunkards. The sleeping woman in Duck's *The Pipe-drunk Woman* (Pl. 88) still holds her pipe and tobacco-tin in her lap; in a picture in the Hermitage in Leningrad ascribed to Jan Steen, but presumably by Duck, the same woman is depicted once more pipe-drunk with the pipe fallen at her feet on the floor, and her husband is seated beside her, pipe in hand; also the pipe in the hand of the sleeping woman in Jan Steen's *After the Carouse* (Pl. 89) suggests that she has been smoking the strong or doped tobacco while the old rake has been drinking.

gentleman and an artist, and compelled to justify his claim to both titles. As Brouwer studied the tobacco-drunkards, so Lautrec studied the harlots, their clients, and their exploiters; and some of his pictures are the same kind of documents as the records of tobacco-drunkards by Brouwer. The mental attitude of such men to such subjects bears no resemblance to the attitude of the ordinary citizen or to that of the popular artist or to that of the satirical moralist. The moment Lautrec took his pencil in hand he was impersonal and detached. But he came at the end of the romantic movement of the nineteenth century, and his work for that reason shows the romantic preoccupation with characteristic rather than with architectural form. Brouwer died before Rembrandt had built the foundation of romantic art, and he was able not only to remain as impersonal as Lautrec, but also to remain free from the romantic attitude that would have given a different complexion to his art.

Brouwer's work has another characteristic. If we compare it with that of the Dutch popular gay-life painters, we observe at once the almost total absence of figures of young women. In the tobacco pictures the rare women who appear are old, middle-aged and invariably ill-favoured. His other genre pictures depict scenes in ordinary taverns where peasants drink or quarrel, and in village surgeries where they grimace in agony while the village doctor lances an ulcer or performs some other operation with a knife; and here the women who very occasionally appear are also old and ugly. In Haarlem there is a picture of soldiers smoking, with a good-looking young woman holding a glass of wine; but this picture was probably painted wholly or largely by Brouwer's pupil Joost Van Craesbeck; there is also a figure, *Idleness*, of a fairly young, not ill-favoured woman from a series which Brouwer painted to symbolize *The Seven Cardinal Vices*; and I have seen an engraving after a picture said, quite incredibly, to be by his hand, which represents a young and attractive woman, perhaps made younger and more attractive by the engraver, engaged in lascivious sky-larking with a group of peasants in a tavern-yard. But with these exceptions young women are entirely absent from the Brouwer *œuvre*.

In his tobacco pictures Brouwer must, therefore, be accounted an exceptional figure in Dutch Art. But in his scenes of normal peasant life he approximates to the low-life popular painters whose works I am about to consider, and he must for that reason be accounted one of the founders of that school.

Brouwer also painted landscapes, and the National Gallery has

153

an interesting landscape *Tobias and the Angel.* Sir Charles Holmes is of opinion that the figures in this picture and the foreground may have been added by a follower of Rembrandt, and that Reynolds, who once owned the picture, also worked on certain parts.[1]

Brouwer sold his pictures in his lifetime for small sums. But his unusual power was perceived by the great artists of the period, for Hals, Rubens and Rembrandt all owned examples of his work. Rembrandt, in fact, is said to have had six of his pictures and a sketch, and Rubens no less than seventeen pictures. Van Dyck, moreover, is said to have painted his portrait.

(*b*) ADRIAEN VAN OSTADE

Born Haarlem 1610, *died Haarlem* 1685

CHARACTERISTIC PICTURES

London—National Gallery	*Peasants Drinking (Room with many figures)*
London—National Gallery	*The Cobbler*
London—National Gallery	*Courtship*
London—Wallace Collection	*Buying Fish*
Paris—Louvre	*The Schoolmaster*
The Hague—Mauritshuis	*Peasants in an Inn*
The Hague—Mauritshuis	*The Village Fiddler*
Amsterdam—Rijks Museum	*The Painter in his Studio*
Amsterdam—Rijks Museum	*The Quack Doctor*
Amsterdam—Rijks Museum	*The Baker blowing his Horn*
Amsterdam—Rijks Museum	*Peasants round a Fire*
Dresden Gallery	*Peasants at an Inn Table*
Dresden Gallery	*A Painter in his Studio*
Dresden Gallery	*Peasants Eating*

Adriaen van Ostade was the son of a weaver. He was a fellow-pupil with Brouwer in Frans Hals's studio, and he was the most typical painter of the Dutch low-life school. Van Ostade's pictures portray the lowest grade of normal Dutch peasants in their normal sur-roundings, and they are more sordid and gloomy than Brouwer's pictures, because whereas in Brouwer's case we feel that the poverty and degeneration of his models, and the dirt, dilapidation and gloom of their surroundings, are exceptional, in Van Ostade's, where we are confronted with the same poverty and gloom, we feel that these conditions were the order of the day.

[1] This *Tobias and the Angel* was formerly ascribed by de Groot to Rembrandt. Professor van Dyke ascribes it to Roeland Roghman, who was a friend of both Hercules Seghers and Rembrandt and painter of a number of landscapes in the Seghers-Rembrandt style. Other students believe the picture to be an English Rembrandtesque *pastiche* of the eighteenth century.

Van Ostade shows us the normal Dutch peasants as poor, stunted, ill-formed, ill-clad, unwashed creatures, passing their life in dark hovels where everything is filthy and broken and where no flower or breeze ever enters. The normal peasants in Holland in the first half of the seventeenth century were doubtless, in fact, the grimy and pathetic dwarfs he sets before us. Seventy years of wars had left their mark most heavily on the poorest classes. The men and women that Ostade painted were the grandsons of the starved thousands in the Haarlem siege—indeed the oldest were born while their parents were eating grass and leather. No share of Holland's new prosperity had come the way of these submerged classes, who had not yet aspired to the domestic orderliness of the Dutch bourgeois classes. Ostade shows us under-men ignorant of the amenities of life. Holland had founded her republic and was putting her house in order with the money that flowed in from her world-trade. But no reflection of this prosperity reached the dim interiors where Ostade's figures gather in huddled groups; and when Ostade painted his peasants out of doors they still cling to the walls of their hovels as though afraid to venture far into the light. There is, moreover, something peculiarly shocking and pathetic in the many pictures by Van Ostade where we see peasants looking out over half-doors where they appear like dogs in their kennels. This effect can be seen in a still more pronounced form in *The Cobbler* (Pl. 92); for the cobbler is shown working in a structure in front of his house— a structure that in size and character is exactly the modern kennel with two compartments; and the fact that a dog in this picture lies upon the roof suggests that the man and the dog share the kennel upon equal terms. The same quality is observable in *Peasants Eating* (Pl. 90), where the man, dog-like, is gnawing at a bone. Such pictures are profoundly depressing, because there is no revolt or protest in these people and no revolt or protest in the painter's attitude of mind.

No pictures portraying such scenes in such a way had ever been painted before and—with the exception, of course, of the thousands of low-life pictures of the same kind painted by followers and imitators of Van Ostade—no such pictures have ever been painted since. For Hogarth's *Gin Lane* and his other low-life pictures burn with protest or are enlivened with comment; and peasant pictures by Teniers and nineteenth-century low-life pictures by Wilkie and so on are not comparable with Van Ostade's as personal records of social experience.

Van Ostade, it is clear, was happy in the normal gloom and grime of the poorest peasant's home; and he recorded in tonal language the faint vitality of these unfortunates who ate and slept and sat and mumbled, who chewed, spat, were sick, and relieved themselves, who made sad jokes and laughed without gaiety, and produced children of the same character.

As a painter he was exceedingly unequal. He shows light and shade effects at times in delicate tones, but his painting is generally poor in texture and gloomy and lifeless in colour. On the other hand, he took over from Brouwer the compositional motif of the small pyramid group as in *Peasants Eating* (Pl. 90) and he seems to have appreciated Rembrandt's conception of space. There are pictures of his, like the *Peasants at an Inn Table* (Pl. 91), where the groups of figures have a definite architectural relation to surrounding space, and where, as in works by Rembrandt, the spectator is led through open windows to space beyond the dark interior.

Like most Dutch popular painters, Van Ostade, who had to compete in an overcrowded market, was industrious and prolific. De Groot gives him about nine hundred pictures (of which he has himself examined about four hundred) and also a large number of water-colours and etchings. I make no comment on these attributions. But I must, however, point out that it was not difficult to paint pictures that bear a general resemblance to those of Van Ostade, and that thousands of Van Ostade *pastiches* have been produced at various times.

(c) JAN STEEN

Born Leyden 1626, died Leyden 1679

CHARACTERISTIC PICTURES

London—National Gallery	*Terrace Scene*
London—National Gallery	*Skittle Players*
London—National Gallery	*Grace before Meat*
London—Lord Lonsdale Collection	*The Artist eating Oysters*
England—Wellington Collection	*The Dissolute Family*
England—Wellington Collection	*The Wedding*
London—Buckingham Palace	*The Morning Toilet*
London—Wallace Collection	*The Christening*
London—Wallace Collection	*Lute Player on a Terrace*
London—Wallace Collection	*The Harpsichord Lesson*
Paris—Louvre	*The Prodigal Son (Bad Company)*
The Hague—Mauritshuis	*Doctor and Sick Girl*
The Hague—Mauritshuis	*The Happy Family*
The Hague—Mauritshuis	*The Cabaret*

The Hague—Mauritshuis	*The Poultry Yard*
Amsterdam—Rijks Museum	*The Quack Doctor*
Amsterdam—Rijks Museum	*The Return Home by Boat*
Amsterdam—Rijks Museum	*Merry Company*
Amsterdam—Rijks Museum	*After the Carouse*
Amsterdam—Rijks Museum	*The Parrot*
Amsterdam—Rijks Museum	*The Supper at Emmaus*
Berlin—Kaiser-Friedrich Museum	*The Prodigal Father (Bad Company)*
Cassel Gallery	*Twelfth Night*
Dresden Gallery	*The Marriage at Cana*
Dresden Gallery	*Abraham dismissing Hagar*
Brussels Gallery	*The Gallant Offering*
Lugano—Thyssen Collection	*The Lute Player*

With Jan Steen we are in a different world. He was the son of a brewer of some means, and the life he depicts in his most characteristic pictures is the life of the Dutch small shopkeeper and his family in numerous aspects.

As already noted, he painted a number of gay-life pictures, but the men in these scenes are not the moneyed sparks we know from paintings by Dirck Hals or Buytewech or the soldiers depicted by Duyster or Palamedes. In Steen's *The Prodigal Son (Bad Company)* (Pl. 78) the young man whose pocket is being picked is scarcely more than a boy—perhaps the son of some chemist or tradesman who is imitating with disastrous results the recreations of those richer than himself; the old man in *The Prodigal Father (Bad Company)* (Pl. 79), who suffers the same fate for all his enterprise and experience, probably kept a small greengrocer's shop; and the old drunkard in *After the Carouse* (Pl. 89) was a man of the same class. Steen also produced a number of other pictures in which relations between the sexes, courtships and advances of various kinds, some timid and decorous, and some crude, are the subject; and there is also a series portraying visits from a doctor to a young woman whose malady, it is hinted, is the result of indiscretion or is of the kind explained by the catch which the artist sometimes pins upon the wall: '*Hier helpt geen medesyn, want het is minnepyn.*'

But the great majority of Steen's works depict jovial scenes in the homes of the shopkeeping class, in respectable taverns and so forth. It is by these pictures, examples of which are in all the more important galleries, that he is mainly known. The life Steen sets before us in these works is quite different from the dismal life depicted by Van Ostade. The men, women, and children of all ages who crowd his canvases have lifted themselves from want to the possibilities of decent life. They are not refined or fastidious. They are illiterate, and they know nothing about art. But their lives are no longer depressed and sordid, they work and enjoy their leisure, and when they get drunk, or drunkish, it is because they are thirsty and because the beer is good.

Steen is essentially the painter of lower middle-class family life. He thinks of the family as a unit, and sees significance in a group of three generations gathered round a table in a home which is to them the centre of the world. The *Happy Family* (Pl. 98), inscribed '*Soo de ouden sigen, so pipjen de jonghen*', and said to represent himself (the figure facing smoking a pipe) and his family, is a pictorial equivalent of Shakespeare's 'The Seven Ages of Man'.

If we compare Jan Steen's interiors of this kind with the pictures of Dutch peasants in their homes by Van Ostade, and with the pictures of Flemish shopkeepers round the family table by Jordaens (in the Brussels Gallery and elsewhere), we cannot fail to be struck by a kinship between Steen and Jordaens that is absent between Steen and Van Ostade. The explanation is, perhaps, that Steen was a Roman Catholic and had roots in that older racial life of the Netherlands which still persists in Belgium. But he was at the same time a Dutchman, and a Dutchman living in Protestant Holland; and these factors also had their effects.

Jan Steen has been represented by the older biographers as a dissipated bohemian. There is no doubt that much beer flowed down that capacious throat—(the *Lute Player* (Pl. 94) is said to be a self-portrait)—but his very large output (de Groot's catalogue describes about a thousand pictures) proves that he was not idle; and pictures like *The Happy Family* and *Twelfth Night* (Pl. 95) show that he was essentially a bourgeois and a family man.

He was, in fact, as already noted, the son of a brewer of Leyden, and he seems to have attended the famous University in that town—perhaps as a training for the law—before he took to painting popular pictures as a trade. He was actually entered as a student in the University in 1646 and he has left a whole series of pictures, presumably early ones, depicting historical and mythological subjects such as the *Antony and Cleopatra* in the Göttingen Museum, which are among the curiosities of art. He also painted at various times a number of religious subjects from the Old and New Testaments and from the Apocrypha. A *Wrath of Ahasuerus* from the Rodolphe Kann Collection was shown in the Steen Exhibition in Leyden in 1926, and it is interesting to observe in this picture the well-known features of his favourite model—always assumed to be his wife—in unaccustomed garb as Esther. In this picture also the model for the girl in *The Harpsichord Lesson* (Pl. 96) appears as a serving-maid, while Ahasuerus appears in turban and osprey as Orientals appear in the pictures by Lastman and Rembrandt, and there is a peacock pie in its dish as in the parties in Dutch pictures of rich bourgeois life and in Rembrandt's *Rembrandt and Saskia* (Pl. 49). Other Old Testament subjects painted by Steen illustrate the stories of Samson, of David and Bathsheba, of Lot and his daughters; and his *Abraham dismissing Hagar* (Pl. 99) should be compared with the pictures of the same subjects (Pls. 65 and 33) by Van der Werff and Rembrandt. The New Testament subjects include *The Adoration of the Shepherds*, *The Flight into Egypt*, *The Supper at Emmaus*, *The Return of the Prodigal*, and *The Marriage at Cana* where a typical Dutch tavern-keeper, with a white apron, keys and knife round his waist and a napkin over his shoulder, dispenses the wines.

Steen's first master in painting is said to have been one Nicholas Knupfer, who worked normally in Utrecht but was for some time in Leyden. His second master was Van Goyen, whose daughter he married. In 1649 Steen moved from Leyden to The Hague. In 1654, as he found it difficult to live and support his family by the sale of his pictures, he moved to Delft and leased a brewery—a venture in which, it would seem, he lost money, doubtless because he spent too much time painting and too little in looking after his subsidiary business.

From 1661–9 he lived in Haarlem, and the splendid *Lute Player* (Pl. 94) is clearly the result of his contact with the work of Hals. At the end of 1669 he returned to Leyden, where in 1672 he took out a licence as a publican, and where for the rest of his life he kept the *openbare herbergh* represented in the famous picture called *The Cabaret* (Pl. 124).

Steen had great difficulty in selling his pictures. When he died he is said to have left five hundred unsold. In 1669 he was unable to pay a chemist a debt of ten gulden and had to suffer the creditor to distrain for the money on his goods and pictures; and he never seems to have been able to count on even the low prices that prevailed for most popular pictures in Holland in his time.

De Groot mentions Jan Molenaer, Esaias van de Velde, Joost Droochsloot and Pieter de Bloot, as well as Knupfer and Van Goyen, as painters who influenced Jan Steen in his early years when he painted outdoor popular scenes with small figures like *The Poultry Yard* in The Hague, and the *Skittle Players* in the National Gallery; Sir Charles Holmes sees the influence of Paul Potter in the *Skittle Players*, that of Metsu in the *The Music Master* in the National

Gallery and *The Harpsichord Lesson* (Pl. 96) in the Wallace Collection, and that of Gerard Dou in the pictures of his later years. Dr. Bode says some of his pictures call to mind those by Vermeer of Delft, Nicolas Maes, Frans van Mieris, Jacob de Wet, Isaack van Ostade, Frans Hals, Judith Leyster, as well as those by Dou, Metsu and so on. In addition I would point out (*a*) that the composition in Steen's *Quack Doctor* (Pl. 97) bears resemblance to Bamboche's *Quack Doctor* (Pl. 70), and that of *Skittle Players* to Bamboche's picture (Pl. 69); (*b*) that Steen in some of his feasting scenes took on the motif of the kneeling servants in the foreground which occurs in the pictures of bourgeois parties by Dirck Hals, Palamedes and so on, and which had appeared before in Venetian pictures by Tintoretto and Bassano; and (*c*) that the woman and child in Steen's *Merry Company* (Pl. 100) in Amsterdam is based on some engraving after an Italian *Virgin and Child* such as Steen, being a Catholic, might well have had hanging on his bedroom wall.

Steen was thus an unusually eclectic artist, even in seventeenth-century Holland where all artists made use of engravings and other artists' pictures as a matter of course; and he never attained to any personal distinction as a designer of pictures. Compared even with Ostade his architectural sense was rudimentary, and the figures in many of his pictures are too large or too small in architectural relation to surrounding space. On the other hand he had a lively sense of colour, and he could handle oil paint dexterously, and in works like *The Harpsichord Lesson* and *The Lute Player on a Terrace* in the Wallace Collection he attained to a richness of surface and colour orchestration that is almost Venetian. He had, moreover, a feeling for large form which comes out in his figures of women, and some of his seated figures attain a majesty that brings them in line with the figures in Duck's *Pipe-drunk Woman* (Pl. 88), and De Hooch's *The Mother* (Pl. 116).

But the majesty of these figures in Steen's work was largely accidental and had a descriptive not an architectural origin. The women from whom he made the drawings for his pictures (he never obviously painted from nature) were heavy and large-limbed, and the imposing attitude of the central figure in the *Twelfth Night* (Pl. 95) was the habitual attitude of women using a foot-warmer at the time. This attitude dictated by the foot-warmer occurs in Duck's *Pipe-drunk Woman* (Pl. 88), and in Brouwer's *The Pipe Drunkard* (Pl. 87); it occurs with genteel variations in Molenaer's *Musical Pastime* and Terborch's *The Guitar Lesson* in the National Gallery, and Metsu's *The Oyster Lunch* (Pl. 107A) and it is consciously

New York, Metropolitan Museum (Bache Collection)

Plate 105. TERBORCH: 'Curiosity'

Plate 106. METSU: 'The Family of Koopman Geelvinck'

Plate 107A. Metsu: 'The Oyster Lunch'

Plate 107B. Metsu: 'Charity'

Plate 108. METSU: 'Lovers of Music'

Plate 109. P. JANSSENS: 'Interior with Woman reading'

The Hague—Mauritshuis

Bruckmann Photo

Plate 110. SAMUEL VAN HOOGSTRATEN: 'Young Lady in a Courtyard'

Private Collection

Plate 111. SAMUEL VAN HOOGSTRATEN: 'Peepshow Cabinet'

Plate 112. VERMEER OF DELFT: 'Lady seated at the Virginals'
(*Cf. Plate* 17)

Plate 113 VERMEER OF DELFT: 'Head of a Young Girl'

Plate 114. CAREL FABRITIUS: 'A View of Delft'

Plate 115 PIETER DE HOOCH: 'Interior of a Dutch House'

Plate 116. PIETER DE HOOCH: 'The Mother'

Plate 117. PIETER DE HOOCH: 'Conversation out of doors'

Plate 118. SAMUEL VAN HOOGSTRATEN: 'Peepshow Cabinet'

Plate 119. VERMEER OF DELFT: 'Girl reading a Letter'

Plate 120. VERMEER OF DELFT: 'The Painter and his Model'

used for its architectural character by Vermeer in his *Allegory of The Faith* (Pl. 122), where the foot-warmer has given place to a globe.

Steen, in a word, must be regarded as fundamentally a descriptive and popular artist; and in the ranks of such artists he takes a distinguished place by reason of his good humour, his varied observation, his genial affection for family life, and his technical skill.

(d) JAN MIENSE MOLENAER

Born Haarlem 1600–10, *died Haarlem* 1668

CHARACTERISTIC PICTURES

London—National Gallery	*Musical Pastime*
The Hague—Mauritshuis	*Fête in a Tavern*
The Hague—Mauritshuis	*The Senses*
Amsterdam—Rijks Museum	*Young Woman at the Virginals*
Amsterdam—Van Loon Collection	*Family Group*
Amsterdam—Van Loon Collection	*The Family Feast*
Brunswick Gallery	*The Dentist*
Brunswick Gallery	*The Oyster Feast*
Ghent Gallery	*Kermesse*
Carlsruhe Gallery	*The Peasant Wedding*
Dresden Gallery	*Violin Player in a Tavern*
Budapest Gallery	*Auberge à la Demi-Lune*
Budapest Gallery	*La Main Chaude*

Jan Molenaer has already been referred to as the husband of Judith Leyster. He was born at Haarlem, where he was probably a pupil of Frans Hals. His marriage took place in 1633 or '36, and in 1637 he established himself in Amsterdam. Later he retired to Heemstede, near Haarlem, and he was in Haarlem when he died.

Molenaer must be regarded both as a painter of low life and of bourgeois life. In the first category we have works like *The Dentist* (Pl. 93), the *Fête in a Tavern* in The Hague, and the *Violin Player in a Tavern* in Dresden.

If *The Dentist* be compared with Honthorst's picture of the same subject (Pl. 27), we see at once the difference between the mental attitudes of the two artists. Honthorst was merely flirting with popular art, and he made the subject an excuse for a composition exhibiting a trick effect of artificial light. Molenaer was entirely concerned with illustrating the incident, and even in that field he cuts a poor figure; for the scene is unconvincing—surely someone in the company would have noticed that the patient was certain to knock over the eggs?

In his tavern pictures, which belong to his later years, Molenaer was influenced by Rembrandt's light and shade and by Van Ostade's compositions; also the touch in these later works is lighter and more nervous. In these pictures the peasants are often shown embracing more amorously than is usual in Dutch low-life works; and Molenaer seems, in fact, to have had trouble with the authorities about the subjects in some cases.

In his Amsterdam period he seems to have had portrait commissions from rich bourgeois, and in executing them he bore in mind the wedding parties by Dirck Hals and Duyster and portraits by Dirck Santvoort (1610–1680), who was the favourite portrait painter of the Amsterdam upper classes. The *Family Feast* (Pl. 102) is one of his most ambitious efforts in this field, and an interesting record of a rich interior of the time; the student will note the handsome panelled room with its picture by some Dutch Romanist or Rembrandt pupil, the marble floor, the musicians in the gallery, the maid bringing in the peacock pie in the centre, the negro attendant in the corner, the pages placing the wine in coolers (the old motif from Tintoretto and Bassano) and the expensive clothes of the company. If we look at the lady listening to a love poem from a kneeling cavalier on the left of the picture (Pl. 103), and observe both the lady's clothes and those of her admirer, we can understand the satires of the Dutch moralists on the extravagance of the new rich, and believe the story of the young lady who threw her lace handkerchief into the fire to make it burn more merrily, in the same way that a young Venetian lady a century earlier, when her pearl necklace broke while she was dancing, merely kicked the falling jewels to a corner of the room.

In a picture of this kind and in the *Young Woman at the Virginals* in Amsterdam and the *Musical Pastime* in the National Gallery (where we see a boy and girl of a bourgeois family practising their 'piece' for the next party) Molenaer is a real ancestor of the Dutch painters of *tableaux de modes* whose works I must now discuss.

iv. Tableaux de Modes

Writing half a century ago of Terborch's *Paternal Advice* in Berlin, round which Goethe wove romance in his *Wahlverwandtschaften*, Lord Ronald Gower said:

'With all due deference to the great German poet's description of Terborch's "satin-gown" picture, we cannot but think that he has magnified a very clever portrait group into a work of pathos, and coloured with his poetical sense a group in which the painter had only wished to show his marvellous power of rendering the quality and texture of a white satin gown on a graceful female form, relieved by the black dress of another lady and by the buff jerkin of a cavalier, who neither appears old enough to be the father of the lady in the satin gown, nor does his attitude or his expression convey in the least the idea of correction.

'It is, in fact, merely one of the many *genre* pictures (or as the old art books called them, *tableaux de modes*) which the Mierises and the Metsus were wont to paint.'

Here is the key to the art of Terborch, Metsu and Mieris. These men record the clothes and to some extent the furniture of the well-to-do Dutch bourgeois. They show us Dutch ladies writing letters, playing the lute, seated or standing in a room; sometimes there is a gentleman or a music master, a servant or a lover in attendance, but there is rarely any revealing action, or much that throws light on the particular habits of the people portrayed. We know a good deal of Dutch gay life from the *bordeeltjes* and *corte-gaardjes*, and of Dutch low life and lower middle-class family life from the pictures by Van Ostade and Jan Steen. But from the 'con-versation' pieces by Terborch and Metsu we learn much less of Dutch bourgeois life than we learn about French life of the same class from the engravings by Abraham Bosse at the same period, or about French eighteenth-century life from *Le Monument du Costume* by Moreau le Jeune, or of English life in Hogarth's day from his *Marriage à la Mode*. We are not informed about Dutch habits by Terborch and Metsu in the way that we are informed about French habits by Abraham Bosse's picture *L'Elégante Accouchée*, where the lady is shown in bed surrounded by her women friends, one of whom blows her nose, while the others chatter and pass their needles in and out of the embroidery they have brought with them.

If we seek information about Dutch life of this class at this period we find it in Duyster's *Wedding Party* (Pl. 101), in Molenaer's *Family Feast* (Pls. 102 and 103) already referred to, and in Van Deelen's *Salons de Conversation*, where we see groups of young gentleman paying formal calls on ladies in characteristic rooms hung with prints and pictures of the picturesque and other kinds. But there is much less information even in these pictures than in the prints in which this type of picture had its origin. Take for example the illustrations to works by the Dutch poet Cats. One shows us a country gentleman being helped to bed by a group of lackeys in the fashion spread abroad by the ceremonies of the French Court; two of the lackeys are taking off his coat, while another removes his boots and socks, a fourth prepares the bed, a fifth brings toilet water, and so forth. Other prints, ascribed to Crispin de Passe, show a lady sitting up in bed startled by some noise or kept awake by jealousy, and we note that she wears a nightcap and a blanket tied round her throat, her night attire and bedclothes being evidently all one, and that the machinery of the elaborate costumes of the time is scattered about the floor; other prints again show us a bourgeois company playing a round game of the character of hunt-the-slipper, a similar company playing the famous game called *La Main Chaude*, a bourgeois making her child's evening toilet, with the child's socks drying on trees before the fire, a bourgeois child in lace cap and collar screaming with rage because it cannot reach the doll and other toys which it has thrown on the ground from the tray of the baby-chair in which it has been imprisoned, or a gentleman at his barber's —an establishment which was as full of bottles as the modern equivalent and where the victim was enveloped in exactly the same kind of sheet as is used to-day.

As social commentators Terborch, Metsu and their school were thus less original and adventurous than the contemporary engravers who worked as illustrators. They concocted their pictures in their studios by naturalistic copying of clothes placed on models or lay figures; and the range of their interest was small.

(a) GERARD TERBORCH

Born Zwolle 1617, *died Deventer* 1681

CHARACTERISTIC PICTURES

London—Buckingham Palace	*The Letter*
London—National Gallery	*The Guitar Lesson*
London—National Gallery	*The Peace of Münster*
London—National Gallery	*Portrait of a Gentleman*
London—Wallace Collection	*A Lady at her Toilet*
London—Wallace Collection	*A Lady reading a Letter*
Paris—Louvre	*Soldier and Woman (Le Galant Militaire)*
The Hague—Mauritshuis	*The Despatch*
Amsterdam—Rijks Museum	*Paternal Advice*
Amsterdam—Rijks Museum	*Portrait of François de Vicq*
Amsterdam—Rijks Museum	*Portrait of Aletta Pancras*

TABLEAUX DE MODES

Amsterdam—Rijks Museum	*Boy picking Fleas from a Dog*
Berlin—Kaiser-Friedrich Museum	*The Concert*
Cassel Gallery	*The Lute Player*
Dresden Gallery	*Trumpeter, and Officer writing*
New York—Metropolitan Museum	*Curiosity*
(Bache Collection)	

Gerard Terborch was the son of a tax-collector of Zwolle, who painted pictures in his spare time, and who seems also to have had the means and leisure to travel in Germany, Italy and France. He thus belonged to a grade of Dutch society above that of Jan Steen, and he never seems to have been in need of money or to have suffered from the surplus of pictorial production in Holland. He travelled a good deal and was able to make money abroad by painting portraits; and he seems on his travels to have been well provided with introductions and to have mixed in good society all his life.

He received his first artistic training from his father. When he was fifteen he went to Amsterdam and there, as already noted, he probably worked with Duyster, though there is no record of the fact. His earliest pictures were *cortegaardjes*, and the influence of the Duyster-Duck-Palamedes school of military gay-life painters is seen in *The Despatch* (Pl. 85), though this was painted as late as 1653. Both the general composition of the *Trumpeter, and Officer writing* in Dresden and the stance of the trumpeter in that picture are moreover quite clearly based on Duyster's *Young Officer* (Pl. 82). It was also, as I have already pointed out, from Duyster that Terborch presumably acquired the trick of painting glittering silks and satins which has caused his pictures to be so much admired by those who enjoy illusionist texture-painting of this kind.

In 1634 Terborch was in Haarlem, where he worked with Pieter Molyn, and came for a time, in the view of Dr. Bode, under the influence of Frans Hals or one of his pupils. When he was eighteen he went to London, where his father sent him a lay figure. No pictures painted on this London visit are known. In 1641 he went to Rome and painted some portraits; in 1645 he was back in Amsterdam; and in 1646 he was at Münster, where he painted *The Peace of Münster* portrait group in the National Gallery. After the Peace of Münster he was taken by the Conde de Penaranda, who appears in the picture, to Madrid, and there he met Velasquez and is said to have painted the King.

The influence on Terborch of the Velasquez formula for full-length portraits, as exemplified in his *Philip IV as a Young Man* in the Prado, is clearly seen in the *Portrait of a Gentleman* (Pl. 104).

The Terborch picture is only twenty-six inches by twenty-one, while the Prado picture is life-size; but the little work has all the dignity and repose of the larger one, because it is based on a coherent principle of design. When Terborch was following this model, his powers as an imitative miniaturist were well directed and controlled; but he did not always keep Velasquez in his mind; too often he fell back on his father's present—the lay figure. In 1664 he married in Deventer and he died there in 1681 at the age of sixty-four.

It is not hard to understand why Terborch's portraits were a success in his lifetime. They were, doubtless, excellent likenesses, their scale made them portable and adapted to a small room, and the Dutch bourgeoisie placed them about their houses in the same way that the bourgeoisie place portrait photographs in the modern world. One can understand, too, that he had success with his *tableaux de modes*; for in craftsmanship these pictures are excellent—as excellent as pictures by Pynacker or by Berchem; and craftsmanship used to achieve illusionist imitation of textures is always accepted by the uninstructed as evidence of art. But to modern eyes Terborch seems little more than a painter of attractive miniature portraits and a craftsman who excelled in eye-and-hand naturalism. His pictures lack the architecture of Vermeer, the descriptive gusto of Jan Steen, and the romance of Rembrandt. The figures in his works are often too big or too small architecturally for the scale of his canvas, and spot passages like a white satin dress often 'jump' right out of the picture's tone.

Terborch, nevertheless, was capable of higher achievement in the architectural field. His instinct for form is seen in his treatment of the human head as an egg-like shape on which hair and features are imposed; and his instinct for composition is seen in the Berlin picture *The Concert* which shows, as Sir Charles Holmes has pointed out, the influence of Vermeer. But he usually preferred the applause of bourgeois patrons to the hard task of architectural research.

Hofstede de Groot's catalogue gives Terborch about five hundred pictures. He mentions Caspar Netscher, Barthold Berentsen, Antoni Jordens, Roelof Koets as among his pupils; Hendrik Ten Oever, Pieter van Anraadt as among those who modelled themselves on his style; and Jacob Ochtervelt, Johannes Verkolje, Eglon Hendrik van der Neer, Michiel van Musscher and Barent Graat as among those responsible for works wrongly ascribed at different times to him. It should be noted that Terborch's sister, Gesina, started to learn drawing and painting from her father at the same time as her brother, and that some of the replicas and variants of Terborch's

Plate C. MIERIS: 'Lady with a Parrot'

tableaux de modes were probably produced in his workshop by her. De Groot concludes his note on Terborch's pictures as follows:

'The careful student of Terborch's pictures, both of his genre-pieces and of his portraits, will be surprised to note how often the painter repeats himself in details; many figures in his genre-pieces occur again and again, either copied exactly or repeated with slight variations. The folds of the costumes in his portraits are often copied with such precision that one may almost conclude that the painter kept pictures of dresses ready in stock, to which he added the heads and hands as required. The articles of furniture in his interiors, the chimney-pieces, beds, tables and chairs, are very often the same. This habit of repeating himself, which is astonishing in the case of an artist of such importance, makes it very difficult to know what attitude to take up in regard to the many old replicas of Terborch's pictures. On the one hand, it must be taken as proved that the painter copied his own work much more often than most of his equally distinguished contemporaries. On the other hand, many of these replicas are not of equal merit, and there is usually one example—such as the *Paternal Advice* at Amsterdam—which so far surpasses all the others that one can scarcely regard those others as repetitions from Terborch's own hand. In numerous cases the question is not yet ripe for solution and still needs a very careful inquiry.'

(b) GABRIEL METSU

Born Leyden 1629, died Amsterdam 1667

CHARACTERISTIC PICTURES

London—National Gallery	*The Duet*
London—National Gallery	*The Music Lesson*
London—National Gallery	*The Drowsy Landlady*
London—National Gallery	*The Forge*
London—Wallace Collection	*A Lady at her Toilet*
London—Wallace Collection	*The Letterwriter Surprised*
London—Wallace Collection	*The Sleeping Sportsman*
London—Wallace Collection	*An Old Woman selling Fish*
London—Wallace Collection	*An Old Woman Asleep*
London—Beit Collection	*The Letter Writer*
London—Beit Collection	*The Letter Reader*
Paris—Louvre	*The Vegetable Market at Amsterdam*
The Hague—Mauritshuis	*Lovers of Music*
The Hague—Mauritshuis	*The Huntsman*
Amsterdam—Rijks Museum	*The Breakfast*

Amsterdam—Rijks Museum	*The Sick Child*
Amsterdam—Rijks Museum	*The Huntsman's Gift*
Berlin—Kaiser-Friedrich Museum	*The Family of Koopman Geelvinck*
Dresden Gallery	*The Bird Seller*
Dresden Gallery	*The Prodigal Son (The Painter and his Wife)*
Cassel Gallery	*Charity*
Leningrad—Hermitage	*The Prodigal Son*
Leningrad—Hermitage	*The Oyster Lunch*

Gabriel Metsu was the son of Jacques Metsu, an artist, and his mother's father, Guilliam Fremault, was also a painter. By the age of fourteen he was a pupil of Gerard Dou in Leyden, and certain of his works like the *Old Woman at a Window* in the National Gallery are plainly influenced by Dou's misunderstanding of the art of Rembrandt and by what M. Louis Gillet calls '*l'incroyable fini des peintures de Gerard Dou, la nacre des surfaces, l'imitation futile et stupéfiante des riens, la minutie à perte de vue . . .*' But Metsu soon escaped from Dou's illusionist triviality, and developed a more virile technique of his own. He painted a few gay-life pictures—there is a *Prodigal Son* by his hand in Leningrad and another in Dresden (usually called *The Painter and his Wife*), and *The Forge* in the National Gallery is in the *cortegaardje* tradition; he also apparently painted a few religious subjects; but he eventually specialized in bourgeois *tableaux de modes*. He moved to Amsterdam when he was twenty-five, and died there at the age of thirty-eight.

Most of Metsu's pictures, like those by Terborch, present a Dutch bourgeoise in a Dutch interior, frequently with a second figure. As a rule the mistress of the house is the central figure but sometimes the central figure is a young serving maid or an old woman. The figures are depicted at a moment of arrested movement, and the movement itself is generally restrained. Metsu shows us a Dutch bourgeoise eating oysters passed to her on a dish by a young man (Pl. 107A), another receiving a present of game just shot by her husband (Amsterdam), a third writing a letter while her husband looks over her shoulder and a young woman plays the lute (Pl. 108), a fourth receiving her music lesson (National Gallery), and so on. The models were posed in the painter's studio where the furniture and accessories were also set up, though some details were doubtless painted from other painters' pictures or engravings and the artist's own drawings. Occasionally Metsu provides his bourgeoise with an outdoor setting. In a picture at Cassel (Pl. 107B) she sits on a seat outside her front door and gives a penny to a poor boy; in a picture at Dresden we see her buying a cock for her chicken-run from an old man who sells poultry at a corner by one of the Amsterdam canals; and in a famous picture in the Louvre we have a general impression of a vegetable-market in that city.

Metsu's bourgeoises are less 'dressed up' than those of Terborch. The young women's clothes were never, I think, painted on a lay figure but always from the living model. Many of his pictures (Pls. 107A and 107B for example) were painted from a particular rather delicately featured model, who evidently sat with exemplary patience, and to whom, I suspect, he was personally attached. As a recorder of Dutch bourgeois life he tells us more than Terborch, but still not very much. The most convincing document he has left is *The Family of Koopman Geelvinck* (Pl. 106); this is more than a *tableaux de modes* put together from a model and odd accessories in the artist's studio; it is a genuine interior with a group of portraits highly satisfactory and complete; the father and mother, the nurse and baby and the older children, one playing with a parrot, another with a dog, and a third kept amused by a toy, are all clearly enlargements of the artist's experience, and the carefully painted interior is part of the record.

De Groot mentions Joost van Greel as an artist whose work is often mistaken for that of Metsu; and Daniel Vertangen, whom I have already recorded as a *pasticheur* of Van Poelenburgh, as also a *pasticheur* of Metsu.

Part VI

VERMEER AND HIS CIRCLE

i. Dutch Architectural Art

When we get to the work of Vermeer of Delft and the artists who must be grouped round him we are dealing with pictures of a different kind.

The descriptive popular artists I have been discussing were concerned with describing their familiar experience of everyday life. It was this experience that constituted their jumping-off board and their main preoccupation. In such pictures the artists first established the figures or groups of figures and then proceeded to put round them as much of an interior or *décor* as was required for the descriptive purpose; they had no need, for their purpose, to concern themselves with the picture-space as an æsthetic problem; and, in fact, from the architectural standpoint, the Dutch popular painters, as I have indicated, often made their figures too large or too small for the surrounding area. Van Ostade alone had a picture-space concept which can be compared with that of the intellectual picturesque painters on the one hand and that of Rembrandt on the other—but, of course, even in Van Ostade's pictures the social description provides the jumping-off point and remains the central preoccupation throughout the work.

To the untrained eye the resemblance of a bourgeois interior by Metsu or Molenaer to a bourgeois interior by Vermeer is much closer than the resemblance of an interior by Vermeer to a landscape by Claude or to a modern architectural Cubist picture. But to the trained eye a picture of a woman at a harpsichord by Metsu and a picture of a woman at a harpsichord by Vermeer are different forms of art; and the picture *A Woman Reading* by Pieter Janssens (Pl. 109) in Munich is the same form of art as Claude's *Queen of Sheba* in the National Gallery or the pictures by the leading artists of the classical renaissance of our time.

Vermeer was primarily concerned with the architectural aspect of the content of his pictures; and the same is true, in varying degrees, of the artists associated with him. Vermeer was concerned with the

170

enlargement of his architectural experience, and with the creation of an architectural picture in which all the details, whether figures, furniture, walls, windows or what not, are of equal importance and all equally organic parts of an architectural *ensemble*; and that *ensemble* was his preoccupation from the start.[1]

The Dutch painters of *tableaux de modes*, as I have indicated, tell us relatively little about the life they purport to describe, and since their work must be judged from the descriptive standpoint this small range must be accounted a defect. But in the case of the architectural painters this restricted range is, on the contrary, a merit, because, whereas the cumulation of social details in an illustration of daily life adds to the subject of the picture, the cumulation of such details in architectural pictures may destroy the formal unity and create confusion.

The artists of the architectural school were intensely interested in problems of optics, and their pictures are characterized both by the clarity of the artists' automatic vision and by the concept of a finite picture-space. The little portraits and *tableaux de modes* by Terborch and Metsu compared with the pictures of the Elsheimer-Lastman-Pynas-Rembrandt tradition are clearly realized in detail; but they are not realized clearly as architectural constructions. A picture by Vermeer, or Janssens, is, however, realized with great clarity not only in respect of the details but also as an architectural construction and as a synthesis with architectural meaning. That is why I have compared the art of Vermeer to the art of Claude, and why the works by Vermeer and the artists associated with him both embody and differ from the art produced by the Dutch popular painters of the same nominal subjects, and are the culmination of the Dutch classical-picturesque art of men like Berchem and Pynacker who were influenced by Claude.

The clarity in the architectural synthesis achieved by this school, which surpasses anything achieved by the Dutch picturesque artists, has led Sir Charles Holmes to describe the Dutch architectural pictures as in the nature of scenes observed through a window opening into a room or from a room to a courtyard. In my view the pictures partake of the nature of scenes observed through a reducing

---

[1] *Cf.* Preface, note p. 12. I use the word architectural here in the wide sense that I have used it throughout the *Modern Movement in Art*—a sense which some critics of that book have suggested would be better expressed by the word 'architectonic'. The interiors of churches, etc., by the Steenwycks and similar artists must, of course, be ranked as descriptive paintings of buildings and have no relation to architectural art in my sense.

lens or reflected in a mirror; and I suggest that the clarity was achieved by several of these artists in many of their pictures by some mechanical device—such as a reducing glass, or the use of one or more mirrors. I shall discuss this suggestion in the section headed 'Vermeer's Mirrors' in this Part.

But whether the architectural synthesis and clarity was or was not achieved with mechanical assistance, it derived, of course, primarily from the artist's attitude of mind. Vermeer's automatic vision was doubtless much the same as that of Dou or Rembrandt. But whereas Dou's mind was merely the servant of his eye and Rembrandt's was romantic, Vermeer's was architectural. Hence the fundamental differences between the types of picture they produced.

Vermeer was so much the most brilliant Dutch architectural artist that we tend to think of the whole school as grouped round him. But students have not yet been able to determine the exact relations one to another of the various artists. Vermeer was almost certainly a pupil of Carel Fabritius. De Hooch, an impressionable artist, much inferior to Vermeer as an architect, and always to some extent descriptive and popular in his attitude, was undoubtedly influenced first by the popular gay-life painters, then by Vermeer, and at some time, I fancy, by Hoogstraten; Janssens was purely an architect but not a very good one; and Hoogstraten, who, I suspect, had contact with Vermeer, was a scientific theoretician.

To modern students of Dutch art the works of this school are only second in interest to the works of Rembrandt; and many modern artists who feel ill at ease with Rembrandt's romantic renderings of emotive fragments set in relation to symbols of infinity, can apprehend with delighted interest the classical concept of a clearly defined and architecturally controlled picture-space which distinguishes the pictures by Vermeer. But in their lifetime these artists were not appreciated to this extent. They were able, it is true, to sell their pictures, and Vermeer, who was well known in Delft, received reasonably high prices. But they did not enjoy the wide celebrity of the Romanists or the picturesque painters; their works were probably not distinguished by many of their contemporaries from the descriptive popular pictures or *tableaux de modes*; and after their deaths all these artists seem to have been so rapidly forgotten that in the first half of the eighteenth century their very names were unknown.

As was natural, the transitional figure of de Hooch first emerged from obscurity, and English collectors in the later years of the eighteenth century and the beginning of the nineteenth began to exhibit a marked pleasure in his work which they regarded quite correctly as superior to the common run of Dutch popular pictures of everyday or bourgeois life. When de Hooch thus became a 'good selling line'[1] with the dealers, other pictures of the school were ascribed to him. Nearly all the pictures that we know by Janssens were thus labelled 'de Hooch' till very recent years, and de Hooch was also credited with pictures by Vermeer and Hoogstraten. Vermeer's name is not mentioned by Descamps, who wrote of the Dutch artists in 1763; he was not 'discovered' till 1842 by Theophile Thoré (W. Bürger), who published in 1866 an essay on his art ascribing to him seventy-six pictures, a list now reduced—including later ascriptions—to approximately half that number; and as late as 1882 his *Head of a Young Girl* (Pl. 113), now in the Mauritshuis, was bought at an auction in The Hague for two and a half gulden— about five shillings. Hoogstraten, as far as England is concerned, was rediscovered even later; his name was almost unknown here till Sir Robert Witt presented the *Peepshow* to the National Gallery through the National Art Collections Fund in 1924.

(a) CAREL FABRITIUS

Born The Beemster 1614, died Delft 1654

CHARACTERISTIC PICTURES

London—National Gallery	*Man in a Fur Cap* (perhaps a self-portrait)
London—National Gallery	*View of Delft, with a Musical Instrument Dealer*
The Hague—Mauritshuis	*The Goldfinch*
Rotterdam—Boymans Museum	*Man with Long Hair* (perhaps a self-portrait)
Amsterdam—Rijks Museum	*Abraham van Notte*
Amsterdam—Rijks Museum	*Beheading of St. John the Baptist*
Brussels Gallery	*Man in large Black Hat*
Munich—Alte Pinakothek	*Man in Black Hat* (perhaps a self-portrait)
Innsbruck—Ferdinandeum	*Tobias and his Wife*
Schwerin Museum	*The Sentinel*

Very little is known of the life of Carel Fabritius. The only quite certain fact is that he was killed in an explosion of a powder magazine

---

[1] In 1765 one of his pictures was sold in Holland for 450 gulden; in 1817 the same work made 4,000 gulden. The *Interior of a Dutch House* (Pl. 115) in the National Gallery was sold in Paris in 1804 for £220. *The Courtyard* in the same gallery made £187 in 1810, and the *Courtyard of a Dutch House* (Pl. A.) £1,722 in 1869. The Berlin Gallery paid £6,000 for a de Hooch in 1876, and one was sold for £11,000 in the Secretan sale in 1889.

in Delft on October 12th, 1654. A contemporary chronicler named Bleijswijck, describing Delft in 1667, says that Fabritius was about thirty at the time of the explosion; but the Boymans Museum portrait is inscribed *C. Fabritius aet Ao* 31, 1645, which would place his birth as 1614. Hoogstraten states that he was a pupil of Rembrandt about 1641, and there is evidence that he was living in Amsterdam in 1643, that he was married in Delft in 1650, that he was a member of the Delft Guild in 1652, that in 1653 and 1654 he was in financial difficulties and borrowing money, that he was buried two days after the explosion in the Oude Kerk in Delft, and that his widow described him as 'painter to the Prince of Orange'. Bleijswijck's account of Delft includes a poem on the death of Fabritius which refers to the artist as a phœnix that reappeared in the art of Vermeer. From this it would seem that Vermeer, who was twenty-two at the time of the explosion and who had been admitted to the Delft Guild the year before, was already known as Carel's brilliant pupil.[1]

Many pictures by Carel Fabritius were doubtless destroyed by the explosion. So few in fact survive that the list given above includes the majority of those known, and even in respect of these there is some doubt in certain cases whether they are the work of Carel or of his brother Barent Fabritius who was also probably a pupil of Rembrandt.

The earliest known picture is the portrait *Abraham de Notte* which is signed and dated 1640, and was thus painted before the artist was twenty, and probably before he went to Rembrandt. It is a clear unromantic portrait silhouetted against a light wall defining the back of the picture-space. The result of Carel's stay with Rembrandt is seen in the *Beheading of St. John the Baptist*, a characteristic light and shade composition of the Rembrandt school. But Carel's mind was not of the Rembrandt type; it was fundamentally architectural and out of sympathy with the metaphysical basis of the chiaroscuro and infinite recession in Rembrandt's pictures. In the *Tobias and his Wife* at Innsbruck, which was probably painted a little later, we see a composition in the Elsheimer-Lastman-Rembrandt tradition, with an opening on to a light landscape with buildings on one side of the central group and a doorway leading into darkness on the other,

---

[1] The poem is by Arnold Bon. The passage reads:

> Soo doov' dan desen Phenix t'onser schade
> En 't midden en in 't beste van zijn swier
> Maar weer gelukkig rees er uyt zijn vier
> Vermeer die meesterlijk betrad zijn paden.

and we observe that the artist has moved a step from Rembrandt by defining the areas of light and darkness and lightening the tonality throughout.

To this period of transition we must presumably assign the romantic portrait of a man in a Rembrandtesque hat—possibly a self-portrait—in Munich.[1] But the Brussels portrait of a *Man with a large black hat*[2] brings us back to the personal style of *Abraham van Notte* with the figure conceived as a well-disposed silhouette against a light background closing the picture space.

, Four pictures of his last period survive: the *View of Delft, with a Musical Instrument Dealer* (Pl. 114) which is dated 1652, and three pictures dated the year of his death: the *Man in a Fur Cap* (which may be a self-portrait) in the National Gallery, *The Goldfinch* in The Hague, and *The Sentinel* in the Schwerin Museum. The National Gallery portrait, like the van Notte and the Brussels portraits, shows a feeling for a silhouette against a light background, and the same feeling is seen in *The Goldfinch*. In *The Sentinel* the artist, while retaining a compositional structure derived from the Rembrandt school, has broken away still further than in the *Tobias* from Rembrandtesque obscurity, and the picture has something of the architectural clarity which distinguishes in varying degrees the works of Vermeer, de Hooch and Janssens.

The *View of Delft, with a Musical Instrument Dealer* (Pl. 114) is the most curious of the surviving pictures by this artist. As a composition it is unique. Sir Charles Holmes has offered an explanation of this singularity:

'Was it a mere coincidence that at this very time the pottery which was the great industry of Delft suddenly changed its character? . . . The importation of Chinese porcelain by the Dutch East India Company had begun to compete seriously with the native industry. Then one Aelbrecht de Kiezer . . . set about imitating the decoration and modelling of the Chinese pieces, and with such success that in a very few years the Delft ware in the Oriental style became widely famous. It was inevitable that Fabritius at Delft . . . should come into close contact with the leading potters and with the Oriental art which they were then studying so closely.'

But is the composition really Chinese in character? It does not

[1] Dr. Schmidt Degener ascribes this picture to Barent Fabritius. It was formerly ascribed to Rembrandt.

[2] Ascribed to Carel Fabritius by Mr. Percy Moore Turner. The ascription is endorsed by Professor Van Dyke.

appear so to my eyes; and I later explain it as a picture achieved by the aid of one or more mirrors. It is clear, at any rate, from this picture that Carel was keenly concerned with architectural composition and with problems of optics—and of this last preoccupation there is further evidence in the statement by Hoogstraten that he painted a wall decoration with perspective vistas which was preserved in 1678 in the house of one Pastor Valentius of Delft.

To the modern student Carel Fabritius is thus a most interesting artist. He had a natural feeling for the classical defined picture-space which was overruled for a time by his association with Rembrandt and reasserted itself in his later years; and this classical cast of his mind and his concern with optics are of special significance since Vermeer was probably his pupil at some time.

(b) PIETER DE HOOCH

Born Rotterdam 1629, *died Amsterdam c.* 1683

CHARACTERISTIC PICTURES

London—National Gallery	*Courtyard of a Dutch House* (Pl. A.)
London—National Gallery	*Interior of a Dutch House*
London—National Gallery	*The Courtyard*
London—Wallace Collection	*A Woman peeling Apples*
London—Wallace Collection	*A Boy bringing Pomegranates*
Paris—Louvre	*Interior of a Dutch House*
Amsterdam—Rijks Museum	*Mother Care*
Amsterdam—Rijks Museum	*Conversation Out-of-Doors*
Amsterdam—Rijks Museum	*Mother and Child*
Brussels—Arenburg Collection	*Dutch Interior*
Berlin—Kaiser-Friedrich Museum	*The Mother*

Nothing is known of Pieter de Hooch before the age of twenty-four except that he was the son of a butcher and that he is said to have been a pupil of Berchem, presumably in Haarlem. But at twenty-four it is recorded that he was attached as 'painter and footman' to the establishment of one Justus La Grange, who is described by Dr. de Groot as a 'distinguished man' and by Dr. Bode as a merchant and a rich adventurer.

In La Grange's service de Hooch lived in Leyden, The Hague, and in Delft where doubtless he met his wife Jannetje van der Burch of that town. He remained with La Grange till he was twenty-six, and the pictures assigned to this period—of which La Grange had ten in his collection—are of the gay-life character depicting soldiers with women, interiors of stables, and so forth. From this we may assume that, after his first apprenticeship to Berchem,

Plate 121. Vermeer of Delft: 'The Love Letter'

Plate 122. VERMEER OF DELFT: 'Allegory of the Faith'

Plate 123. SAMUEL VAN HOOGSTRATEN(?) : 'Refusing the Glass'

Plate 124. JAN STEEN: 'The Cabaret'

Plate 125. REMBRANDT (?): 'The Holy Family'

Plate 126. PAUL MOREELSE (?): 'Vanity'

Madrid—Prado

Plate 127. VELASQUEZ: 'Las Meninas'

Plate 128. GERARD DOU: 'Self-Portrait'

he was recommended by that master to one of the painters of *cortegaardjes* who had been his pupil earlier—perhaps to Jacob Duck. An *Interior of a Stable* in the National Gallery is perhaps an example of his work at this period.

In Delft he may have come in contact with Carel Fabritius before 1654 and he doubtless had contact with Vermeer, who was twenty-two when de Hooch was admitted to the guild. The pictures on which his reputation mainly rests were painted in Delft and they include the *Interior of a Dutch House* (Pl. 115), the *Courtyard of a Dutch House* (Pl. A.) in the National Gallery (*cf.* p. 28), the examples in the Wallace Collection, the Berlin picture called *The Mother* (Pl. 116), and other pictures of the kind.

We have but to examine these pictures and to compare them on the one hand with the Dutch popular pictures discussed in Part V, and on the other with works by Vermeer, to realize that de Hooch was an artist who stood midway between the two attitudes and was influenced by both. I am not acquainted with any picture by de Hooch, after he had worked through his gay-life period, which is purely a record of the clothes and social aspects of the persons represented. He does not begin his pictures with the figures. He begins by the architectural structure of the picture and fits the figures in afterwards. But he is never completely captured by the archi-tectural attitude, and he never achieves really adequate architectural results. In the other National Gallery picture of a Dutch courtyard the gesture of the woman with her back turned leads the eye to the kneeling figure; and the side of the house, with the pump, basket, broom and open doorway lead it back to the right-hand front corner of the picture; this triangular rhythm fits, moreover, into another architectural motif—a Z-shaped recession starting from the open door on the right to the fence, across the fence and away down the path to the little figure of the man at the far end. But de Hooch has not forgotten that the figure with her back turned is the mistress of the house and that the kneeling woman is the servant; nor has he forgotten that the servant is about to use the pump to wash the fish as instructed by her mistress. In the same way the colour is neither entirely naturalistic nor entirely part of an architectural design. It is thus possible to regard the picture either as a description of everyday life and so 'national' and popular, or as an architectural work of art; and because of this dual character it is not quite integral from either point of view.

The same applies, I think, to all de Hooch's pictures of this Delft period, not even excepting the *Conversation Out-of-Doors* (Pl. 117) with its clever solution of problems of aerial perspective, or *The Mother* (Pl. 116), where the figure has a majesty already observed in the *Pipe-drunk Woman* by Jacob Duck (Pl. 88) and in certain figures by Jan Steen (Pl. 95).

In 1667 de Hooch removed to Amsterdam, and there, or perhaps earlier in Delft or elsewhere, he presumably had contact with Hoogstraten. The picture called *La Collation* in the National Gallery is characteristic of the works ascribed to this last period which represent the Amsterdam upper bourgeoisie in handsome apartments and colonnaded courtyards of the kind depicted in Hoogstraten's *Young Lady in a Courtyard* (Pl. 110).

Most critics assert that de Hooch's Delft standards were not maintained in his Amsterdam period. But the truth is, I fancy, that the later pictures, being more romantic, should be judged by romantic and not architectural or descriptive standards.

(c) SAMUEL VAN HOOGSTRATEN

Born Dordrecht 1627, died Dordrecht 1678

CHARACTERISTIC PICTURES

London—National Gallery	*Dutch Interior (Peepshow Cabinet)*
London—National Gallery	*Refusing the Glass*
England—Finch Collection	*Young Gentleman in a Courtyard*
England—Blathwayt Collection	*Perspective of a Corridor*
England—Godrey-Faussett Collection	*Thomas Godfrey*
The Hague—Mauritshuis	*Young Lady in a Courtyard*
Amsterdam—Rijks Museum	*Doctor and Dropsical Woman*
Dordrecht Museum	*Group of Dordrecht Mint-Masters*
Vienna Gallery	*Burgplatz at Vienna*
Vienna Gallery	*The Man at the Window*
Bamberg Gallery	*Christ crowned with Thorns*
Formerly Sabin Gallery	*Soldier and Woman at Spinet*

Samuel van Hoogstraten, like most of the artists of this group, worked in different manners at different times; but he is mainly of interest by reason of his experiments in optics and his probable contact with de Hooch and Vermeer.

He was undoubtedly a man of considerable parts and of great intellectual curiosity. He was at first a pupil of his father Dirck van Hoogstraten, who was a jeweller and painter, and had established himself in Dordrecht after his father Jan van Hoogstraten had been obliged to leave Antwerp for his religious opinions. Dirck van Hoogstraten died in 1640 and after that Samuel went to Amsterdam and studied with Rembrandt.

178

The Rembrandt influence in Hoogstraten's work is evident in his drawings, which are executed in a technique closely modelled on the master's, and it is also evident in certain pictures such as the *Man at the Window* in Vienna. But Hoogstraten had far too lively a mind to be a *pasticheur* or even to remain quietly in Dordrecht where he returned from Amsterdam in 1648; and two years later he set out on foreign travels. In 1651 we find him in Vienna painting for the Emperor; from Vienna he went to Rome, and after another year in Vienna he returned to Dordrecht in 1654. Here he soon attracted attention by his accomplishments which had been increased by the experience of his foreign travels. He wrote a poem on the death of Mathijs Pompe van Slingeland, and he caused a nine days' scandal in his native town when he was expelled in 1656 from the Mennonite community, to which he belonged, for marrying without the community's approval and for wearing a sword. After this it may be presumed that he visited other cities—including Delft, where he perhaps had contact with de Hooch and Vermeer. In 1662 he came to London. The only surviving picture known to have been painted by him in London is *Thomas Godfrey*—a portrait of Thomas Godfrey of Burton Aleph dated 1663, though Walpole speaks of a still-life and a self-portrait. He remained here till the Great Fire, which he is said to have witnessed. He then returned to Holland, and two years later, in 1668, he became a member of The Hague painters' guild. He lived in The Hague for three years and wrote a play called 'Dierik and Dorothé' which was performed there. In 1671 he was appointed Director of the Dordrecht Mint and he returned to his native town. He had already painted a *Group of Dordrecht Mint-Masters* in the year of his marriage, and his connexion with that institution is also recorded in a *History of Currency* which he wrote, presumably while he was director. At various periods he had a number of pupils who included Aert de Gelder, Godfried Schalcken, and the art-historian Arnold Houbraken; and he composed in his old age for the benefit of students an elaborate treatise on painting called '*Inleydinghe tot de Hooge Schoole der Schilderkonst, anders de Zichtbare Werelt*' which he illustrated with engravings by himself.

Houbraken bears witness to Hoogstraten's passionate interest in optics, and he relates that his house was full of cut cardboard representations of fruit, fish and so forth which appeared to have three dimensions. This interest is seen in his *Peepshow* (Pl. 118) in the National Gallery where the perspective effects are obtained with astonishing science—tiles, two chairs and a dog being painted partly on the wall and partly on the floor, and a table being painted entirely on the floor. On the top of this cabinet, moreover, there is an elongated Venus and Cupid group intended to be looked at from an angle which would restore the natural proportions.

I reproduce also his *Young Lady in a Courtyard* (Pl. 110) in the Mauritshuis, which is a pendant to a picture showing a gentleman sitting reading in a similar courtyard with a dog and cat which is in the Finch Collection at Burley-on-the-Hill. In the Mauritshuis picture we have a relation between the dog in the foreground and the figure beyond which in my view suggests that the dog was standing in front of a mirror in which the scene behind was reflected, and in a picture at one time in the Sabin Gallery showing a soldier in the foreground and a woman further back playing a clavichord—which has been ascribed to Hoogstraten—we have a similar effect produced possibly by the same means.

One other work which is probably by this interesting artist calls for mention—the picture called *Refusing the Glass* (Pl. 123) in the National Gallery. This, formerly ascribed to de Hooch, is now ascribed by some students to H. van der Burch. I refer to it in the section headed 'Vermeer's Mirrors' where I suggest that it depicts the actual position of the artist in front of a mirror when his models were grouped behind him as he worked.[1]

(d) PIETER JANSSENS

Born before 1640, *died before* 1682(?)

CHARACTERISTIC PICTURES

Frankfort Museum	*Interior with Woman and Dog* (A Man seen in an Inner Room)[2]
Munich—Alte Pinakothek	*Interior with Woman Reading*[2]
Strasbourg Gallery	*The Promenade* (Renaissance portico with lady and gentleman followed by nurse and baby. Homely interior seen beyond)[2]

Hardly anything is known of Pieter Janssens, who signed P. Janssens E. He is presumed by some identical with one Pieter Janssens Elinga. He painted still-life; and a number of interiors, most of which were previously labelled de Hooch, are now ascribed to him.

[1] *Cf.* pp. 188–194. For colour plate *cf. Dutch Indoor Subjects* in Faber Gallery.
[2] Formerly ascribed to de Hooch.

DUTCH ARCHITECTURAL ART

Janssens, as can be seen from the example reproduced (Pl. 109), certainly had contact with de Hooch and probably with Van Hoogstraten as well. The interiors now assigned to him are all of the character of this example except the curious work at Strasbourg which has a foreground of the character of Hoogstraten's *Young Lady in a Courtyard* (Pl. 110), and shows, through a door beyond, a homely interior in the manner of de Hooch. All the other pictures show interiors with the lower windows shuttered and all show one or more mirrors on the wall. The Frankfort picture shows a room with a large gold mirror between the windows and a woman with her back turned at a table; through a door a man also with his back turned is seen in a room beyond. Another of his pictures shows the same woman with her back turned at a table and a second woman sweeping the floor.

Janssens appears in fact to have taken conspicuously little interest in descriptive and social aspects of the interiors he describes, and when he introduces a figure it is nearly always with its back to the spectator.[1] As compared with de Hooch, who was always concerned to some extent with social description, he was as purely concerned with architectural problems as Hoogstraten was concerned with them in his peepshows. But he was not, of course, an architect of the quality of Vermeer. He often failed, for example, to define the front plane of his pictures. In the *Interior with Woman Reading* (Pl. 109) he has tried to define this plane by the fragment of a chair-back and what was possibly his own puffed sleeve as he painted in a mirror,[2] but the form thus produced has no architectural coherence with the rest of the picture and serves only to complete a semicircle, with the shoes and chest, surrounding the figure of the reading girl; and in this picture, moreover, the left side of the picture-box is undefined.

Janssens was thus not a first-rate artist of this school; but it is important to realize the character of his endeavour because, when we consider his work together with the experiments by Carel Fabritius, Hoogstraten, and with the pictures by de Hooch, it is clear that Vermeer was not the only Dutch artist of the period to react completely from Rembrandt's romantic concept of picture space but that there was, on the contrary, a definite movement pursuing this aim.

[1] I have already pointed out that this characteristic also occurs in Berchem's classical-picturesque compositions; but the purpose there is rather different (*cf.* p. 117).

[2] *Cf.* p. 192.

ii. Vermeer of Delft

Born Delft 1632, died Delft 1675

London—National Gallery	*Lady standing at the Virginals* (Pl. D.) (*s*)
London—National Gallery	*Lady seated at the Virginals* (*s*)
London—Royal Collection	*Lady and Gentleman at a Clavichord* (*s*)
London—Beit Collection	*Lady writing a Letter, and Maid*[1] (*s*)
Edinburgh—N.G. Scotland	*Christ with Mary and Martha*[1] (*s*)
Paris—Louvre	*The Lace Maker*[1] (*s*)
Paris—Private Collection	*The Astronomer* (*s* and 1668)
The Hague—Mauritshuis	*Diana and her Companions* (*s* ?)
The Hague—Mauritshuis	*View of Delft* (*s*)
The Hague—Mauritshuis	*Head of a Young Girl*[1] (*s*)
Amsterdam—Rijks Museum	*Woman reading a Letter*
Amsterdam—Rijks Museum	*The Little Street*[1] (*s*)
Amsterdam—Rijks Museum	*The Love Letter, Lady and Maid* (*s*)
Amsterdam—Rijks Museum	*The Milk Girl* (*The Cook*)[1]
Vienna—Kunsthistorisches Museum	*The Painter and his Model*[1] (*s*)
Dresden Gallery	*Girl reading a Letter* (*s* ?)
Dresden Gallery	*The Procuress* (*s* and 1656)
Berlin—Kaiser-Friedrich Museum	*The Pearl Necklace* (*s*)
Berlin—Kaiser-Friedrich Museum	*A Glass of Wine*
Frankfort—Staedel Institute	*The Geographer* (*s*)
Boston—Gardner Collection	*The Concert*
Washington—N.G. of Art	*Woman in a Chinese Hat with flute*
Washington—N.G. of Art	*Young Woman weighing Gold*[1]
Washington—N.G. of Art	*Woman with a Red Hat*[1]
New York—Frick Collection	*Soldier and Laughing Girl*
New York—Metropolitan Museum	*Woman with Jug and Platter*
New York—Metropolitan Musuem	*Young Woman Asleep*
New York—Metropolitan Museum	*Allegory of the Faith*

The facts of Vermeer's life can be very briefly told. The dates of his birth and death in Delft are recorded, and there are no records that he ever lived or worked in any other town or visited any other country. He was, as noted, almost certainly a pupil of Carel Fabritius. He married in 1652 at the age of twenty and had eight children. He was admitted to the Delft painters' guild in 1653, was on the guild's committee in 1662, 1663, and 1670, and he was the guild's 'doyen' in 1670. He died at the age of forty-three.

[1] Reproduced in colour in Faber Gallery 'Vermeer'.

Plate D. VERMEER: 'Lady standing at the Virginals'

VERMEER OF DELFT

Less than forty pictures are now assigned to him by even the most optimistic students. The neglect of his work in the eighteenth and early nineteenth centuries, when he was vaguely confused with the landscape painter Vermeer of Haarlem and with de Hooch, may account in some measure for the shortness of the list. But it may be that he did in fact produce unusually few pictures; M. de Monconys, who visited Holland in 1663, relates that he called upon him in Delft and that the artist had no pictures to show him (though he was able to see one in a baker's house). Many of Vermeer's pictures seem to have passed into the hands of a painter and art dealer named Jan Coelembier of Haarlem, who had twenty-six in 1676, and of a printer named J. A. Dissius of Delft, who left nineteen when he died in 1682. A few seem to have remained the property of Vermeer's widow who, after his death, pawned *The Painter and his Model* (Pl. 120) to her mother, and two others, *The Lady writing a Letter, and Maid* (Beit Collection) and a *Guitar Player* to a baker for 617 gulden.

On May 16th, 1696, the following twenty-one pictures by Vermeer were sold by auction in Amsterdam in a sale of a hundred and thirty-four pictures by various artists:

1. *Young Woman weighing Gold.*[1] (155 gulden.)
2. *The Milk Girl.*[1] (175 gulden.)
3. *Picture of Vermeer in an Interior.*[2] (45 gulden.)
4. *Young Woman playing the Guitar.*[3] (70 gulden.)
5. *A Gentleman in an Interior washing his hands.*[4] (95 gulden.)
6. *Lady and Gentleman at a Clavichord.*[1] (30 gulden.)
7. *Young Woman receiving a Letter from Her Servant.* (*The Love Letter, Lady and Maid.*)[1] (70 gulden.)
8. *Drunken Servant asleep at a Table.* (*Woman Asleep.*)[1] (62 gulden.)
9. *Merry Company in an Interior.*[5] (73 gulden.)
10. *A Lady and Gentleman making Music.*[4] (81 gulden.)
11. *Soldier and Laughing Girl.*[1] (44 gulden.)
12. *The Lace Maker.*[1] (28 gulden.)
13. *View of Delft.*[1] (200 gulden.)
14. *A House at Delft.*[4] (72 gulden.)
15. *View of some Houses.*[6] (48 gulden.)
16. *Young Woman Writing.*[4] (63 gulden.)

[1] For footnote references, see p. 184.

17. *Young Woman at Her Toilet.* (*The Pearl Necklace.*)[1] (30 gulden.)

18. *Lady at the Virginals.*[1] (42 gulden.)

19. *A Portrait in Antique Costume.*[4] (38 gulden.)

20 and 21. *Two Pendants.*[4] (34 gulden.)

Vermeer seems to have received what were high prices at the time for his pictures and M. de Monconys recorded that the baker had paid 600 gulden for his picture. But he was in financial difficulties from a year or two after his marriage, partly perhaps because he produced few pictures, and also, doubtless, because he found his large family an expense and because he spent money on buying pictures—witness those on his studio walls that occur in his paintings. When he died he was barely solvent, if not actually bankrupt, and a trustee was appointed to administer his estate.

The chronological order of Vermeer's existing pictures is unknown. Only two, *The Procuress* and *The Astronomer*, bear dates. It seems to me possible, however, if doubtful pictures be left aside, to divide Vermeer's works into several groups.[7]

We have in the first place some works probably painted before *The Procuress*. These include *Christ with Mary and Martha*, formerly in the Coats Collection and now in the Edinburgh Gallery; and possibly the *Diana and her Companions* in the Mauritshuis which most students regard as an early work. Dr. Tancred Borenius has suggested that the *Christ with Mary and Martha* bears a resemblance to *The Death of St. Joseph*, ascribed to Bernardo Cavallino, in Naples. But, as I see it, we have in Vermeer's picture what would seem to be the influence of the Caravaggio-Honthorst tradition. Is it possible that there was a contact about 1649–50 between Vermeer and Dirck Baburen, whose picture *The Procuress* (Pl. 17) appears in Vermeer's *Lady seated at the Virginals* (Pl. 112) and in *The Concert* in the Gardner Collection, Boston? As already noted, Baburen went to

[1] For present whereabouts see list of characteristic pictures, p. 182.

[2] Perhaps the Vienna picture (Pl. 120) pawned by the artist's widow.

[3] Perhaps the picture now in the Huntingdon Collection in New York or the picture of which versions exist in the Johnson Collection in Philadelphia and the Iveagh Collection at Ken Wood. Probably the picture pawned by the artist's widow.

[4] Present whereabouts unknown.

[5] Perhaps *The Procuress*.

[6] Perhaps *The Little Street*.

[7] Other grouping has been suggested by L. Gowing in his 'Vermeer' (Faber) 1953.

Italy and was known to have been impressed by Caravaggio, and his *Procuress* is in the Caravaggio-Honthorst tradition. If such a contact were established, we might have an explanation of Vermeer's style in his *Christ with Mary and Martha*, of the choice of subject in *The Procuress*—a subject unique in Vermeer's *œuvre* as we know it—and of the way the figures fill the canvas in both Vermeer's and Baburen's versions of the subject. Is there not, moreover, a definite resemblance between the sharp angular folds in Baburen's picture and those in the skirt of the Vermeer *Lady seated at the Virginals* and Baburen's picture? Dr. Bode suggested a relation between the *Diana and her companions* and a picture of the subject dated 1648 by the Amsterdam eclectic Jacob van Loo.

In a second group come pictures painted perhaps soon after *The Procuress*. These, I suggest, include the *Woman Asleep* and *Woman with Jug and Platter*, in the New York Metropolitan Museum, the *Young Woman weighing Gold*, in the Washington National Gallery, *The Geographer* in Frankfort, and probably the *Lady and Gentleman at a Clavichord* in the Royal collection.

Since this book was first published the Rotterdam Museum acquired a painting with a Vermeer signature: *The Supper at Emmaus*. I have not seen this picture, which has now been proved a modern forgery. The composition is an obvious variant of Caravaggio's *The Supper at Emmaus* (Pl. 26)—the main change being the shifting of the attendant figure from left to right. It is thus very directly in what I have called here the Caravaggio-Honthorst tradition which influenced the pictures in the first group and also *The Procuress*. It also resembles the pictures I have allotted to the second group. The figure of the attendant has the face of the beautiful young woman who sat for the young woman in *The Procuress*, for the *Young Woman weighing Gold* and for the *Woman with Jug and Platter*. The young man who posed for both disciples resembles the young gentleman in *A Lady and Gentleman at the Clavichord* and for *The Geographer*. The earthenware jug is in the Queen's picture, in the *Woman Asleep* and in some other pictures. Also as a detail the armchair which occurs in *The Supper at Emmaus* is the same as the chair in *Christ with Mary and Martha* and armchairs in later pictures by Vermeer.[1]

[1] The history of the acquisition of *The Supper at Emmaus* by the Rotterdam Museum is as follows. The picture was said to have belonged to a Parisian gentleman married to a Dutch lady who had inherited it. In 1937 it appeared in the sale room. Then Doctor Bredius wrote about it in the *Burlington Magazine*, a Dutch dealer acquired it and in 1938 Mr. Hannema, Director of the Rotterdam Museum, raised funds to secure it for his gallery. The forger's name was Van Meegeren.

In a third group may come the *Milk Girl* and the *Little Street* in Amsterdam, the Louvre *Lace Maker*, and the *View of Delft* in The Hague. They are less broadly and freely painted than the works here assigned to the earlier phases. The paint is solid, and the touch small, though the effect—for this type of handling—is broad. They strike me as works of a man who is subjecting himself to a period of naturalistic discipline, who is determined to get, as it were, the last ounce of what Ruskin used to call 'fact' into his work, and who, to secure this end, has surrendered his mind to a large extent to his eye and hand. They correspond to Rembrandt's *Head of an Old Woman* in the National Gallery, and they must, in my view, be assigned the character of elaborate and conscientious studies.[1]

This group was followed perhaps by a fourth which includes the *Soldier and Laughing Girl* in the Frick Collection, the Dresden *Girl reading a Letter* (Pl 119) and *The Astronomer* dated 1668. The model for the girl in the first two pictures is the same, and she wears the same type of dress. The technique of the Dresden picture is similar to that of the studies just referred to, but there is now more interest in architectural problems of the picture-space, and the pictures, I think, are a bridge to the next group—the final phase.

This fifth group contains works where Vermeer is primarily concerned with the architecture of his picture-space and where he developed the smooth, lustrous handling which we associate especially with his name. This group includes the *Painter and his Model* (Pl. 120), the *Love Letter* (Pl. 121), the *Allegory of The Faith* (Pl. 122), the *Lady standing at the Virginals* (Pl. D),[2] and the *Lady writing a Letter, and Maid* in the Beit Collection.

Another group which preceded the foregoing or followed it includes the *Lady seated at the Virginals* (Pl. 112), the *Head of a Young Girl*[3] (Pl. 113), and the *Pearl Necklace* in Berlin.

Vermeer, in my view, must be judged a great master by the pictures in the fifth group, each of which is an original creation. As social descriptions the pictures in many cases are not only eccentric but definitely 'bizarre'. The lady and her maid are unaccountably placed in *The Love Letter* (Pl. 121); from internal evidence it is difficult

[1]Charles Blanc, writing of the famous *View in Delft* in 1861, said: 'L'exécution en est grossière, l'empâtement brutal et l'aspect monotone.'

[2]*Cf.* pp. 29, 30.

[3]When this head was bought at auction in The Hague in 1882 for two and a half gulden it was in a bad condition. It has since been restored and in, parts, repainted.

to discover what the *Allegory of The Faith* is about[1]; and who can tell us why the *Lady standing by the Virginals* does not take the chair in the foreground and sit upon it if she wants to play the instrument?[2] But such considerations, which would be appropriate in the case of descriptive works by Jan Steen or Van Ostade, are obviously quite beside the point in front of such pictures by Vermeer. For Vermeer started these pictures as Claude and Janssens started theirs, by the concept of his picture-space as an empty box, the four sides of which it was his first preoccupation to define. In these pictures by Vermeer we are always conscious of the front plane indicated by a curtain or some other device and the background is always a flat surface—wherein, it may be observed in passing, Vermeer differs from de Hooch, whose space concept was a compromise between the classical cube and the infinite recessions of the Rembrandt school, and who felt accordingly impelled to open doors and windows in the backcloth which in Vermeer's most characteristic pictures is always a closing plane. This feeling for architectural form which dictated Vermeer's initial compositions was extended to the objects disposed within the box. With the nature of these objects Vermeer was as little concerned as Claude was with Abraham and Hagar[3] or Janssens was with the face of his reading woman, or a modern cubist is with the species of a tree. He regarded all the objects which he arranged in his picture-space as architectural data to be formally related one to another and to the box as a whole. In this architectural form he included light and colour which he treated in the same constructive and essentially architectural way. He included in it also the science of perspective which he used, not in the manner of illusionist naturalists like Dou, but as an architectural factor in itself; the perspective in Vermeer's pictures is, in fact, in many cases too sudden for verisimilitude, and it only convinces us because it is consistent with itself and evidently part of an architectural synthesis. In the same way the portrait heads are conceived

[1] The subject has in fact some relation to a description of *Faith* in a work published in Holland in 1644 called *Iconologie of Uytbeeldinghe des Verstants* translated by Dirck Pietersz Pers from Cesare Ripa. In this iconology *The Faith* is described as a 'woman seated with a chalice in her right hand, her left hand on a book and her feet on the earth: on the ground a serpent crushed by an angular stone, and an apple representing sin; behind the woman a crown of thorns suspended on a nail; in the background a picture of the Sacrifice of Abraham'. Vermeer's picture was sold by a Berlin dealer to Dr. Bredius for 700 marks as a work by E. H. Van der Neer.

[2] Though people did sometimes stand to play this instrument, as is pointed out by Mr. Lawrence Haward in the Faber Gallery volume *Music in Painting*.

[3] *Cf.* note, pp. 107, 108.

as filling the picture box, and no artist has ever set portraits more perfectly within the picture's frame.

In these paintings Vermeer absorbs the art of the Dutch picturesque painters, the clothes-painting by Duyster, Terborch and Metsu, the architectural efforts of Janssens, the optical science of Hoogstraten and the compositional experiments by Carel Fabritius. He triumphs over them all because as an architect he is, at his best, immensely their superior. Confronted with a picture of his best period the whole structure seems final and inevitable. It is impossible to imagine the slightest modification of a line, a tone, a colour or a recession that would not destroy the perfect poise and balance of the whole.

iii. Vermeer's Mirrors

(In the Dutch painters' studios) 'among various objects with bright reflecting surfaces we often see a convex mirror or a crystal ball. Artists seem to have made some use of this object. . . .'—DR. W. MARTIN, Director of the Mauritshuis, The Hague.

'It is possible that it is to him (Gerard Dou) that we must attribute an invention — to some extent ingenious but fraught with certain drawbacks—which reduces large objects to a small scale. Dou used a kind of screen fixed to his foot; in the screen he had inserted and framed a concave glass at the height of his eye when he was seated at his easel. This screen formed a species of partition between the object to be represented and the artist. The object was seen in a reduced scale in the concave glass and the artist had only to copy its form and colour. . . . Dou then drew the objects on to his canvas which was divided into equal squares corresponding to threads on a little frame of the exact size of the circumference of the concave glass, in such a way that when the frame was attached to the glass it represented a square drawn within a circle.'[1]—DESCAMPS, *La Vie des Peintres Flamands, Allemands et Hollandais*, 1763.

[1] 'Je ne scais si ce n'est pas à lui que l'on doit une invention assez ingénieuse, mais sujette pourtant a quelques inconvénients, de réduire en un petit espace de grands objets: Il se servoit d'une espèce d'écran sur son pied, dans lequel il avoit pratiqué et encadré un miroir concave à la hauteur de sa vue, quand il étoit assis. Cet écran etoit une sorte de cloison entre l'objet à représenter et lui; Cet objet se traçoit en petit dans ce verre concave, et le Peintre n'avoit plus à en imiter que le trait et la couleur.

'Sa composition étant disposée, il portoit sur sa toile, divisée en plusiers quarreaux égaux entr'eux, les objets dont il avoit besoin: Cette division étoit repétée avec des fils sur un petit chassis qui étoit de la grandeur de la circonférence du verre concave; de façon que lorsqu'il attachoit le chassis sur le verre, ce chassis représentoit un quarré inscrit dans un cercle.'

VERMEER'S MIRRORS

There can be no doubt that some of the Dutch artists made use of mechanical contrivances to assist them in naturalistic imitation in their pictures; and the instrument described by Descamps would certainly have appealed to Dou, who was primarily concerned with achieving illusionist effects. If the use of such contrivances had been confined to artists of Dou's calibre it would be of no present interest. But it is, I think, more than probable that artists like Carel Fabritius, Hoogstraten and Janssens, with their great interest in optics, used some analogous procedure, and that this procedure was also used for his architectural purposes by Vermeer himself.

Vermeer, I believe, frequently worked out his compositions and perhaps actually painted his pictures with the aid of one, or two, mirrors.

Take for example *The Love Letter* (Pl. 121). This is always regarded as a view through a doorway into another room with two women in the middle of it. The curtain and chair in the foreground are presumed to be in a front room or passage where the painter was working. I suggest that the doorway (attached to which is no sign of a door) was a *mirror* reflecting the figures in another part of the room in which Vermeer was working. The curtain was perhaps used to cover the mirror when not in use. The chair stands in front of the wall next to the mirror which seems to be placed in a corner of the room. Vermeer sat with his back to the curtain, chair, and mirror, looking into another mirror by the side of or above his canvas. Reflected in this second mirror the curtain, chair and mirror become the *foreground* and the rest of the picture is the reflection in the back mirror. Vermeer sat a little to the left of the back mirror with his back probably a little to the left of the chair. The models were either on a level with him facing the back mirror, or behind him and between him and the curtain, chair and back mirror, or possibly in front and to the right of him. The broom which appears to be leaning across the entrance to the second room was probably substituted at the last minute for the leg of the artist's easel which was reflected in the back mirror at this point.

The shoes in the foreground of this picture recall the shoes in Van Eyck's *Jan Arnolfini and his Wife* in the National Gallery. Is it too fantastic to suppose that Jan Eyck's picture also was painted with two mirrors, that Vermeer knew it, and that the shoes are a challenge to the older master in the same way that the figure of Goya at his easel in his Royal Group in the Prado is a challenge to *Las Meninas* by Velasquez? Is it too fantastic to suppose that when

Jan Eyck wrote on the wall above his mirror *Johannes de Eyck fuit hic* he meant what he said—'*was here*'—i.e. at the back of the room, and not '*fecit hoc*', i.e. painted this picture?[1]

Now let us look at Vermeer's *The Painter and his Model* (Pl. 120). Here, I suggest, the back mirror reflected the artist's back and easel as he sat at work and his model in front of him against the wall, and that he painted all this as re-reflected in the front mirror. He also painted the chair *behind his back* up against the back mirror and the mirror-covering curtain, partly pulled aside—details added to the reflection in the back mirror by the front one, which accordingly form the foreground of the picture.

Now consider *Girl reading a Letter* (Pl. 119). Here on the left is a window and a wall at right angles to it facing the spectator. The window is almost in the corner of the room and a chair with brass lions' heads stands cornerways across the corner. Beneath the window is a table covered with a bunched-up cloth and still life. Between the table and the wall, almost touching the table and the chair and the wall, stands a girl. A curtain hanging on a rod by rings hangs in the foreground; it reaches from the rod which is high above the window to the top of the table. The disposition here is as strange as in the case of *The Love Letter* in Amsterdam. What is the ordinary function of this curtain which cuts across the room at right angles to the window and a few feet from the wall? It cannot keep out the draught as it stops short with a fringe about four feet from the ground. The explanation I submit is that the picture was painted in a mirror and that the curtain used to cover the mirror was painted in by the artist. The curtain came down to the bottom of the mirror, which is also the bottom of the picture, and no further; and the artist has painted in not only the curtain partly pulled across the mirror but also the rod on which it was hung.

In the Queen's *Lady and Gentleman at a Clavichord*, we do not see the curtain in the foreground; but the whole picture, I believe, was painted in a mirror, and the artist with his back to his models sat close to the mirror, perhaps level with the front of the table-cloth which forms the foreground. This picture, moreover, shows one of Vermeer's small mirrors on the wall. It is not an ornamental mirror but a working mirror in a plain black frame. It is placed above the clavichord, and tilted forward on a string, and it shows how much Vermeer was intrigued by the effects of reflection because

---

[1] The shoes occur also in Janssens's *Interior with a Woman Reading* (Pl. 109) and Janssens, as noted, was certainly associated with the optical experiments of the Vermeer circle.

he has set down how the mirror reflects the lady's face and the tessellated floor in juxtaposition owing to the tilt.

Mirrors are also shown on the wall in the *Woman Asleep* and *The Pearl Necklace*. They occur also in pictures by de Hooch and in, as already noted, all interiors ascribed to Janssens.

Vermeer did not, I think, use mirrors for all his pictures, but he used them at all periods of his career. The *Woman Asleep*, the *Soldier and Laughing Girl*, the *Allegory of The Faith* (Pl. 122) and *The Pearl Necklace* were probably painted in some such way. This would account for the large scale of the objects in the foreground in compositions like the *Soldier and Laughing Girl* where the figure of the soldier in the foreground is quite out of scale. This peculiarity in composition we find nowhere else in European art (except in Hoogstraten) till we get to Degas and the other nineteenth-century artists who exploited similar effects observed in photographs; and it is perhaps one of the ironies of art history that with a Kodak any child might now produce by accident a composition that a great artist like Vermeer had to use all his ingenuity and perhaps the aid of mirrors to achieve.

Vermeer, I think, also used a mirror in portraits like the *Woman in Chinese Hat with Flute* and *Woman with a Red Hat*. I saw the *Woman with a Red Hat* in London before it went to the United States. I was struck first by its vitreous quality which is evident in all the mirror pictures—and by a conviction that the picture was painted in a mirror. I was then struck by the circumstance that the lions' heads on the chair on which the young woman is sitting are turned towards the spectator, whereas on Vermeer's lion chair, which occurs in other pictures, and indeed on all such chairs, the lions' heads face the front of the chair. I thought at first that the original description of this picture (*Gazette des Beaux Arts*, 1866) as 'Portrait of a Young Man' was the correct one, and that it was a self-portrait by Vermeer. Then I saw a reproduction of the *Woman in a Chinese Hat*, obviously the same sitter, and obviously a woman, holding what I took to be the handles of two paint brushes in her hand, and I thought that these two pictures were self-portraits by some woman pupil of Vermeer. But I now think that both pictures must be included in Vermeer's mirror experiments.

As already noted I believe that the curious composition of the *View in Delft with a Musical Instrument Dealer* (Pl. 114) by Carel Fabritius in the National Gallery, derives from some use of mirrors. Here possibly the artist used one of those mirrors which the Dutch had fixed outside their windows to reflect the passers-by; and the

Refusing the Glass (Pl. 123) in the National Gallery, formerly ascribed to de Hooch or Hoogstraten, and now to H. van der Burch, seems to me another interesting example of a mirror picture by a member of Vermeer's circle. For here we see the artist at work before his front mirror with his back to the group of the man, woman and boy in the foreground who are reflected in the second mirror behind him. It is, when one comes to think of it, an incredible composition unless we accept this explanation.

In regard to this work, *Refusing the Glass*, it should also be noted that the Amsterdam Rijks Museum contains a picture by J. Ekels the Younger (1759–93) which is called *The Writer* but which is obviously the artist drawing himself in a mirror. In this picture the artist's back is turned towards us and his face is reflected in just the same way as in Hoogstraten's picture, and it would thus seem that the tradition of this procedure continued into the eighteenth century.

I do not think that any of de Hooch's pictures were painted in this way—though the *Interior of a Dutch House* (Pl. 115) may be an example—but Hoogstraten's *Young Lady in a Courtyard* (Pl. 110) and Janssen's *Interior with Woman Reading* (Pl. 109) are, I believe, mirror pictures, and it may be that all Janssen's interiors were so painted.

Experiments in mirror painting were also made, I think, outside the Vermeer-Hoogstraten-Janssens circle—witness *The Cabaret* (Pl. 124) by Jan Steen, the *Holy Family* (Pl. 125) ascribed to Rembrandt, the *Self-Portrait* (Pl. 128) by Dou, and *Vanity* (Pl. 126) ascribed to Moreelse.

In Jan Steen's picture we see the top of the mirror frame and the curtain looped up above it; and it is noteworthy that this is the only interior that I know by Jan Steen where the problem of picture-space with considerable recession is adequately solved. The scene is lumbered with detail because Steen was essentially a descriptive not an architectural artist, but I do feel here that Steen has achieved an architectural framework by the aid of the mirrors which he would not have been able to compass without their aid. It also seems to me possible that the picture on the wall at the back was in fact the mirror in which Steen saw the whole scene re-reflected from the other mirror with the curtain behind his back.

In the *Holy Family* (Pl. 125) in Cassel we have the whole frame of the mirror with the curtain half pulled across on its rod. I do not know if this picture is by Rembrandt. It is ascribed by Professor Van Dyke to Van der Pluym.

In Dou's *Self-Portrait* (Pl. 128) we again have the whole frame of the mirror and the curtain on its rod; and Dou, I am convinced,

Oxford—Ashmolean Museum

Plate 129. BALTHASAR VAN DER AST: 'Flowers in a Porcelain Vase'

Plate 130. WILLEM VAN AELST: 'Flowers in a Gilt Vase on a Marble Slab'

Collection of Major the Hon. H. R. Broughton

Plate 131. NICOLAES LACHTROPIUS: 'Flowers in a Glass Vase on a Marble Slab'

Plate 132. MATHIAS WITHOOS: 'The Hedgehog'

Collection of Major the Hon. H. R. Broughton

Plate 133. RACHEL RUYSCH: 'The Lizard'

London—Victoria and Albert Museum

Plate 134. JACOB VAN WALSCAPELLE: 'Flowers in a Glass Vase on a Marble Table'

Oxford—Ashmolean Museum

Plate 135. SIMON VERELST: 'Apple Blossom and Poppies'

Plate 136. COENRAET ROEPEL: 'White-purple Tulips, Narcissi, Poppies and Polyanthus'

used mirrors for many of his pictures when he was not using the diminishing device which Descamps described.

The *Vanity* (Pl. 126) ascribed to Moreelse strikes me as a self-portrait with two mirrors by some woman artist. I suggest Judith Leyster as the painter because the picture has a relation to the school of Hals and it shows her particular feeling for design, as seen in *The Merry Toper* (Pl. 47).[1] What, incidentally, is the curious object that resembles a watch-case in this picture? Has it a connexion with the procedure here in question?

I submit the whole problem of the use of mirrors by the seventeenth-century painters for investigation. The practice was not, of course, confined to Holland. Velasquez probably used one mirror, perhaps two, for *Las Meninas* (Pl. 127), and I fancy that what appears to be a door next to the mirror reflecting the King and Queen was also possibly a mirror reflecting a figure in some other part of the room. In *The House of Martha* by Velasquez (in the National Gallery) there is evidently a mirror reflecting a scene in the adjacent room.

In the Vienna Gallery there is a picture called *The Family of the Artist* by J. B. del Mazo, the pupil and son-in-law of Velasquez. In this picture the family, consisting of nine persons, is disposed across the foreground; on the wall behind there is a mirror reflecting the *back* of the artist painting at his easel, and the backs also of a woman and child who are looking on.

The use of mirrors doubtless began in Venice, where they were first made, and they occur in pictures by Titian and other Venetian masters. But the little genre scene reflected in the mirror in Titian's *Vanitas* in Munich is admitted to be a seventeenth-century addition, and probably, I imagine, the work of a Dutch hand.

The mirrors used by the Dutch painters were probably relatively small in size, because large mirrors were still rare and expensive in the seventeenth century and because, owing to the small scale on which most of the artists worked, small mirrors served their purpose very well. But the main mirror required by Velasquez for *Las Meninas* which has life-size figures must, however, have been a large one; and the mirror seen in his *House of Martha* is also large.

Students with whom I have discussed the pictures have expressed the view that the curtains shown hanging on rods were not used to cover mirrors as I suggest, but were illusionist representations of curtains used by the Dutch to cover their pictures, and that the

---

[1] *Cf.* pp. 84–86. The *Vanity* is however stated in the Amsterdam Catalogue to be signed with the monogram P.M.

artists were attempting to deceive the spectator into imagining that
he was looking at a picture with its curtain covering already fixed.
It is true that the creation of an illusion of this kind would have
appealed to the mind of Dou. It is also true that the Dutch sometimes
used curtains to cover their pictures, because, although the vast
majority of pictures shown on the walls in Dutch paintings have no
such covering, we do, in fact, find a curtain on a rod in front of
a picture shown in Metsu's *The Family of Koopman Geelvinck* (Pl. 106)
and again in front of a picture shown in Metsu's *Music Lesson* in
the National Gallery, and in certain other works. But it is impossible
to believe that Vermeer would have been interested in a trick of this
kind, and indeed, in his Dresden picture (Pl. 119) the rod continues
behind the frame and there is a space above, in the original, showing
the continuation of the window and the curtain, which unfortunately
cannot be seen in the reproduction. It may be that the curtains in
the Dou picture and in the picture ascribed to Rembrandt were
intended to suggest curtains hanging on frames within the real
frame, but there was certainly no attempt to create such an illusion
in the picture by Vermeer; and in Jan Steen's picture (Pl. 124) if
the curtain is not covering a mirror it is thrown up over a gallery or
balustrade.

In any case, these curtain pictures are of a character which is
different from that of the other pictures in which I suggest Vermeer
used mirrors for the purpose of building up his architectural compositions; and whether my suggestion is valid or not, the character
and the value of Vermeer's achievement remain precisely the same,
just as the character and value of the works of a modern artist who
uses photographs for an architectural purpose remain unaltered by
this mechanical aid. Nor, on the other hand, if Janssens and Hoogstraten, as I believe, and perhaps de Hooch, used similar procedures,
do they thereby enter the same category of artists as Vermeer.
For their pictures, however produced, remain architecturally less
brilliant. Vermeer, if he used mirrors, as I suggest, was doubtless
helped thereby to achieve that classical symbolic synthesis which
was the purpose of his work; but this help would not have enabled
him to achieve more than Hoogstraten or the others had it not been
guided by his powers as an architect; and his pictures remain masterpieces because he had a master-architect's mind.[1]

---

[1] Another explanation of the characters here explained by the use of mirrors is
put forward by L. Gowing in his 'Vermeer' 1953, already referred to (Footnote
p. 184). Mr. Gowing suggests that Vermeer used a camera obscura.

Part VII
DUTCH FLOWER PAINTING

i. Some outstanding painters

'A Dutchman, newly come over, one Verelst . . . did show us a little flower pot of his drawing, the finest thing that ever, I think, I saw in my life; the drops of dew hanging on the leaves, so as I was forced, again and again, to put my finger to it, to feel whether my eyes were deceived or no.'—PEPYS.

'The most perfect ideas and pleasures of imitation are when one sense is contradicted by another . . . as when the eye says a thing is round and the finger says it is flat. . . . These ideas and pleasures are the most contemptible which can be received from art.'—RUSKIN.

'As to you, dear old Jan van Huysum . . . your pearly dewdrops on the fresh-gathered green things of the earth refresh me.'—JAMES SMETHAM.

'The Dutchman never got a wet flower to paint from. He had his exquisite and exemplary poppy or tulip brought in from the market . . . and put on its dew-drops for it as a lady's dressing-maid puts on her diamonds, merely for state.'—RUSKIN.

'Painters should go to the Dutch school to learn the art of painting, as they would go to a grammar school to learn languages. . . . A clearness and brilliancy of colouring may be learned by examining the flower pieces of De Heem, Huysum and Mignon; and a short time employed in painting flowers would make no improper part of a painter's study.'—SIR JOSHUA REYNOLDS.

Flower painting, as distinguished from other forms of still-life, deals with objects which make an aesthetic visual appeal to laymen. You have to be an artist to take pleasure in the form and colour of pots and pans and herrings, dead game, asparagus and clay pipes, but every layman looks aesthetically at apple blossom, roses, columbines, forget-me-nots and tulips. The Dutch flower-painters, like other flower-painters, thus started with an evident advantage. In seventeenth century Holland, moreover, there was a second factor aiding these painters to material success; for the cultivation of exhibition flora was a local passion, and flower-paintings thus had special meaning for an audience of people who grew flowers in gardens and watched the bees and butterflies upon them or bought the finest flowers from florists and had them in glass or faience vases in their rooms. Many of the best-known characters in Dutch flower-painting were, in fact, due to these conditions, because to satisfy the flower-connoisseurs the painters were led to study the form and colour of what Ruskin called 'exquisite and exemplary' specimens and to use the extreme of *trompe l'oeil* technique in their representation; and these technical procedures in their turn brought many of the artists a further measure of material success because the richest collectors of works of art have always shown a tendency to pay large sums for pictures which have clearly taken a long time to produce. But the success-stories of the most famous and diligent flower-painters are only one aspect of the history of this art which was much more varied in seventeenth century Holland than is commonly supposed; for there were also minor artists whose work now seems to us intriguing or affective; and it is probable that many pictures ascribed to the names most favoured in the international art trade were actually painted by these less successful artists whose signatures have been removed at some time by unscrupulous dealers.

Some of these Dutch flower-painters are alive for us as personalities because contemporary or near-contemporary writers (Arnold Houbraken, for example, J. Campo Weyerman, and Jan van Gool) have indicated their characters, temperaments and ways of working by revealing notes and anecdotes; of others we know only the towns they lived in, the time of their marriage and similar data from civic records; but from the one source and the other we know enough to follow their action in successive decades.

We have first some painters born at the turn of the sixteenth to the seventeenth century and active before 1640; these included Balthasar van der Ast, and Hans Bollongier and also Jan Davidsz de Heem who belongs more properly to the Flemish school. Then come some painters working from the end of the 'forties or the middle of the 'fifties including Otto Marseus van Schrieck, Mathias Withoos and Cornelis Kick who were followed from the middle 'sixties by Willem van Aelst, Maria van Oosterwijck, Nicolaes Lachtropius, Jacob can Walscapelle and Simon Verelst. Two eclectics, Abraham Mignon and Elias van den Broeck, bridge the years between this and the final period—the last years of the seventeenth and the first half of the eighteenth century—when Rachel Ruysch and Jan van Huysum were the most famous and Conraet Roepel was one of the minor and intriguing figures.

In the first group both Balthasar van der Ast and Hans Bollongier seem to have been influenced by the Antwerp-trained Ambrosius Bosschaert who worked in Holland from 1593 till 1645 and painted flowers more or less symmetrically arranged in faience pots placed centrally on tables or in glasses placed in niches, sometimes with shells and insects at the base; and also by the gifted Clara Peeters who went to Holland from Antwerp in 1612 and often included flowers in vases among plates of fruit, cakes and vessels in her still-life compositions. Balthasar van der Ast, said to have been a nephew or brother-in-law of Bosschaert, was in Utrecht till 1632 and then moved to Delft; Bollongier is known to have worked in Haarlem; but both are shadowy personalities for us today as no contemporary has informed us about them. Both are believed to have built up their flower arrangements from water colour studies of individual blossoms or from prints by botanical experts; and the picture reproduced by Balthasar van der Ast (Pl. 129), dated 1623, may indeed have been constructed in that way. But one of the few surviving pictures by Hans Bollongier suggests that he had the flowers before him as the tones seem studied in relation to the pale grey background. Jan Davidsz de Heem, who may have been Van der Ast's pupil in Utrecht about 1623, goes out of our story soon after, as he painted mainly miscellaneous still-life and only occasional flower-pieces in various Antwerp manners after moving to Antwerp in the 'thirties.

We are well-informed about Otto Marseus van Schrieck and Mathias Withoos (Pl. 132) because Houbraken knew the widow of of the first and a daughter of the second. Both painted plants and flowers growing on the outskirts of woods, with a distant landscape, and snakes, lizards and other reptiles, often fighting, among fungi in the foreground. There is a strange fascination in these concepts which suggest a drama of nature in the undergrowths; and as many of these pictures have darkened with time the sense of mystery and drama is increased. These two artists went to Italy together and had success among the collectors in Florence and also in Rome where Withoos was known in the artists' colony as Calzetta Bianca (the Italian translation of his name) and Marseus as Snuffelaer (Ferret) because he was always ferreting round for reptiles and strange plants; and Marseus was visited in Rome by Samuel van Hoogstraten (referred to earlier in this book) and had Willem van Aelst for a time as his assistant. Back in Holland in the 'fifties Withoos lived at Amersfoort till the French besieged it in 1672 when, fearing for the safety of his daughters (two of whom were later flower painters), he moved to Hoorn in Friesland where he worked quietly till his hands became crippled with gout or rheumatoid arthritis and his fingers were contracted like an eagle's claws (*'zoo krom als arentsklauwen aan de handen stonden'*). Marseus, who also returned in the 'fifties, had his own woodland on the outskirts of Amsterdam where he kept many reptiles, some of which (his widow told Houbraken) were so tame that he could push them this way or that with his mahlstick and they would stay thus till he had drawn them; and when he died there were hundreds of drawings of snakes and lizards and so forth in his studio.

Cornelis Kick, who painted flowers in glass vases, had a flower garden belonging to his father-in-law at his disposal; but he made little use of it being a slow worker and indolent, though highly regarded in his day; Elias van den Broeck and Jacob van Walscapelle (Pl. 134) were his pupils in Amsterdam about 1666. Flowers in vases were also painted by Willem van Aelst (Pl. 130), Maria van Oosterwijck and Nicolas Lachtropius (Pl. 131) who all showed a tendency to mass their flowers diagonally from the lower left hand corner upwards, to increase this movement by light and shade effects and to use darker backgrounds than the earlier painters. Willem van Aelst had a boy and girl romance in Delft with Maria van Ooster-wijck when he was twenty and she about fifteen; but she teased him and refused his offer of marriage and he went instead via France to Rome where he had high jinks in the evenings with Marseus; on his return he established himself in Amsterdam, became arrogant, aggressive and exceedingly successful and eventually married a fat German girl (*een dikke moffekop*) who had been his maid-servant and mistress. Maria van Oosterwijck, daughter of a Protestant pastor, remained all her life a spinster and won such international repute that Louis XIV, the Emperor Leopold, William and Mary of England and the King of Poland all bought her flower pictures for large sums; she gave painting lessons to her servant Geertje Pieters who signed a flower-piece now owned by the Fitzwilliam Museum in Cambridge.

Nicolaes Lachtropius seems to have painted flowers for his pleasure and to have earned his living first as a coach-painter in Amsterdam and later as a brewer in Alphen; his work has points of contact with paintings by Van Aelst and Walscapelle; but he was none the less an individual artist with a daring and unusual colour sense and a feeling for nice balance; in his picture reproduced here (Pl. 131), for ex-ample, lilac blue and wine-colour form the basis of the colour scheme and the flowers were probably painted from an actual cluster with the butterflies added to complete the design.

Jacob van Walscapelle seems also to have combined his flower-painting with another occupation; Houbraken tells us that he actually abandoned painting; but he seems in fact to have painted for some fifteen years from 1667 and then to have taken an administrative post in the textile world which left him some leisure to paint when the spirit moved him. His picture reproduced here (Pl. 134), with its blue-green leaves and yellow butterfly as foil to the scarlet poppy and pink rose against the dark gradated background, is most delicately painted. Fine workmanship marks indeed the majority of surviving pieces by the flower painters of this epoch. For these artists underpainted with most patient care, building up each leaf and flower and tendril in a delicate impasto and adding the final tints in a series of transparent glazes which alas! are often destroyed by cleaning and renewed, with a difference, by restorers; and restorers, it must be added, have also renewed the dark backgrounds of many of these pictures to 'make the flowers stand out' thus destroying the original edges painted wet into the background by artists with a sense of tone.

Simon Verelst was among these artists with a sense of tone; and tonal qualities give poetic charm to his picture reproduced here (Pl. 135); and there is perhaps an influence of the Rembrandt school in the way the light flowers, rising mysteriously from nowhere, are embraced by surrounding darkness. Verelst, whose dewdrops delighted Pepys, spent most of his life in England, as he came here aged twenty-five in 1669; he was taken up by the malicious Second Duke of Buckingham who incited him to portraiture; and he painted the Duke in a picture 'crowded with fruits and sunflowers'; he also painted the Duchess of Portsmouth as 'Flora' and a portrait of the Duchess of Norfolk who offered him a purse of gold if he would claim as his own a shirt and waistcoat left behind by her lover and discovered by the Duke; his contemporary Vertue tells us that he was extravagantly conceited, calling himself the 'King of Painters' and 'the God of Flowers' and had, in the end, a mental collapse.

Abraham Mignon, though generally grouped with the Dutch school, was actually a German who came to Utrecht in the later 'sixties and returned to Germany about 1675; he worked for a time as assistant to Jan Davidsz de Heem (who was in Utrecht, from Antwerp, in 1669 and fled back to Antwerp before the French invasion of 1672); he stole efficiently from Van Aelst and Maria van Oosterwijck, and he also imitated the wood-with-plants-and-reptiles pieces of Otto Marseus and Mathias Withoos. All these influences are also seen in paintings by Elias van den Broeck a pupil, as noted, of Cornelis Kick in Amsterdam. Van den Broeck moved to Antwerp in the early 'seventies, worked there probably for a time with Jan Davidsz de Heem, and is known to have received there a yearly salary from a dealer; he then fell into disrepute as a result of a rumour that he stuck living butterflies to his flowerpieces, and he returned to Amsterdam where, following Marseus, he cultivated flowers and reptiles in a private garden and enclosure.

Houbraken, writing in their lifetime, said that Rachel Ruysch and Jan van Huysum outshone the preceding flower-painters 'as the sun the moon'; and his judgment held in the eighteenth and the nineteenth centuries, though taste today takes more pleasure in the earlier and mid-century painters.

Rachel Ruysch, daughter of an Amsterdam professor of anatomy and grand-daughter of an architect, was one of Willem van Aelst's last pupils. Though technically most skilful she was fundamentally an eclectic imitating not only Willem van Aelst and his successors but also Otto Marseus and Mathias Withoos, as her picture reproduced here (Pl. 133) shows. Unlike Maria van Oosterwijck she married and had ten children. Her husband Jurriaen Pool painted portraits till middle life and then went into commerce, perhaps in unconscious envy of his wife's success—for in 1708, when she was forty-four, Rachel Ruysch became a Court painter to Johann Wilhelm, the Elector Palatine (mentioned earlier in this book as patron of Adriaen van der Werff and other artists); and despite the claims of her large family, she found time to visit him in Düsseldorf on several occasions before 1716 when he died. In those eight years the Elector bought her entire production and gave her in addition a set of twenty-eight silver toilet appointments for her dressing room. She lived to the age of eighty-six and was still painting at eighty. Some pictures ascribed to her may be by her sister Anna Ruysch who signed an extant flower piece in 1685 and is said to have lived beyond 1741.

Jan van Huysum, fourteen years younger than Rachel Ruysch, predeceased her by a year. He began as pupil and assistant of his father Justus van Huysum who ran a decorating business supplying flower-pieces and other subjects for over-doors and so forth; and his own later pictures, with their light-coloured backgrounds, always make a decorative effect—as can be seen from the example reproduced here (Frontispiece). He claimed to paint each flower in his elaborate compositions from specimen blooms supplied to him by growers; and when he wished to show flowers of different seasons together in one composition he would wait for the appropriate time to insert that particular detail in the cluster. Contemporaries describe him as secretive and suspicious, admitting no one to his studio when he was painting; his only known pupil was Margareta Haverman whose adaptation of his style can be seen in the New York Metropolitan Museum; and he soon found occasion to quarrel with her and dismiss her. In his later years he was much chagrined by the misconduct of one of his sons; and in the end he became melancholic and, some assert, insane. Though he never went to Italy he painted some Italianate landscapes (and examples are preserved in Amsterdam, The Hague, Dresden and the Louvre). Some of his flower-pieces were copied by his brother Jacob van Huysum, who came to London in 1721 and also copied various pictures for Horace Walpole until Walpole could no longer endure his drunkenness.

Conraet Roepel, an almost exact contemporary of Jan van Huysum, began as a portrait painter in The Hague; but ill-health drove him to the country where he cultivated flowers in a garden belonging to his father. The Elector Palatine bought some of his pictures; and others were bought later by Prince Wilhelm of Hesse. An extreme sensibility, perhaps the result of his ill-health, marks his flower-piece reproduced here (Pl. 136); the flowers grow partly from the ground and partly from a pot; and both the colour-scheme and the chiaroscuro are so curiously affective that Van Huysum's work, if set beside it, would seem all technique and parade.

ii. Some characteristic pictures

BALTHASAR VAN DER AST
Born Middelburg before 1590, died Delft (?) after 1656

Oxford—Ashmolean	Carnations, columbines and rose in blue and white gilt-mounted Chinese porcelain vase; butterfly and spider; in front, two beetles; behind, a dragon fly on a sprig of oak. Signed and dated 1623. (Pl. 129.)
England—Major the Hon. H. R. Broughton	Flowers in a basket; in front on a slab, shells, insects, an iris and wild strawberries. Signed.
Amsterdam—Rijksmuseum	Flowers in a Chinese porcelain vase; shells, flowers; a butterfly and beetle in the foreground; a plate of fruit and autumnal leaves behind. Signed (twice) and dated 1620 and 1621.

Other signed examples are in Dessau and Pommersfelden. Cambridge (Fitzwilliam) has a fruit piece.

JAN DAVIDSZ DE HEEM
Born Utrecht 1606, died Antwerp 1683

Antwerp Gallery	Roses, tulips, a peony, a cluster of cherries on a branch of ivy; a grasshopper and two butterfles on the flowers. Signed.
Brussels Gallery	Flowers in a glass vase on a slab; butterflies and and snail. Signed.
Hague—Mauritshuis	Garland of flowers and fruit across a niche; butterflies, caterpillars, mice, earwigs and other insects. Signed.

Other signed flower pieces are in Cambridge (Fitzwilliam), Dresden, Munich and Berlin.

DUTCH FLOWER PAINTING

HANS BOLLONGIER

Born Haarlem (?) c. 1600, *died Haarlem c.* 1660 (?)

Amsterdam—Rijksmuseum	Round glass vase with tulips, roses and other flowers; snail and lizard on slab. Signed and dated 1639.
Haarlem Gallery	Flowers. Signed and dated 1644.
Oxford—Ashmolean	Round glass vase with tulips, roses and honeysuckle; snail and grasshopper on slab. Monogrammed and dated 1636.

OTTO MARSEUS VAN SCHRIECK

Born Nymwegen 1619, *died Amsterdam* 1678

Montpellier—Musée Fabre	Snake and lizard attacking butterfly; other butterflies round a thistle. Signed and dated 1664.
Amsterdam—Rijksmuseum	Against a wooded background two lizards fighting at the foot of a birch tree; in middle distance a butterfly and a snake. Monogrammed.
The Hague—Mauritshuis	Snake attacking a lizard at the foot of an oak tree; butterflies and a bird in flight; hills in the background. Signed and dated 1665.

Other signed examples are in Brunswick (dated 1662), Dresden (dated 1671 and 1673) and Stockholm.

MATHIAS WITHOOS

Born Amersfoort 1621 *or* 1627, *died Hoorn* 1703

London—Captain E. C. Palmer, M.C.	*The Hedgehog:* Thistles, honeysuckle and other flowers and butterflies in a landscape with distant hills; in the foreground a hedgehog, a mouse and a frog. Signed and dated Amersfoort 1669. (Pl. 132.)
Hampton Court—Royal Collection	Brambles, thistles, a lily and a rose; in the foreground a hedgehog and various insects. Signed.
Hampton Court—Royal Collection	Table with roses, marigolds, nasturtia, and other flowers in a glass vase; also a skull, an enamelled watch with gold chain, and old book with vellum binding. Signed.
Hampton Court—Royal Collection	White butterflies on blue convolvulus; in the foreground a small green snake. Signed.
Nottingham Castle Museum	Thistles and butterflies round the base of a tree. Monogrammed.

SOME CHARACTERISTIC PICTURES

WILLEM VAN AELST

Born Delft c. 1625, *died Amsterdam after* 1683

Oxford—Ashmolean	Roses, poppies, hollyhocks, carnations and a tulip in a gilt vase on a marble slab; round the flowers, butterflies and a dragon fly; on the slab a snail. Signed and dated 1663. (Pl. 130.)
Cambridge—Fitzwilliam	Roses and carnations on a reddish grey-veined marble slap; a fly, a caterpillar and a spider on the flowers. Signed and dated 1675.
The Hague—Mauritshuis	Roses, carnations, lilac, snowballs, callendulas, poppies and other flowers in a silver vase on a red and white marble slab; butterflies and a dragon fly round the flowers; on the slab a watch with blue ribbon and crystal box. Signed and dated 1663.
Rotterdam—Boymans	Flowerpiece with watch (similar to the Hague example). Signed and dated 1662.

MARIA VAN OOSTERWIJCK

Born Nootdorp (near Delft) 1630, *died Uitdam* 1693

Hampton Court—Royal	Roses, nasturtia and other flowers in a glass vase on a table. Signed and dated 1686.
Hampton Court—Royal	Roses, carnations and other flowers in a glass on a marble table, with a shell. Signed and dated 1689.
The Hague—Mauritshuis	Roses, carnations, a sunflower, leaves, grass, etc., in an ivory vase on which are carved nude children playing with a goat; butterflies, bees and a beetle; on the marble table the lid of the vase surmounted by a kneeling Venus. Signed.

Other signed examples are in Copenhagen, Vienna and Dresden.

NICOLAES LACHTROPIUS

Born Amsterdam (?) before 1640, *died Alfen (?) after* 1700

England—Major the Hon. H. R. Broughton	Hollyhock, sunflower, convolvulus, mallows, marigold and thistle in a glass vase on a wine coloured marble slab; butterflies round the flowers; insect on the slab. Signed and dated 1685. (Pl. 131)
Amsterdam—Rijksmuseum	Roses, poppies and other flowers in a vase on a marble table; insects on some flowers and a snail on the edge of the table. Signed and dated 1667.

DUTCH FLOWER PAINTING
ABRAHAM MIGNON

Born Frankfort 1640, *died Wedzlar* 1679

Brussels Gallery	Flowers round a tree-trunk; birds and butterfles; in foreground fungi, a serpent and a mouse. Signed.
Oxford—Ashmolean	Tulips, poppies, roses, marigolds, carnations and other flowers in a glass vase on a stone sill within a niche. Signed.
Paris—Louvre	The chaffinch's nest. Signed.

Other signed examples in London (National Gallery) and Amsterdam (Rijksmuseum).

JACOB VAN WALSCAPELLE

Born Dordrecht 1644, *died Amsterdam* 1727

London—Victoria & Albert Museum	Scarlet poppy, pink rose, carnation, kingcup, snowballs and other flowers with leaves and ear of corn in glass vase on reddish-brown marble table; a fly on the rose; a ladybird on a leaf; a snail on the table; butterflies on various flowers. Signed and dated 1667. (Pl. 134.)
London—National Gallery	Tulips, lilies, roses, a tulip and other flowers in a glass bowl on a table; insects on flowers; strawberries, a carnation and ear of corn on table. Signed.
Frankfort—Staedel Institute	Flowers in a vase decorated with relief figures. Signed and dated 1677.

Other signed examples are in Berlin and Breslau (1685).

SIMON VERELST

Born The Hague 1644, *died London* 1721

Oxford—Ashmolean	Apple blossom, poppies and foliage against a dark ground, Signed. (Pl. 135.)
The Hague—Bredius Museum	Pink roses, purplish-white tulip, red poppy and flowers in a glass vase on a table; a butterfly on the vase in which the studio window is reflected. Signed and dated 1669.

Other signed examples are in Stockholm, Brunswick, Pommersfelden and Boston Museum of Fine Arts.

SOME CHARACTERISTIC PICTURES

ELIAS VAN DEN BROECK

Born Amsterdam 1650 (*or Antwerp* 1653), *died Amsterdam* 1708

Oxford—Ashmolean	Tulip, poppies, roses, marigolds, narcissi and other flowers in a vase on a stone slab. Signed.
Amsterdam—Rijksmuseum	A rose and other flowers on a stone slab; a butterfly on a leaf and two snails on the slab. Signed.
Amsterdam—Rijksmuseum	A sprig with flowers and fruit; on a stone a snail and a lizard. Signed.
Vienna—Kunsthistorisches Museum	Tulip, roses, poppies, carnations and other flowers in a glass pot reflecting a window, on a stone slab; insects and butterfly on flowers; a stag-beetle on the slab. Signed.

Other signed examples in Rotterdam and Copenhagen.

RACHEL RUYSCH

Born Amsterdam 1664, *died Amsterdam* 1750

England—Major the Hon. H. R. Broughton	*The Lizard:* Plants and flowers against wooded background with distant hills; butterflies, a lizard, a snail and other insects. Signed. (Pl. 133.)
Glasgow—Art Gallery	Flowers and plants against the trunk of a tree; caterpillars, butterflies, a snail and a lizard. Signed.
Glasgow—Art Gallery	Roses, honeysuckle and other flowers in a terra-cotta vase. Signed and dated 1723.
Oxford—Ashmolean	Poppies, marigolds, cyclamen, plum blossom, polyanthus and morning glory at the foot of a tree trunk; fungi in foreground; butterflies. Signed and dated 1687.
England—Major the Hon. H. R. Broughton	Flowers in a vase. Signed and dated 1701.

Other signed examples in Amsterdam (1716), The Hague (1700), Rotterdam (1685), Dresden, and Vienna (1706).

JAN VAN HUYSUM

Born Amsterdam 1682, *died Amsterdam* 1749

London—Wallace Collection	Flowers in a vase with cupid in relief; butterflies and insects; on the pedestal a bird's nest. Landscape background. Signed and dated 1726. (Frontispiece.)

DUTCH FLOWER PAINTING

London—National Gallery   Poppies, peonies, iris, hollyhocks, narcissi, apple-blossom and other flowers in a vase with bas reliefs; on the pedestal roses, grapes, peaches and a bird's nest; dull golden background. Signed and dated '1736 and 1737'.

Dulwich—Gallery   Tulips, roses, French marigolds, poppies, auriculas, salvias, orange-blossom, forget-me-not, London pride, iris, larkspur, verconia, flax and convolvulus minor in a vase on a marble slab; insects and dewdrops on the leaves; a bird's nest with hedgesparrow's eggs and one cuckoo's egg; blue grey background. Signed.

Amsterdam—Rijksmuseum   Lilies, carnations, poppies and other flowers in an earthenware vase with classical bas-relief on a marble slab; grey curtain against a golden brown wall as background. Signed.

Other signed examples in The Hague, Paris (Louvre), Stockholm, Copenhagen, Vienna and German galleries.

COENRAET ROEPEL

Born The Hague 1678, *died The Hague* 1748

England—Miss K. McDouall   White-purple tulips and narcissi, poppies and polyanthus; dark background. Signed and dated 1715. (Pl. 136.)

Amsterdam—Rijksmuseum   Flowers in a metal vase placed in a niche. Signed and dated 1721.

Other signed examples in Cassel (1722 and 1723) and Dresden.

INDEX

207

INDEX

INDEX

INDEX

INDEX